D1538818

CHRONICLE OF THE CHINESE EMPERORS

ANN PALUDAN

CHRONICLE OF THE CHINESE EMPERORS

THE REIGN-BY-REIGN RECORD OF THE RULERS OF IMPERIAL CHINA

WITH 368 ILLUSTRATIONS
126 IN COLOR

Thames & Hudson

Author's Note
There are great variations in Chinese dates, reflecting the variety of sources and methods of dating. I have used the dates given in the official Chinese date list for emperors, published in Beijing, 1993, supplemented by the Cambridge History of China (where available – not all volumes are published yet). The *pinyin* system of romanization is used throughout. With a few exceptions, listed below, this is pronounced as it looks. The exceptions are: c = ts; q = ch; j=r. Where the consonant break is not clear an apostrophe is used, i.e. Xi'an not Xian.

(Half-title) An 18th-century embroidered satin medallion showing a five-clawed dragon chasing a pearl (Victoria and Albert Museum, London). The dragon represents the emperor and the pearl is a symbol of infinite wisdom.

(Frontispiece) Anonymous portrait of the Ming emperor Yongle who reigned from 1403 to 1424 (National Place Museum, Taiwan).

© 1998 Thames & Hudson Ltd, London

All Rights Reserved. No part of this publication may be reproduced or transmitted in any form or by any means, electronic or mechanical, including photocopy, recording or any other information storage and retrieval system, without prior permission in writing from the publisher.

First published in the United States of America in hardcover in 1998 by Thames & Hudson Inc., 500 Fifth Avenue, New York, New York 10110

thamesandhudsonusa.com

First paperback edition 2008

Library of Congress Catalog Card Number 98-60041

ISBN 978-0-500-28764-4

Printed and bound in Singapore by Craft Print International Ltd

CONTENTS

pages 6–7
Preface
pages 8–13
Introduction
pp. 10–11 Map of Imperial China

pages 14–61

THE EARLY EMPIRES
221 BC–AD 220

Qin Shihuangdi unifies feudal states thus creating the Chinese empire; the Qin dynasty collapses; the Han re-establish, expand and consolidate the imperial system; the decline and fall of the Han dynasty

Special Features

pp. 18–19 The Great Wall
pp. 24–25 The Terracotta Army of the First Emperor of China
pp. 34–35 Western Han Tombs
pp. 46–47 Stone Sculpture
pp. 56–57 The Silk Roads
pp. 58–59 Tomb Figurines

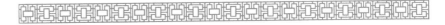

pages 60–117

CONFUSION, REUNIFICATION AND THE GOLDEN AGE
AD 220–907

The Three Kingdoms and the start of the 'Period of Disunion' in which China is divided into the Northern and Southern Dynasties; Southern Dynasties at Nanjing fend off northern invaders; the reunification of north and south under the Sui and the Tang

Special Features

pp. 78–79 Buddhism
pp. 80–81 The Northern Dynasties
pp. 84–85 The Grand Canal
pp. 94–95 Horses
pp. 102–103 Tang Mausolea
p. 106 Chang'an
pp.110–111 Buddhist Art and Architecture

Taizong (626–649)

pages 118–157

CHAOS, DIPLOMACY AND INVASION

AD 907–1368

Half a century of instability during the Five Dynasties period; peace and intense intellectual and artistic activity under the Song; the Jin kingdom invades northern China forcing the Song south; Mongol incursions; Khubilai Khan becomes emperor of China

Special Features

p. 127 Northern Song Imperial Tombs
pp. 140–141 Song Painting
p. 152 The Mongols

Taizu (960–976)

pages 158–217

REVIVAL AND COLLAPSE

AD 1368–1911

The Ming Dynasty restores the Chinese imperial tradition; imperial capital moved to Beijing, the Forbidden City built; Manchus invade Beijing after Ming dynasty collapses; Manchus establish the last imperial dynasty – the Qing; European contact, internal rebellion and the fall of imperial China

Special Features

pp. 164–165 The Forbidden City in Beijing
p.166 Maritime Expeditions
p. 168 The Temple of Heaven
pp. 184–185 The Ming Tombs
p. 186 Jesuits in China
pp. 188–189 Ming Porcelain
p. 197 The Jesuits and the Summer Palace
p. 200 Commercial Trade and Expansion
p. 203 Macartney's Embassy
p. 207 The Opium War
p. 215 The Boxer Rebellion

Khaishan (1308–1311)

page 218
Select Bibliography

page 219
Illustration and Text Credits

pages 220–224
Index

Kangxi (1662–1722)

PREFACE: HEIRS TO THE MANTLE OF HEAVEN

(*Above*) Statue of Confucius in the Bamboo temple, Kunming.

The Chinese empire lasted from the 3rd century BC at the time of the Roman Republic until the 20th century. In 221 BC, the victorious king of one of the early Chinese states declared himself First Emperor; in 1911, the last emperor was overthrown and replaced by a republic. The empire inherited some 1,500 years of pre-imperial historically recorded states, stretching back to the time of the Minoan civilization of the 2nd millennium BC. For virtually the entire period of recorded European history there was thus a Chinese emperor on the throne.

The mystery and attraction that China holds for the West, partly inspired by its distance and vast size, has been magnified by this continuity with the distant past. The Egyptian and Mesopotamian civilizations were earlier, the Roman empire covered as large an area, but we see these periods through a telescope across the ages. We have no first-hand experience of their ways of thought and daily habits. In China, however, not only was the emperor still ruling within living memory, but Chinese beliefs and customs had survived from the dawn of the imperial period. Government and general conduct were based on the teachings of Confucius (*c.* 551–*c.* 479 BC), a contemporary of the Greek statesman Pericles (*c.*490–*c.*429 BC); the fundamental aspects of the Chinese imperial administration system evolved at the time of the Roman empire.

(*Right*) The Qing dynasty painting *Spring Dawn in the Palaces of the Han* illustrates the wealth and luxury of imperial palaces from early times (National Palace Museum, Taiwan).

(*Above*) Ming watercolour of the emperor Wanli from an 18th-century album of imperial portraits (British Library).

Early European knowledge of China was indirect, passed by word of mouth along the trade routes, and as always, the retelling led to increasingly fanciful accounts woven round the only certainty – that this large country was ruled by an emperor of fabulous wealth. The emperor's unique position as mediator between this world and the spirit world was recognized by his title 'Son of Heaven'. He lived in a vast palace filled with beautiful women; in his parks were rare trees, flowers and exotic beasts, tribute from distant peoples. His cities were fortified with high walls, and his officials administered an area as large as the whole of Europe. The first popular account of China by a Westerner, Marco Polo's *The Travels*, confirmed this impression of luxury. His descriptions of the wonders he had seen and the opulence of 13th-century China contained so many superlatives that he was mockingly referred to as *il Millione*.

Drawing on contemporary accounts, historical records and archaeological discoveries, *Chronicle of the Chinese Emperors* traces the chequered lives of the 157 emperors of China. They are, by any standards, an unusual collection of individuals whose virtues, vices and eccentricities were exaggerated by their position of supreme power. Two emperors were born commoners,

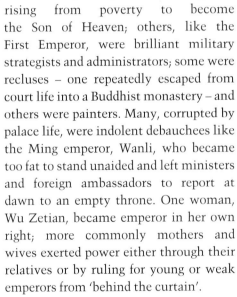

rising from poverty to become the Son of Heaven; others, like the First Emperor, were brilliant military strategists and administrators; some were recluses – one repeatedly escaped from court life into a Buddhist monastery – and others were painters. Many, corrupted by palace life, were indolent debauchees like the Ming emperor, Wanli, who became too fat to stand unaided and left ministers and foreign ambassadors to report at dawn to an empty throne. One woman, Wu Zetian, became emperor in her own right; more commonly mothers and wives exerted power either through their relatives or by ruling for young or weak emperors from 'behind the curtain'.

Weak or strong, young or old, all these emperors played an essential role. They were the hub of a vast administrative system and the all-powerful mediator between heaven and earth. This connection provided a moral base: if things went badly, the emperor had clearly lost heaven's trust and revolution was justified. With such a safety valve, the imperial system remained unchallenged until the 20th century.

INTRODUCTION: THE BIRTH OF IMPERIAL CHINA

(*Above*) The legendary sovereign Shennong, inventor of agriculture. Woodcut from the Ming encyclopedia *Sancai tuhui*, 1607.

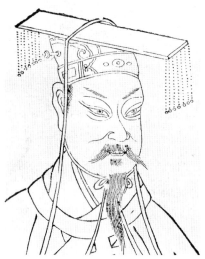

(*Above*) King Yu of the Xia dynasty (National Palace Museum, Taiwan).

The First Emperor created 'China'. Before him, the states in the north China plain and Yellow River basin were known by the name of their ruling family. Traditional Chinese histories record the names of kings going back to the 27th century BC belonging to the Xia, Shang and Zhou dynasties. For the last two dynasties, spanning the great Chinese Bronze Age, there is abundant archaeological evidence, but only recently has evidence of a pre-Shang state, the Xia, appeared. When the First Emperor established the empire in 221 BC, he deliberately crushed the nationalism of his defeated rivals by taking a title without geographical limitation or family significance. He was not 'Emperor of China' but 'First Emperor', and it was his intention that his descendants would follow with the correct numerical appellations. 'China' was a word the outside world created, derived from the name of the First Emperor's home state – Qin (pronounced Chin); the Chinese refer to their own country as the 'Middle Kingdom' or 'Central Country'. In early periods the civilized world was called *Tian Xia*, meaning 'all under heaven', and this phrase was also used to denote the empire.

The empire inherited many thousands of years of social and technological development. From earliest times the Chinese had valued practical ability above abstract virtue. According to legends, Pan Ku, the Chinese creator of the universe, separated heaven and earth and after 18,000 years the various parts of his body were transformed into the sun and moon, the earth, wind, mountains and seas with all their minerals and living creatures; the parasites which infected his body became the human race. Pan was followed by three sets of Supreme Sovereigns corresponding to the three elements in the cosmos: heaven, earth and man. The 12 celestial, 11 terrestrial and 9 human sovereigns were succeeded by 5 Model Rulers or Sages – Huangdi (the Yellow Emperor), Zhuan Xiu, Ku, Yao and Shun – who laid the foundations of Chinese civilization. To them were attributed the inventions of fire, fishing, hunting, agriculture, housebuilding, medicine, calendars and writing. Huangdi, the mythical Yellow Emperor, was regarded as the founding deity of the philosophical school of Daoism; his wife introduced the arts of cultivating and spinning silk. The last two Sages, Yao and Shun, set an example by choosing their successor on merit, not birth; Shun choosing the great Yu, who controlled floods and founded the Xia dynasty, thus bridging the gap between legend and history.

The achievements of the legendary rulers are reflected in Neolithic remains which include evidence of widespread silk production, jade carvings of amulets and ritual weapons and a privileged class of pottery workers with their own living quarters. During the Bronze Age which followed (from the mid-2nd millennium BC onwards) the use of writing became widespread. From the 8th century BC onwards there are fairly detailed and reliable records; the great literary and philosophical works of the 5th century BC were later to form the basis of the imperial educational system. The techniques of metalworking were highly developed and the demand for huge quantities of bronze ritual vessels led to the

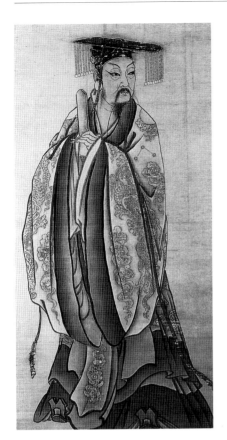

(*Above*) Huangdi, the legendary Yellow Emperor. Painting by Ma Lin (National Palace Museum, Taiwan).

world's first mass-production system based on the conveyor belt pattern.

These Bronze Age nation states were urban states in which the basic form of later Chinese cities – walled with corner and gate-towers and a grid-pattern of streets with buildings consisting of south-facing rectangular halls with a wooden framework and rammed-earth foundations – was already well established. The palaces had large gardens and hunting parks, and some idea of the luxury and level of craftsmanship can be gauged from the exquisite artifacts found in wealthy aristocratic tombs. As well as inscribed ritual bronzes, these include delicate jades, metal and ivory inlaid ornaments, beakers and weapons, and fine lacquer objects for personal use.

Of all these skills, it was writing that proved the most important. The empire was created by military conquest, but it was perpetuated through its written heritage. The Chinese empire was the product of two conflicting ideas: that unity and order depended on the sword, but, in the long run, government could only survive if it benefited and was accepted by the people. The First Emperor proved the truth of the Chinese saying that a kingdom can be won but not ruled from horseback. His authoritarian rule alienated the populace to such an extent that three years after his death in 210 BC, his son, the Second Emperor, was put to death with all members of the imperial family. It was his successors, the Han emperors, who gave the imperial system its lasting shape. Drawing on the works of the great 5th-century BC philosopher, Confucius, the Han adopted a political theory based on social and moral considerations. By the end of the Han dynasty's four centuries of rule, the First Emperor's ideas of unity and a strongly centralized empire were firmly associated with an administrative and educational system which was based on a belief in the perfection of society through education.

(*Right*) The Chinese developed a unique form of bronze casting based on the use of mass-produced clay moulds made from a finished dried clay model of the desired object. The moulds were removed in pieces and then re-assembled around a hard core, leaving a space to pour in the metal alloy which when set, formed the vessel. This method enabled the Chinese to make very large vessels with extremely elaborate decoration. The flanges which resulted from the mould joins were used as decorative features. Bronze ritual vessel (British Museum).

PRINCIPAL DYNASTIES

Qin (221–207 BC)

Han (206 BC–AD 220)

Sui (581–618)

Tang (618–907)

Song (960–1279)

Yuan (1279–1368)

Ming (1368–1644)

Qing (1644–1911)

Extent of Qin empire
Extent of Qing empire
Present international boundaries
Present provincial boundaries

0   500 km
0   500 miles

KAZAKHSTAN

KYRGYZSTAN

TAJIKISTAN

Urumqi

Kashgar

Xinjiang

Dunhuang

PAKISTAN

Khotan

Qinghai

Tibet

NEPAL

Lhasa

INDIA

BANGLADESH

BURMA

Bay
of
Bengal

RUSSIAN FEDERATION

MONGOLIA

Heilongjiang

• Harbin

Changchun

Inner Mongolia

• Jilin

M A N C H U R I A

Yellow R

Hohhot •

Chengde (Jehol) •

Shenyang
(Mukden) •

Liaoning

NORTH
KOREA

• Yinchuan

Ningxia

Shanhaiguan •
Beijing •

Mt Wu Tai ▲

Yungang •
Taiyuan •

Hebei

Tianjin
(Tientsin)

*Liaodong
Peninsula*

• Dalien

JAPAN

SOUTH KOREA

Xining •

• Lanzhou

Shaanxi

Shanxi

Shijiazhuang •

• Weihaiwei

Qufu •

Qingdao •

gang

Gansu

Lintong •
Xianyang •

Luoyang• Gongxian
Longmen• Dengfeng •Kaifeng
Xi'an
(Chang'an)

• Jinan
▲*Mt Tai*

Shandong

Jiangsu

• Xining

Henan

Hubei

Yangzi

Wuhan •

Anhui

Hefei •

Yangzhou
•Nanjing
Suzhou

• Shanghai

• Ningpo

Sichuan

Guanxian •
•Chengdu

Dazu •

Changsha •

Nanchang •

Hunan

Jiangxi

Hangzhou
(Lin'an)

Zhejiang

East
China
Sea

Guizhou

• Guiyang

Fujian

Fuzhou •

Taipei •

Kunming •

Guilin •

Guangdong

Guangzhou
(Canton)

•Kowloon

Xiamen
(Amoy)

Taiwan

Yunnan

Guangxi

• Nanning

•
•Hong Kong
Macao

VIETNAM

LAOS

Haikou •

Hainan

AND

gang

Many local maps from the 17th century have survived in provincial records. This shows a single prefecture in Jiangsu; the large town is the administrative centre (British Library).

Thousands of oracle bones have been recovered from Shang dynasty sites. Characters were inscribed on tortoise shells and shoulder bones of cattle; when heated, the bones cracked and the diviner then interpreted the result.

This was the distinctive characteristic of the Chinese empire. The empire had no natural unity. Its creation was based on the destruction of national identities and the peoples of the Chinese empire, like those of the Peoples' Republic of China today, were a mixture of nationalities and ethnic types. Physically, there is little in common between the heavy Chinese of the north and the lithe southerner, and today there are reckoned to be 55 minorities, each with their own language and many with their own script. Nor is China a natural geographical entity. Its vast area, some 3,400 miles (5,500 km) from north to south and 3,200 miles (5,200 km) from east to west is broken up by some of the world's highest mountains and longest rivers, creating formidable barriers to transport and communication. Not until 1960, for example, was it possible to bridge the lower Yangzi River, and trains from north to south China had to cross by ferry. Today it is the world's most populous nation but over half the land is high plateau or mountains and only 11 per cent is suitable for cultivation.

In its long history, China's frontiers have not been stable. From the core of central states in the Yellow River area, it spread southwards into the Yangzi Valley and hence as far as Thailand in the southwest and Vietnam to the south; at times it reached well into Central Asia, dominating the trade routes and oases leading to the West. A similar expansion took its boundaries across the Great Wall into Mongolia in the northwest and former Manchuria in the northeast, but all this expansion was a fluctuating process. When the empire was strong and stable, it expanded; in times of weakness it retreated before the incursions of powerful border peoples. Conflict with the nomadic tribes on the steppes was a permanent feature in imperial history leading to periodic occupation of the north by non-Chinese. For over 100 years the whole empire was under the alien rule of Khubilai Khan and his Mongol successors. And yet the imperial system survived. With the exception of the Mongols, for whom China was merely part of a much wider empire stretching across Asia to the gates of Europe, these successive waves of invaders were assimilated by the Chinese, bringing new blood and energy into an often flagging society.

What held this disparate region together was neither race nor military power but a common cultural heritage. Military expansion brought Chinese civilization with it, and it was the acceptance of a common culture and intellectual background spread by the use of a common script

IMPERIAL NAMES

Chinese emperors had many names – a family name, reign titles, and a temple name as well as a multitude of honorary titles. The first Ming emperor, for example, was born Zhu Yuanzhang (Zhu was his family name). When he declared himself emperor he took the reign title Hongwu ('Vast Military Power') and was known after death by his temple name, Taizu ('Supreme Progenitor'). Strictly speaking the reign title refers to a number of years and the correct usage is therefore 'emperor of the Hongwu period'. Ming and Qing emperors kept one reign title throughout their reign but many earlier emperors changed them to mark an auspicious event or the start of a new era and years were then dated from the start of such reign eras rather than from the emperor's date of accession.

For simplicity I will adopt Western usage, using the name by which the particular emperor is best known, i.e. the emperor Huizong (temple name), Khubilai Khan (birth name), Qianlong (reign title), prefixed where necessary by the dynastic name, Han Wudi being the emperor Wudi of the Han dynasty. The Chinese calligraphy which accompanies each name shows the temple name of the emperor, except for the Ming and Qing periods where the calligraphy shows the more commonly known reign titles.

The exact regulations governing the ranks of women in the imperial household varied. A girl entered the palace as a concubine; if she became an imperial favourite, she was promoted to consort; if the emperor married her, she became empress. Any concubine whose son became emperor became empress on her son's accession (this frequently occurred posthumously). Only the better known empresses and consorts are listed in the fact files.

which formed a bond between peoples throughout the empire. Consciousness of their civilized social behaviour and organization bred the Chinese belief that they were at the centre of the world. The Son of Heaven was the natural ruler of those on earth, and when later Chinese emperors were faced with demands for equality by Western rulers they found these impossible to accept.

Our knowledge of the early Chinese empire is drawn from two main sources: written records and archaeological discoveries. Unlike their Egyptian or Roman counterparts, the Chinese emperors left few imperial monuments above ground. Their lasting works were of a public nature such as the Great Wall, the Grand Canal, and the great irrigation systems of Sichuan. The use of wooden frameworks means that few pre-14th-century wooden buildings have survived, and all that remains of the great cities before that date are the rammed-earth foundations of city walls, towers and terraces. Almost the only stone buildings are tombs, pagodas and bridges; stone monuments are limited to statuary and to memorial features placed on tombs.

This lack of visible remains is more than compensated for by the wealth of written texts. The Chinese have always attached great importance to the written word – an engraved inscription is valued far above any carved statue – and the modern Chinese pictorial script has recognizable links with the earliest hieroglyphs on bones from the 2nd millennium BC. The first Chinese historian, Sima Qian, wrote the *Historical Records* of early Chinese history in the 1st century BC and from that time onwards there exist Dynastic Histories. These were supplemented by local records which like the Dynastic Histories gave information under headings such as Biographies, Ritual and Ceremony (including official dress), Carriages, and Monuments. The very wealth of information, however, brought a danger of historical distortion since it created the impression that all fields of activity were covered and that if something was not mentioned in the texts, it could not have been important. In fact, the scholar-officials of the court presented a selected version of events reflecting contemporary views; history was frequently reinterpreted to suit their rulers and large areas of activity were ignored as being beneath notice. For example, no textual references to the First Emperor's great terracotta army have yet been found, and it was not until the 7th century AD, when the emperors became interested in fine quality porcelain, that China's best-known artifact – china – was mentioned in the texts.

Archaeological discoveries help to overcome these limitations. The ancient tradition of providing the dead with what they might need in the next world means that China's soil is a vast treasure house. There is no other country in the world where archaeological discoveries are taking place so fast and on such a scale as in China, discoveries which are continually expanding our knowledge of the past and reversing previously accepted ideas. What follows, therefore, is an unfinished story still in the process of being revealed.

QIN	WESTERN HAN	EASTERN HAN
Qin Shihuangdi	Gaodi	Guang Wudi
221–210 BC	206–195 BC	25–57
Er Shi	Huidi	Mingdi
210–207 BC	195–188 BC	57–75
	(Lu Hou)	Zhangdi
	(Regent 188–180 BC)	75–88
	Wendi	Hedi
	180–157 BC	88–106
	Jingdi	Shangdi
	157–141 BC	106
	Wudi	Andi
	141–87 BC	106–125
	Zhaodi	Shundi
	87–74 BC	125–144
	Xuandi	Chongdi
	74–49 BC	144–145
	Yuandi	Zhidi
	49–33 BC	145–146
	Chengdi	Huandi
	33–7 BC	146–168
	Aidi	Lingdi
	7–1 BC	168–189
	Pingdi	Xiandi
	1 BC–AD 6	189–220
	Ruzi	
	7–9	
	Wang Mang	
	9–23	

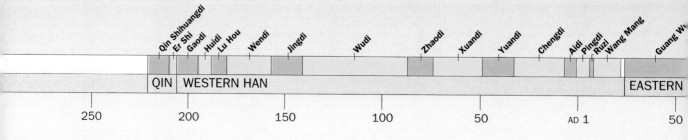

Qin Shihuangdi (221–210BC)

Gaodi (206–195BC)

Wendi (180–157BC)

Guang Wudi (25–57)

THE EARLY EMPIRES
Qin dynasty 221–207 BC
Han dynasty 206 BC–AD 220

QIN SHIHUANGDI UNIFIED THE EMPIRE but the burden of his harsh laws and colossal public works led to the empire's break-up within 15 years. The Han reunified the country, keeping the Qin's centralized system of government, but enlarging the power base by enlisting the support of the scholar class who provided the administration with enlightened officials.

The four centuries of Han rule were divided by an interregnum under an outsider, Wang Mang, and the two halves are known as the Former and Later Han, or, more commonly, Western and Eastern Han after the location of their capitals at Chang'an (modern Xi'an) and Luoyang (further east) respectively.

The history of Western and Eastern Han followed a similar pattern: consolidation, expansion, exhaustion and peasant risings leading to a breakdown of administration. The imperial system was plagued by inherent factional rivalry between officials, consort families, eunuchs and warlords. Succession was seldom secure: only five Western and three Eastern Han emperors were of age on accession; the remainder were children dominated by their mothers or by eunuchs. Despite these problems the Han left a lasting legacy – the ideal of a unified empire whose ruler provided the necessary link between heaven and earth and in which government had a moral duty to promote harmony and prosperity.

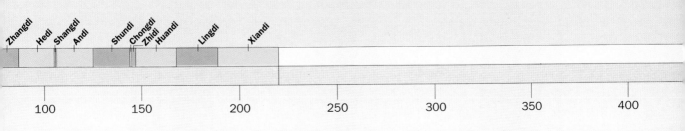

Zhangdi Hedi Shangdi Andi Shundi Chongdi Zhidi Huandi Lingdi Xiandi

100   150   200   250   300   350   400

QIN DYNASTY
221–207 BC

秦始皇帝 **Qin Shihuangdi**
221–210 BC

二世皇帝 **Er Shi**
210–207 BC

帝皇始秦

Shihuangdi. Woodcut from a Ming dynasty encyclopedia, the *Sancai tuhui*, 1607.

QIN SHIHUANGDI	
Born	*Mother*
259 BC, as Zheng ('Correct' or 'Upright')	Zhao Ji, former concubine of wealthy merchant Lu Buwei
Title before accession	*Children*
King Zheng of Qin (246 BC)	more than 20
Accession	*Died*
221 BC, as Shihuangdi ('The First August Emperor')	210 BC
	Tomb
Father	Mount Li, Lintong, Shaanxi
King Zhuang Xiang of Qin	

QIN SHIHUANGDI

He has the proboscis of a hornet and large all-seeing eyes. His chest is like that of a bird of prey and his voice like that of a jackal. He is merciless, with the heart of a tiger or a wolf.

Wei Liao, one of Qin Shihuangdi's advisers, before he fled the court

The future First Emperor was born in 259 BC into a world of war. The Warring States period (475–221 BC) was a time of almost incessant strife between powerful feudal states struggling for supremacy. His father was King Zhuang Xiang of Qin, one of the seven competing states; his mother, Zhao Ji, was the former concubine of the king's wealthy merchant supporter, Lu Buwei. Critics later claimed that the First Emperor was really Lu Buwei's son, but the boy's character – his extraordinary practical and strategic sense coupled with martial vigour – are hallmarks of the earlier Qin rulers. At 13, on his father's death in 246 BC, he became King Zheng of Qin. At first his mother and Lu Buwei acted as regents, but after a court scandal in which Lu and the queen smuggled a famously virile protégé of Lu's into the palace disguised as a eunuch, they were disgraced. From 238, Zheng ruled alone.

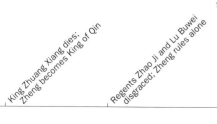

King Zhuang Xiang dies; Zheng becomes King of Qin

Regents Zhao Ji and Lu Buwei disgraced; Zheng rules alone

Jing Ke's assassination attempt

Zheng unifies China and becomes Qin Shihuangdi, 'First Emperor' of China

Hannibal crosses the Alps

Earlier ramparts linked to form Great Wall

The Burning of the Books

Qin Shihuangdi dies; Er Shi emperor

Er Shi commits suicide; Gaodi of Western Han emperor

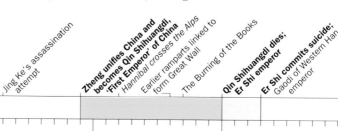

240 230 220 210 200

QIN SHIHUANGDI AND ER SHI 17

(*Above*) Rubbing of the Yishan stele, one of seven large stone tablets which Qin Shihuangdi had erected to mark the extent of his empire.

THE FIRST EMPEROR'S TITLES

In taking the title Shihuangdi, the Qin ruler deliberately claimed equality with the legendary deity-rulers of antiquity such as the Yellow Emperor, Huangdi, whose reign was described as a golden age of peace and good government. *Huang* meant 'sovereign'; *di*, drawn like a bundle of sticks, appears in early Shang oracle bones, apparently referring to the sacrifices in which burnt meats were offered to the ancestral spirits, the chief of whom was the founder-ancestor, Shangdi. Later *di* came to represent the deities themselves. Previously (and in all later dynasties), it was the habit to give a ruler a 'tomb name' or 'temple name' – a posthumous title reflecting his virtues – but in the edict announcing his own title the new emperor specifically forbade this practice.

(*Right*) To keep strict control over his generals, Qin Shihuangdi gave them each half a tally, shaped like a tiger. Orders were only to be obeyed if accompanied by the other half.

Zheng had grown up in a harsh world. The Qin, who originally came from the west, probably from modern Gansu, had brought with them the martial spirit of the steppe peoples. Their natural warlike instincts had been harnessed under the king's grandfather whose chief minister, Shang Yang, created a strongly centralized administration based on the Legalist belief (see p. 20) that man is inherently evil and can only be controlled by fear. 'In an orderly country,' said Shang Yang, 'punishments are numerous and rewards are rare.'

Tantalizingly little is known about the First Emperor's personal life. The only written sources are the history of early China written by Sima Qian a century later and some inscriptions on contemporary stone tablets. We know that he had more than 20 children, but of his wives and concubines nothing is said; no favourites are mentioned and even the name of the Second Emperor's mother is unknown. The only comments on his character refer to his resolution, conscientious attention to detail and energy – continuing late into the night he 'worked without rest, day and night'.

Zheng's meteoric rise was based on meticulous planning. With his chief minister, Li Si, an ardent Legalist, he streamlined the administration and with sweeping land reforms created a sound agricultural base for feeding the troops. The entire population was mobilized into 'productive occupations' and the army was honed into an instrument of attack the like of which has seldom been seen. An elite force, its discipline was legendary and the ferocity of its troops, who slaughtered their prisoners, inspired dread among their opponents. Between 230 and 221 BC, with a skilful mixture of diplomacy, cunning and strategy, the Qin devoured their enemies 'as a silkworm devours a mulberry leaf', and by 221, the Tiger of Qin had eliminated all opposition, unified China and declared himself **Qin Shihuangdi** (221–210 BC) – 'The First August Emperor'. His intention was clear: 'We are the First Emperor, and our successors shall be known as the Second Emperor, Third Emperor, and so on, for endless generations.'

The next 11 years revealed the full extent of his genius. With an iron hand, Qin Shihuangdi forged the previously warring states into a unified empire, creating a centralized administration whose basic outlines were to serve the whole imperial period. At the centre was the emperor,

THE GREAT WALL

The Chinese call it 'the wall of ten thousand *li*'. It stretches as the crow flies for 1,674 miles (2,696 km) from Shanhaiguan on the eastern coast in Shandong to Jiayuguan in Gansu in the west, but its actual length is much longer since there are at least another 1,000 miles (1,600 km) in loops and double lines at the passes. Some sections date from the 4th century BC, built by feudal kingdoms as a defence against the mounted nomads from the west. In 214 BC, Qin Shihuangdi ordered General Meng Jian to join these sections and set up a line of fortresses along the empire's western and northern borders. Later dynasties extended or moved the Great Wall but the basic design remained virtually the same.

Its height varied between 23 and 46 ft (7 and 14 m); the base was 33 ft (10 m) wide and 5 horses could ride side by side along the ramparts. There were turrets and over 2,500 watchtowers for signalling at regular intervals and garrisons stationed on the inside to provide patrols. Those on duty had to exchange tablets with the next post as proof that they had covered the distance. The material varied according to local conditions. In the Gobi desert the original construction of alternate layers of sand, pebbles and tamarisk twigs has survived up to 20 ft (6 m) high; in the northeast the wall is made with planks of pine, fir and oak which provide a casing for rammed earth. The outer and inner walls of the sections near Beijing which were restored by the Ming are faced with stone slabs and filled with cobbles, lime and earth and the

(Below) Sections of surviving Qin dynasty wall in the Ningxia Hui Autonomous Region (east of the Gansu corridor leading to the west) are still between 5 and 6 metres high and the layers of pounded earth from which it was made are clearly visible.

(Above) Detail of the Han wall in the Lop Nor region, showing alternating layers of tied reeds and clay mixed with pebbles.

(Right) Much of the wall which we see today was rebuilt or added by the Ming dynasty who followed the Yuan Mongol occupation and were therefore particularly aware of the need for an effective defence against northern tribes.

surface of the ramparts is made from bricks, weighing 20 lb (10 kg) each, which were fired on the spot. Wide windows in the turrets enabled the defenders to shoot their crossbows.

Its military advantages were inestimable. The wall closed China's only open frontier – the gap between the natural barriers of the Himalayas and high plateaus of Yunnan and Tibet in the southwest and the sea in the northeast – and provided an excellent defence against her traditional enemies – the horse-riding nomads of the steppes and Central Asia.

It was, however, much more than a defence. The wall marked the limits of the civilized world. The character for wall and city is the same in China and carries the idea of a dividing line or enclosure. Early Chinese walled cities were not built for defensive purposes but for administrative reasons, separating city from field. With the wall, Qin Shihuangdi gave the empire an administrative structure reflecting the belief that China was the unique civilization of the world. The wall distinguished order from disorder – the Middle Kingdom from the Barbarians. Those within belonged to the Chinese cultural tradition, observing the rituals and following sedentary occupations; those outside were wild and uneducated, without moral instruction.

The suffering caused by its construction is remembered in countless ballads and legends. Working in arid deserts or up to 6,500 ft (2,000 m) high in the mountains, in bitter winters and blazing summer heat, the men died from exhaustion, disease and hunger, and, far from home, were often buried within the wall itself.

(Below) Map showing remaining sections of the Great Wall. Later dynasties adapted Qin Shihuangdi's Great Wall for their own military and political purposes, extending and reinforcing it where necessary.

The Great Wall
— Qin Dynasty
— Western Han Dynasty
— Ming Dynasty

(Above) The Han dynasty built two long extensions of the wall westwards to Lop Nor in modern Xinjiang, to protect the Silk Road. Han watch-towers have survived in this region and in places the original wall is still more than 3m high and 1m wide.

LEGALISM

Legalism was based on the idea that man is by nature evil and undisciplined and can only be kept in order by fear and harsh punishments. The first great Legalist was Shang Yang, who laid the foundations of the Qin administrative system 361–338 BC. Unlike the other feudal states with their privileged aristocracies, Qin was governed by a centralized military administration which applied the law impartially, regardless of family or religious traditions. All citizens were forced into 'productive occupations' such as agriculture and the army; merchants and intellectuals were harmful: 'In the state of an enlightened ruler, there are no books; the law supplies the only instruction.' By the end of Shang's period, an historian noted: 'The Qin people were acquiescent.... Punishments were numerous, rewards rare.'

Shang Yang's influence persisted long after his death. A century later, one of his disciples, Han Feizi (died 233 BC) wrote a definitive account of Legalism (in the *Han Feizi*) and another, Li Si (died 208 BC) became the First Emperor's close adviser, responsible for much of his success both in conquest and consolidation of the empire. Asked to describe his policies, Li Si replied: 'For four generations now, Qin has won victory. Its armies are the strongest in the world and its authority sways the other feudal lords. It did not reach this position by benevolence and righteousness, but by taking advantage of its opportunities. That is all.'

whose palace and capital – visible symbols of imperial power – formed the hub of a network covering the entire empire. The area of Shihuangdi's A-fang palace foundations is seven times that of the largest hall in the later Ming dynasty's Forbidden City in Beijing; the Qin capital, Xianyang, was rebuilt and included replicas of 270 palaces of the defeated states. Over 120,000 of the defeated states' leading families were forcibly resettled in these replicas.

From this imposing centre of power the entire territory, divided into 36 administrative units, was controlled by imperial officials. The distant provinces were linked to the capital by a network of arterial highways, totalling over 4,700 miles (7,500 km) – some 500 miles (800 km) more than the Romans two centuries later. With regular staging posts, these routes were 50 ft (15 m) wide, tree-lined and with three lanes, the central for imperial use only. Even the width of axles was standardized so that wheeled vehicles moved along the same ruts. Weights and measures were standardized; Shihuangdi imposed a single currency and more important, a single script. Although all the feudal states had used a pictorial script with common features, local variations had developed. Now Qin Shihuangdi simplified the 3,000 most common characters, creating a basic core for all future developments in writing.

He ordered complete disarmament and from the melted down weapons he had bronze bells and 12 colossal bronze giants cast, each weighing 30 tons (30,500 kg), to stand in the palace courtyards. With a passion for order, he marked the boundaries of his empire. The Great

(*Right*) Remains of the Xianyang palace. Archaeologists have found sections of patterned tile flooring painted scarlet and remnants of colourful wall paintings. Some halls had fireplaces and special drains for storm water; beneath the palace were seven large storage cellars.

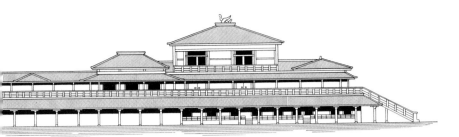

(*Above*) Reconstruction of a Qin palace. The emperor's palace at Xianyang dominated its surroundings. Facing south, on a large raised platform 6m high, 60m wide and 45m deep, it was built in tiers with several large halls linked by covered ways.

(*Above*) This circular eave tile from the A-fang palace is inscribed: 'The Spirit descends from Heaven, so that the court will endure for 10,000 years, and there will be peace and tranquillity on earth below'.

(*Below*) Examples of the standardized weights and measures imposed by Qin Shihuangdi.

Wall, extended and consolidated by the emperor's command, now stretched over 2,500 miles (4,000 km) and delimited the western and northern frontiers, providing a defence against the mounted nomads of the steppes. In the east, large stone tablets recorded his successes and the extent of his domain:

> Wherever the sun and moon shine,
> Wherever one can go by boat or by carriage,
> Men obey the orders
> And satisfy his [the sovereign's] desires...

Finally, Shihuangdi tried to standardize thought. His grandiose projects, reckoned to absorb 15 per cent of the population, were leading to widespread unrest. Nearly three quarters of a million men were conscripted to build his palace and tomb; in Chinese folklore it is said that one man died for every metre of the Great Wall. As criticism mounted, Qin Shihuangdi ordered the Burning of the Books, an act for which he will never be forgiven by Chinese scholars. All the classics, works by the great liberal philosophers of earlier periods which were used to attack his authoritarian rule, were burned; scholars who disobeyed were branded and sent to work on the Great Wall and the 460 most recalcitrant dissenters were buried alive.

Good or evil, these were all the actions of a resolute man following a practical aim – the unification of the empire. There was, however, another side to the emperor's character. He was deeply superstitious and terrified of dying. Three assassination attempts left him with a morbid fear of attack and it was a crime punishable by death to reveal his whereabouts. Each night he slept in a different place, moving from palace to palace along closed corridors, and travelled with two carriages so that would-be assassins would not know where to strike. Seeking immortality he consulted soothsayers and shamans, sought elixirs and life-giving herbs, sacrificed to mountain and river spirits and travelled to the east, sending delegations of young men and virgins to contact the immortals in the fabled Isles of Penglai across the Eastern Sea.

THE TERRACOTTA ARMY OF THE FIRST EMPEROR OF CHINA

The army discovered in 1974 by farmers digging for a well at Lintong, to the east of modern-day Xian in the Shaanxi province, has no comparison in world history. Placed in perfect battle formation, over 7,000 figures are portrayed with such realism that they were at first believed to be individual portraits. Slightly larger than life, the men reflect the ethnic diversity of an army drawn from all over the empire. Every detail of clothing is shown, down to the studs on an archer's shoe to stop him slipping. Their metal weapons, including two-sided swords coated with anti-corrosive substances, are still so sharp that they can cut through a thick leather shield.

The figures were placed in three pits to the east of the First Emperor's tomb. The first pit (*see pp. 22–23*) contained some 6,000 infantry with a few chariots and horses; the second a mixture of 1,400 soldiers and cavalry, the third, the headquarters with 68 senior officers. A fourth pit was empty, unfinished when the emperor died. Confirming the offensive nature of Qin Shihuangdi's army, the vanguard wear neither armour nor shields; lightly clad for swift movement, their survival depends on successful attack with long spears and halberds. Even the rearguard have only half-armour. The officers, with epaulettes showing rank, are taller than the troops, and the horses, with red lips and dilated nostrils, are sturdy and well-fed. The army stands at attention, caught at the moment before battle as if awaiting the command to advance. Even today the sense of pent-up power is overwhelming.

The prime role of this army was not to defend but to complete a three-dimensional picture of the empire below ground. Recent excavations show that this picture spread far beyond the tomb itself. To the north of the army hundreds of small pits with grooms and live horse burials have been found representing the imperial stables and menageries; outside the western entrance to the tomb were two beautiful bronze chariots (*bottom*), each with a charioteer and four horses, waiting to convey the deceased emperor to the land of the immortals. The army was thus an essential part of Qin Shihuangdi's preparations for his life in the next world: no picture of his rule would be complete without his main source of power.

The scale of production is staggering. Modern workers find it difficult to reproduce large quantities of small replicas, let alone full-size figures. The sheer quantity of raw materials, the number and size of kilns, the detailed accuracy and planning and mobilization of a workforce with the

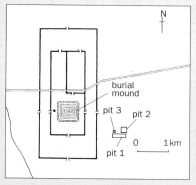

Previous pages: Overall view of the infantry in Pit 1.

(Below) Bronze chariot, charioteer and horses reconstructed from nearly 3,500 pieces and weighing 1,200kg.

(Above, left) Plan of the First Emperor's tomb and view of the tomb's tumulus (above) with Mount Li in the background. After over two millennia, the mound is still nearly 165 ft (50 m) high with a circumference of nearly 1 mile (1.5 km). The tomb lay on an east–west axis; the army pits are close to the eastern approach.

necessary skills imply an extraordinary degree of organization and talent. Production was based on a high degree of specialization within a conveyor belt system – a method developed a thousand years earlier for the mass-production of clay moulds for bronze ritual vessels in the Bronze Age. Bodies were made from two moulds – front and back for humans, left and right for horses; heads and limbs were made separately, with a choice of positions and these were then assembled to create the desired model. This model was then covered with layers of fine clay in which hair, beard, eyes, mouth and muscles were carved Finally, moulded parts such as noses, ears, rivets of armour and straps were added. After firing, the figure was painted in the colours of its section of the army. This process, combining mass-production with individual detail, was so successful that it has been used ever since for clay figures made for tombs.

(Left) Unarmoured officer. Only officers, who were always taller than common soldiers, wore headgear.

(Right) Kneeling archer. The sole of his right shoe is modelled with studs which prevented slipping.

(Right, centre) Lightly armoured soldier from the rearguard.

(Far right) Infantry general with epaulettes. No figure of a commander-in-chief has been found, presumably because the emperor, who could not be portrayed, held this role.

(Right, below) The disparate origins of an army drawn from all over the empire are reflected in the widely differing features and hairstyles.

(Below) The pits had a framework of wooden pillars and crossbeams; the roof of woven matting was covered with clay. When the dynasty fell, rebels set fire to the pits and the intense heat baked the soil hard, thus preserving the warriors.

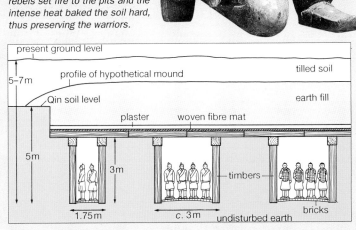

present ground level

profile of hypothetical mound — tilled soil

5–7m

Qin soil level — earth fill

plaster — woven fibre mat

5m — 3m

— timbers —

1.75m — c. 3m — bricks

undisturbed earth

(Right) Ming dynasty woodcuts depicting the Burning of the Books and the burying alive of recalcitrant scholars.

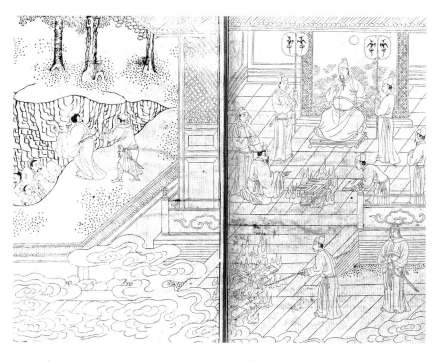

(Below) For the Han dynasty (206BC–220AD), Qin Shihuangdi was a tyrant and numerous tomb reliefs portray the assassination attempt by Jing Ke, minister of Yan, a state threatened by Qin. Jing Ke, seizing the emperor's sleeve, tries to kill him with a poisoned dagger but Qin Shihuangdi pulls his sleeve off and seeks refuge behind a pillar. Rubbing from the Wu family shrines, Shandong, 2nd century BC.

In later years the First Emperor suffered from melancholy. Preoccupied with death, he ordered court poets and musicians to write and play songs about the immortals, and his tomb was designed to safeguard his position in the next world. According to the historian Sima Qian, its underground chamber reproduced the cosmos: the stars and planets were set in pearls in its copper-domed ceiling, a magnificent palace with copper pillars was filled with attendants and every imaginable luxury and around it the great rivers and seas of China were reproduced in mercury. Automatic crossbows guarded the tomb from grave robbers and when the emperor was buried, his son ordered all childless concubines and all the workers who knew the secrets of the tomb to be buried alive with him. Such were the tomb's wonders that the terracotta army which so impresses us today was not even mentioned.

Qin Shihuangdi died whilst on a trip to the eastern shore. The emperor's wily adviser, Li Si, kept his death secret whilst he manipulated the succession, forging an edict ordering the liberal crown prince, Fu Su, to commit suicide. The emperor's body was brought back to the capital in one of the imperial carriages; to avert suspicion (it was summer and the trip took six weeks), a cartload of salted fish was added to the convoy. With a forged will, Li then installed a younger son, the prince Hu Hai, as Er Shi, the Second Emperor.

ER SHI	
Born	*Father*
230 BC, as Prince	Qin Shihuangdi
Hu Hai	(2nd son of)
Accession	*Mother*
210 BC, as Er Shi	Unknown
('The Second	*Died*
Emperor')	207 BC, by suicide

ER SHI

My father began as the king of a single state, yet he founded the empire. He repelled the barbarians, pacified the country, and built palaces to mark his success....Now during the two years of my reign, brigands have been making trouble on all sides....You are neither carrying out the wishes of the First Emperor nor are you working loyally for me. You are unfit for office!

Memorandum from Er Shi to his grand councillor, Li Si, 209 BC

It was a short-lived victory. **Er Shi** (210–207 BC), who acceded at the age of 20, was a dissolute character totally under the thumb of his unscrupulous and ambitious eunuch tutor, Zhao Gao, with whom he swiftly purged possible opponents including Li Si. Ministers, princes, army officers and all their families were killed and 'ten princesses torn limb from limb'.

Whilst Er Shi withdrew from public affairs to a life of extravagant indolence within the palace grounds, Zhao increased taxes and punishments. The already restless population were driven to rebellion by a decision to conscript peasants for military service. The initial spark was lit in 208 BC by a poor peasant, Chen She, in the Yangzi Valley. When the peasant Chen, who had been conscripted, mutinied, his example was followed by thousands in the same plight and trouble spread like wildfire. Writing about this period, the Han scholar Tong Zhongshu noted: 'The poor often wore the clothing of oxen and horses and ate the food of dogs and swine. They were burdened by avaricious and oppressive officials, and executions increased in an arbitrary manner. The people...fled into the mountains and forest and became brigands.' When the leaders of the former feudal states rose against the government, the empire disintegrated.

Er Shi refused to listen to bad news and appears to have been mentally disturbed, suffering from ominous dreams. His humiliation was complete when Zhao, in a vicious display of dominance, confirmed the emperor's fear of delusions by forcing officials to affirm that a stag (which the emperor had recognized as such) was a horse. When Er Shi, with a last flicker of courage, tried to rebuke Zhao in 206 BC, the eunuch occupied the palace with his own troops and forced the emperor to commit suicide. He then installed Er Shi's nephew, prince Ziying, as king of Qin, for by now the empire had ceased to exist.

The new king reigned 46 days, surrendering to Liu Bang, future founder of the Han dynasty; Liu spared his life but a month later, another general, Xiang Yu, had the king and all members of the Qin imperial family beheaded, sacking the capital in a fire that burned for three months. As a later Chinese critic, Jin Yi, commented, the Qin dynasty had fallen because: 'When a man has the rank of the Son of Heaven, and all the wealth of the empire as his riches, and yet cannot escape being massacred, it is because he has failed to distinguish between the means by which power is safeguarded and the causes which lead to disaster.'

What is splendid about possessing an empire is being able to do as you please and satisfy your desires.... In name we are lord of ten thousand chariots, but not in fact. Thus I want a retinue of not a thousand but ten thousand chariots to match my title.

The emperor Er Shi

WESTERN HAN DYNASTY
206–87 BC

 高帝 **Gaodi**
206–195 BC

惠帝 **Huidi**
195–188 BC

吕后 **Lu Hou** (regent)
188–180 BC

文帝 **Wendi**
180–157 BC

景帝 **Jingdi**
157–141 BC

武帝 **Wudi**
141–87 BC

The emperor Han Gaodi. Watercolour from an 18th-century Ming album of imperial portraits (British Library).

GAODI	
Born	*Children*
247 BC, as Liu Bang, also known as Liu Ji	8 sons, 1 daughter
Titles before accession	*Died*
	195 BC; killed by an arrow while fighting against the king of Huainan
Lord of Pei (209 BC); king of Han (206 BC)	
Accession	*Temple name*
206 BC	Gaodi ('High Emperor') or Gaozu ('High Progenitor')
Wife	
empress Lu	*Note on Western Han tombs*
Major concubines	All that remains above ground of the Western Han tombs are the tumuli near Xi'an, Shaanxi.
(1) consort Cao	
(2) consort Zhao	
(3) consort Qi	
(4) consort Bo	

GAODI

If any of the princes or governors discovers a man of talent and virtue under his jurisdiction, he should personally invite him to serve the government...An official who knows a virtuous man within his jurisdiction and chooses not to report it shall lose his position. However, he should not send a man who is either too old or suffering from chronic disease.

Decree by Han Gaodi 196 BC

Liu Bang (later the emperor **Gaodi**) is one of the great heroes of Chinese history. Born a peasant who turned bandit, he became emperor of China and founder of the Han dynasty which ruled for 400 years. As a minor official in central China he rebelled and raised a large following which joined forces with the main anti-Qin army under its leader, Xiang Yu. The two men soon fell out; whereas Liu Bang had urged moderation towards the defeated Qin, forbidding looting and sparing his royal captives, Xiang Yu had the capital Xianyang destroyed and the entire Qin family slaughtered.

Er Shi commits suicide; **Gaodi of Western Han emperor**

Rosetta Stone engraved **Huidi emperor**

Lu Hou regent

Han begin to mint own copper coins; ban on private minting disregarded

Wendi emperor

First state examinations for civil service recruitment

210   200   190   180   170

The conflict between them was more than a question of personalities: it was a battle between old and new, between the aristocrat and the peasant, the former kingdoms and the unified state. The fall of the empire had revived the ambitions and rivalry of the former feudal states and the aristocratic Xiang Yu attempted to restore the former kingdoms under the imperial rule of his own Chu state. Liu Bang, king of Han since 206 BC, opposed this return to feudalism and from his strong base in Sichuan embarked on the conquest of China. By 202 BC, he had defeated Xiang Yu and declared himself as the emperor Gaodi of the Han dynasty. His capital, Chang'an (modern Xi'an), was placed strategically on the banks of the River Wei near the ruins of the old Qin capital Xianyang.

Gaodi's first task was to re-establish the unity of the empire. Slowly he brought the separate provinces and kingdoms back under central control by replacing all but one of their rulers with his brothers or sons.

Five years of war had brought famine and rampant inflation; the economy was in ruins and on his accession Gaodi could not even find four horses of the same colour for his chariot. To restore public finances he practised strict economy, living frugally and avoiding public works and foreign military ventures. When unable to defeat China's traditional enemies in the northwest, the Xiongnu (powerful nomads of Turkic origin), he bought peace by offering their ruler a Han princess in marriage and sending tribute. The worst excesses of the Qin penal code were reformed but the basic Qin administrative system remained in force and merchants, blamed for speculation and profiteering, were taxed heavily and subject to new restrictions, being forbidden to wear silk, ride in carts or hold office.

(*Right*) Remains of the Xuanpingmen, the northernmost of the three gates in the Chang'an city east wall, which was excavated in 1957. Each of the twelve city gates had three gateways 6m wide — enough for four carriages to pass at the same time.

Jingdi emperor

Carthage destroyed by Romans under Scipio

Government monopoly of minting

Wudi emperor

Zhang Qian's first expedition to Central Asia

Canal built linking R. Wei with Yellow River

Introduction of copper wuzhu coins

Sale of military honours to meet war expenses

c.120 Great Wall extended to protect Silk Routes: total length 10,000 km

State monopoly of iron and salt

Zhang Qian's second expedition

160   150   140   130   120   110

CITIES OF THE HAN

The Chinese character for wall and city is the same and the defining characteristic of a Chinese city was its walls, marking an administrative boundary. Planned with straight lines and right-angles, cities were carefully orientated on a north–south axis to place them correctly within the cosmos. The Han capitals Chang'an and Luoyang were destroyed, but from surviving rammed-earth foundations of walls and terraces and literary records it has been possible to reconstruct their plans.

At its peak under Wudi, Chang'an was the largest city in the world, with

walls 15 miles (25 km) long on a rammed-earth base 52 ft (16 m) wide. Luoyang, ancient capital of the Eastern Zhou (8th–3rd centuries BC), was rebuilt by Guang Wudi (AD 25–57).

Its suburbs had a population of 500,000 making it the most populous city in the world. Rectangular, on a north–south axis, it had 12 gates and a grid system of streets; parts of the outer walls have survived to a height of 33 ft (10 m). The city was dominated by the Northern and Southern Palaces, each covering 125 acres (50 ha) and connected by an elevated covered passageway. The remainder of the city was divided into walled wards for offices, ministries and residences for nobles and officials as well as an arsenal, granary and market. The city was supplied by water pumped from a nearby river via a canal into the city moat.

Outside the walls were the imperial observatory (where the brilliant mathematician and scientist, Zhang Heng, the director of astrology, created his seismograph), the Academy (where 30,000 students were trained for the official examinations), two markets and a granary for relief. Beyond these lay the Altar of Heaven, funeral workshops and the imperial mausolea. The city was destroyed in the fighting following the massacre of eunuchs in 189.

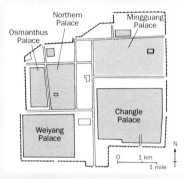

(Above) Map of the Western Han and Wang Mang capital, Chang'an . The irregular shape of the city in the north is due to a tributary of the River Wei.

(Above, centre) Tomb murals give detailed pictures of contemporary architecture. In this manor house complex, the entrance gate, in the southern wall, leads to a main hall at the far end of a long open courtyard; each of the small courtyards served different, specific purposes - private quarters for the women, sleeping quarters, storage rooms, kitchen, pigsty and at the rear, a tall watchtower.

(Left) A modern reconstruction of Zhang Heng's seismograph. The eight dragons on the upper section of the bowl represented eight compass points. When an earth tremor occurred, a ball in the mouth of the dragon facing the origin of the quake fell into the open mouth of the toad below. In this way, the authorities learned of the need for help in a particular region long before messengers from the stricken areas could arrive.

104-102 BC Han army reaches Ferghana; captives include Roman soldiers

Wudi dies; Zhaodi emperor

100   90   80   70   60

Above all, there was a change in attitude towards government. Qin Legalism was slowly replaced by an adaptation of Confucian theories known as Han Confucianism, based on the belief that in the long run, good government depended on consent, not force, a belief expounded by the Confucian saying: 'An empire can be conquered on horseback but not governed from a horse.'

Later historians used Gaodi's rise to power as an illustration of the doctrine of the Mantle of Heaven, endowing him with all the Confucian virtues of a civilized scholar. In fact, he was poorly educated, never lost his rural accent and his earthy vocabulary and behaviour shocked the upper classes. He once expressed his contempt for scholars by urinating in a scholar's formal hat. He was, however, extremely intelligent. A brilliant strategist, brave and generous, his strength lay in his ability to judge men and to accept advice. Against his own inclination for a simple life and his innate mistrust of scholars as impractical theoreticians, he accepted the main tenets of Confucianism, appointed scholars as ministers and agreed to an elaborate court ritual designed to strengthen his claim to legitimacy by associating it with the great Zhou dynasty of the Bronze Age. The Zhou rulers had been the first to call themselves Sons of Heaven and to claim the Mantle of Heaven; their early rule was therefore looked back on as a golden age in which all prospered.

HUIDI AND THE REGENT LU HOU

Gaodi was killed in 195 BC by a stray arrow in a frontier skirmish and the next 16 years were dominated by his widow, the dowager-empress Lu Hou. Said to have murdered four of Gaodi's other sons, mutilating and killing the mother of one, she terrified the new emperor, **Huidi** (Gaodi's eldest son) into submission and when he died without an official heir, she placed two puppet infants, Shaodi Kong and Shaodi Hong, the sons of Huidi's concubines, on the throne. Huidi, a gentle figure, encouraged ancestor worship of the ruler and established shrines to his father throughout the empire; he also eased the harshest Qin laws, repealing the edict ordering the Burning of the Books. Real power, however, rested with his mother, Lu, and her family who embarked on unsuccessful military campaigns in the west and south. On Lu Hou's death in 180 BC, the Lu family tried to seize the throne but Gaodi's three remaining sons foiled the attempt and the entire Lu clan was eliminated.

These events illustrated an inherent weakness in the new imperial system: the backstairs involvement of women in the administration. Once ensconced, an empress or favourite could use her power to further the ambitions of her own family, installing them in high positions. Since her influence usually ceased on her husband's death, however, there was a built-in incentive for these clans to try and seize power. This led to an endless succession of court intrigues often culminating, on the death of the empress, with the extermination of her entire family who would then be replaced by the relations of her successor.

HUIDI	
Born	*Children*
210 BC, as Liu Ying	At least 1 daughter
Accession	(murdered by
195 BC	empress Lu)
Father	*Died*
Gaodi (eldest son	188 BC
of)	*Temple name*
Mother	Huidi ('Beneficial
empress Lu	Emperor')
Wives	
empress Chang	

LU HOU (regent)	
Birth name	the infant rulers
Lu Zhi	Shaodi Kong and
Position	Shaodi Hong – the
empress Lu, wife of	sons of minor
Gaodi; mother of	consorts
the emperor Huidi	*Died*
and regent	180 BC
(188–180 BC) for	

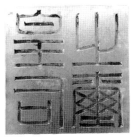

(*Above*) This tiger-shaped jade seal with inscription belonged to the empress Lu Hou and was found in the joint tomb of the empress and the emperor Gaozu.

CHINA'S GREAT PHILOSOPHIES – CONFUCIANISM AND DAOISM

Confucius (551–479 BC) gave China one of the most durable moral-political philosophies ever devised by man. Unsuccessful in worldly terms – a minor official who toured the Warring States vainly seeking a ruler who would adopt his policies – Confucius was recognized during his lifetime as a great thinker and teacher. After his death, his disciples used the *Analects*, a collection of his teachings in question and answer form, to spread the ideas which became the cornerstone of the imperial system, and which still exert influence in Asia today.

A humanist, moralist and political philosopher, Confucius was concerned with man's role in society, defining this in terms of reciprocal duties and obligations between the individual and his family, friends and ruler. Good behaviour depended on education and example since man was inherently good. As adapted by the Han, his doctrines created a highly efficient basis for government with moral and cosmic sanctions. The emperor, as contact between earth and heaven, ruled with the Mandate of Heaven; if things went badly and the people suffered it showed that he had lost this mandate and rebellion was justified. Confucius's emphasis on education provided the ruler with an official class with a common educational background stressing morality, moderation and respect for authority.

Daoism was concerned with the individual's relationship to nature and the other world. The main Daoist texts are the *Dao de Jing* ('The Way and Power Classic'), attributed to Laozi, believed to have lived in the 6th century BC, and a collection of writings known by the name of their author, *Zhuangzi*, from the 3rd to 4th centuries AD. Its doctrines were diffuse, embodying local cults and animistic beliefs, and its fundamental tenet – the existence of a single cosmic force (the *Dao* or 'Way') which animated all matter led to an ideal which complemented but was almost diametrically opposed to Confucianism. The Daoist ideal was to merge like a drop of water in the ocean, and where Confucians preached duty, Daoists urged non-action, harmony depending on acceptance of the Way. Its close association with nature and rejection of social restrictions attracted artists, poets and recluses, while its professed ability to contact the spirit world through magic gave it wide popular appeal. Daoists were China's earliest scientists, studying the physical laws and experimenting with herbs, metals and chemicals in their search for medicines, alchemy and long life.

Tomb relief showing a mythical meeting between Confucius and the legendary founder of Daoism, Laozi.

(Above) Remnants of the oldest known Daoist texts; a silk book from 179BC.

(Below) In Lingdi's reign, the major texts of Confucius were inscribed on 46 large stone slabs 2.3m high in an open-air library for scholars at the state university at Luoyang.

For most Chinese, the two philosophies were seen as complementary rather than opposites. A Confucian official could well be a Daoist in private or in retirement, and the extraordinary complexity and richness of the Han period – in particular, the apparent contrast between a highly practical approach to social and economic problems and an all-pervading preoccupation with the search for immortality – reflect the interaction between the two.

(Left) The ancient Daoist idea of yin/yang – a harmonious whole made up of two complementary opposing forces – is still alive today. In this Ming dynasty ink slab, the yin/yang symbol is surrounded by the Eight Trigrams – 8 groups of broken lines which formed the basis of ancient divination practices.

WENDI	
Born	*Wife*
202 BC, Liu Heng	empress Dou (died
Title before accession	135)
King of Dai (196 BC)	*Children*
Accession	5 sons
180 BC	*Died*
Father	157 BC
Gaodi (5th son of)	*Temple name*
Mother	Wendi ('Literary
consort Bo	Emperor')

JINGDI	
Born	(2) consort Cheng
188 BC, as Liu Qi	(3) consort Deng
Accession	(4) consort Wang
157 BC	*Children*
Father	14 sons, all made
Wendi (5th son of)	kings
Mother	*Died*
empress Dou	141 BC
Wives	*Temple name*
(1) empress Bo	Jingdi ('Admired
(died 150 BC)	Emperor')
(2) empress Wang	
Major concubines	
(1) consort Li	

WENDI AND JINGDI

I have heard that Heaven installs rulers to govern the people it creates and that it will warn a ruler with natural disasters if he has lost virtue or if his rule has become unjust. On the eleventh month of this year there was an eclipse of the sun. No natural disaster can be more serious than this: Heaven has reproached me!

Han Wendi 178 BC

Stability was restored by Gaodi's surviving sons who deliberately chose their half-brother **Wendi** as emperor in 180 BC because his mother had no powerful relatives. Wendi and his son Jingdi firmly established Confucianism as the governing philosophy. Historians describe their reigns as an ideal period in which wise rulers, living with modesty and decorum, consulted and entrusted state affairs to their Confucian-educated ministers, and, under the influence of Wendi's Daoist wife, the empress Dou, avoided wasteful foreign ventures.

The peaceful succession from father to son in 157 BC gave a much needed sense of continuity and permanence to the dynasty. The economy was stabilized, trade prospered and government warehouses were filled with grain for relief in times of flood or famine. The burdens on merchants were reduced and by 168 BC the economy had improved so much that Wendi first halved and then removed the tax on produce, only reimposing it at a reduced rate at the end of his reign. In a move of lasting importance in 165 BC, he introduced recruitment to the civil service through examinations based on knowledge of Confucian texts. Confucianism was thus ensconced at the heart of the education system and, through imperially sponsored institutes, talented scholars were recruited and trained for government service. Under **Jingdi**, the emphasis on moral values in the examinations was strengthened and the importance of agriculture recognized. A contemporary register shows

(Right) Reliefs on tomb bricks illustrate the importance of agriculture. These peasants wear typical cross-over robes over short trousers tied below the knee. Tomb relief, Sichuan, 1st–2nd century AD.

WESTERN HAN TOMBS

The search for immortality and the Confucian emphasis on filial piety which dominated Han life led to an explosion in tomb expenditure. In an age of conspicuous consumption, tombs became status symbols, visible expressions of virtue and wealth, and court officials, large landowners and rich merchants vied with each other in ostentatious burials.

For nearly a century the use of underground armies in pits outside the tomb continued, but unlike the First Emperor's warriors, the figures are miniatures, averaging 24 in (60 cm) in height. Royal tombs from the late 2nd century BC were guarded by armies of 3,000–4,000 warriors and cavalry, and in 1990 a complex covering an area five times that of the Terracotta Army was discovered just south of Yangling, the

joint tomb of the emperor Han Jingdi (praised by historians for his frugality) and his wife, the empress Wang. Twenty-four pits are filled with over 40,000 clay figures, one-third life size, originally with movable arms and clothing of silk and hemp. As well as soldiers, whose loose formations and gentle, often smiling expressions contrast vividly with the stern and disciplined troops of the First Emperor, there are domestic animals, agricultural machinery, carts and tools, weights and measures and storage jars filled with real grain. The weapons and farm implements are of bronze, iron and wood. Excavations are still continuing but already it is clear that this is a picture of a prosperous society based on agriculture.

From c. 140 BC onwards, such 'outside burials' were replaced by costly stone monuments and statuary above ground and a concentration of offerings in the tomb itself. Acting on the maxim 'treat the dead as if alive', tombs were designed like dwellings, either excavated horizontally into the rock or in pits with side chambers and carved or painted windows, doors and roof tiles. Rising standards of living stimulated artistic

(Left) In 1965, over 3,000 miniature cavalry and foot soldiers were found in a Han royal tomb c. 179–141 BC at Yangjiawan, Xianyang. Made from moulds and painted, the figures give a vivid illustration of contemporary cavalry formations (Xianyang Museum, Shaanxi province).

(Right) This perfectly preserved silk painted banner is a unique example of early Han pictorial art. It portrays the journey of the deceased from the land of the living (the central section) to the land of the immortals above. The bottom section represents the underworld. Mawangdui, Changsha.

(Below) It was believed that jade protected the body from decay and Liu Sheng's corpse was clad in a jade suit made from 2,156 jade wafers sewn together with gold thread (Hebei Provincial Museum).

production and the staggering variety of tomb goods reveals very high technical skills. Corpses have been found clad in spectacular jade suits, made from thousands of small plaques sewn with gold or silver thread according to the rank of the deceased, designed to prevent decay. Mid-2nd-century BC tombs at Mawangdui, Changsha, Hebei, contain exquisite silk artifacts: the mummified body of Lady Dai was wrapped in 20 garments bound with silk ribbons and covered with a silk banner – the earliest known Chinese painting – depicting her journey to the land of the immortals. Around her were 46 rolls of silk clothing – plain taffetas and brightly coloured embroidered silks and gauzes. Lacquer objects (prized second only to jade) ranged from lacquer paintings of immortals on coffins to double-eared cups and finely decorated toilet boxes with cosmetics.

As the Western Han period progressed there was a shift in decoration from mystical subjects to reality, reflecting the increasing conviction that life after death was merely an extension of this existence. The deceased were provided with texts of the classics on bamboo and silken slips, with maps, medicines, food and money. The new naturalistic style can be seen in beautiful bronzes with simple flowing lines such as a smoke-free lamp in the form of a kneeling girl. Her sleeve, acting as a chimney, draws the smoke down into the body of the lamp, thus avoiding pollution.

(Above) Plan of Liu Sheng's tomb, Mancheng. The tomb was built like a real house with stables and storerooms flanking the entrance; behind the central hall was the coffin chamber with a bathroom to its left.

(Right) Gilded with bright gold, this lamp in the form of a kneeling palace maid, epitomizes the high technical and artistic standards of the time. Both the strength and direction of the lamp's light are adjustable and the girl's arm acts as a chimney, leaving the room smoke-free. Changxin Palace lamp, from the tomb of princess Dou Wan, Mancheng, Hebei, second half of 2nd century BC.

(Above) In 1968 the tombs of an early Western Han prince, Liu Sheng and his wife, the princess Dou Wan, were found at Mancheng, Hebei. The tombs, tunnelled into the rock, were intact and contained over 2,800 funeral objects including jade shrouds, horses and chariots. Second half of 2nd century BC.

(Right) Han lacquer toiletry box with inlaid silver cloud patterns, 2nd-3rd century AD (British Museum).

(*Right*) In March 1990, a vast miniature terracotta army was discovered in 24 pits south of the mausoleum of Han Jingdi. The pits cover 96,000 square metres, five times the total area of Qin Shihuangdi's four pits; preliminary reports indicate that they include a minimum of 40,000 figures. One third life size, the figures had flexible arms and after being modelled and painted flesh-colour with black hair, eyebrows, and eyes, were clad in silk or hempen clothing.

that 90 per cent of the population lived on the land; peasants were subject to two years' military conscription and one month's corvée labour on public works such as road repairs, bridge building or transporting grain.

Behind this successful and practical approach to social and economic problems, however, burned a passionate interest in the afterlife and a desire for immortality. The wealth uncovered in Western Han tombs (see feature pp. 34–35) belies the official picture of frugality. The excavation of exquisite bronzes, jades, silks and lacquers as well as vast miniature terracotta armies reflects contemporary extravagance. This was an age of luxury which could afford to pamper the dead.

WUDI

WUDI	
Born	*Major concubines*
157 BC, as Liu Che	(1) consort Li
Title before accession	(2) consort Zhao
King of Jiaodong	(3) consort Wang
(153–150 BC)	(4) consort Li
Accession	*Children*
141 BC	at least 1 son, 4
Father	daughters
Jingdi (eldest son	*Died*
of)	87 BC
Wives	*Temple name*
(1) empress Chen	Wudi ('Martial
(deposed 130 BC)	Emperor')
(2) empress Wei	
(suicide 91 BC)	

The prime duty of all ministers is to formulate policies, unify the people, universalize our culture and cultivate good customs. The Five Emperors [the legendary Sages] brought peace and prosperity to the country because they emphasized love and righteousness as the moral foundation of the nation. I never cease to hope that I can attain this goal.

Decree of Han Wudi 128 BC

Wudi had one of the longest reigns in imperial history. King of Jiaodong at four and Heir Apparent at nine, he dominated the history of China for 54 years, and yet information about his personal life is surprisingly scant. What little we have is full of contradictions. He was not a military man, taking no active part in campaigns, yet under his rule China almost doubled the size of her empire. He espoused Confucianism and

REIGN TITLES

Wudi introduced a new system of titles whereby he changed his name every few years. This innovation became a permanent feature and henceforth emperors chose new names for magical reasons, or, like political slogans, to celebrate an auspicious event or mark the beginning of a new era. Previously years were dated by the length of reign, e.g. '3rd year of Han Gaozu'; now they were known by the reign name – '4th year of the New Beginning' or '1st year of Vast Imperial Power'.

founded an Imperial Academy to train future officials in the classics, while exercising his imperial prerogatives to the full, counterbalancing the influence of ministers and officials with his own advisers. Obsessed with the search for immortality, Wudi richly rewarded magicians or alchemists, offering elixirs of longevity, giving one such 'wizard' a marquisate, a fiefdom of 200,000 households, 1,000 slaves and his own eldest daughter as bride with a dowry of 10,000 lb (4,500 kg) of gold. His extravagance and the luxury of his court are legendary – the palaces were filled with rare imports from the West and his famous hunting parks were designed like microcosms of the universe, with artificial lakes and mountains and stone figures to attract wandering spirits.

Wudi had all the characteristics of a despot. While well-educated and fond of literature, he was ruthlessly ambitious and lacked self-discipline, brooking no criticism and subject to violent rages. He was, however, an efficient administrator who believed in maximizing revenues through strict control of the population and economy. Surviving fragments of imperial edicts deal with dates for planting and harvesting, crop types and yields. He encouraged horsebreeding for military purposes, imposed state monopolies of minting, iron, salt and later alcohol and attempted to control prices, using government caravans to trade in border areas. With conscript and convict labour, he repaired the Yellow River dykes and improved grain supplies to Chang'an with a canal 80 miles (125 km) long, linking the capital to the great river.

In the early part of his reign these measures were successful: the treasury was said to be so full that the strings holding the coins together were rotting, warehouses overflowed and villagers enjoyed abundant meat and grain. Once the restraining influence of the Daoist dowager-empress Dou was removed, however, in 135 BC, Wudi embarked on foreign ventures which nearly brought the empire to its knees.

The emperor's reaction to border encroachments was conquest. His armies advanced in the south, the north and the west. The southern coastal states of Zhejiang and Fujian were occupied and their populations moved inland; by 111 BC the independent kingdom of Nanyue (modern Guangdong, Guanxi and North Vietnam) was defeated and brought under Chinese political influence. Wudi invaded Korea, establishing military settlements which survived until the early 4th century – some of the finest of all Han tomb artifacts have been found in tombs in this region. The emperor's main problem, however, was with the Xiongnu in the northwest. These nomadic tribes of the steppes,

(*Below*) Salt mining was a major industry in Sichuan province. Wells, such as the one on the lower left corner, were drilled to extract brine which was led through bamboo pipes to evaporation pans (lower right). Two peasants carry bags of salt on their backs while others, in the typically mountainous Sichuanese countryside, hunt wild game. Relief from a tomb near Chengdu, Sichuan, 2nd century AD.

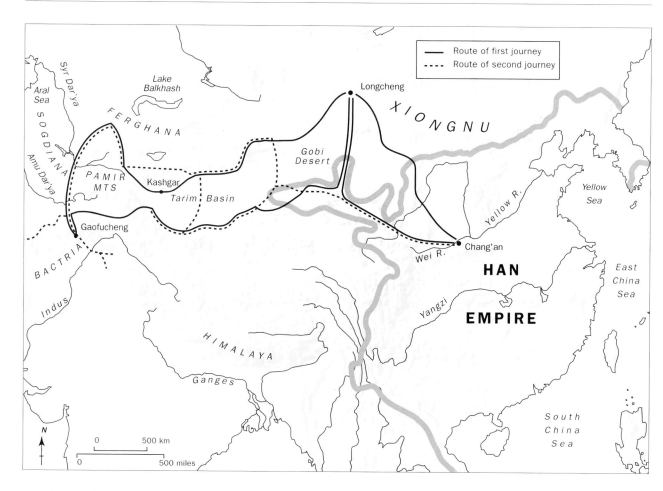

Map showing the routes of Han Wudi's envoy Zhang Qian in 139 BC and 115 BC. His epic journeys, the first lasting over twelve years, brought him to the eastern edges of the Greek world, and the produce and political and cultural information he brought back revolutionized Chinese knowledge of foreign lands, laying the basis for their dramatic expansion westwards.

whose dominion stretched from western Manchuria across Mongolia and southern Siberia into Chinese Turkestan, posed a perpetual threat to the empire whose rich lands acted like a magnet. Despite earlier imperial attempts at appeasement, they repeatedly invaded China, in 166 BC even getting within sight of the capital. Wudi determined to overcome this threat and in a series of massive campaigns drove the Xiongnu back to the Gobi desert. It was a bitter war of attrition – waves of 50,000–100,000 cavalry and men were decimated – but eventually the Chinese succeeded in controlling the approaches to Central Asia, and the Great Wall was extended to enclose the Gansu corridor which was colonized by 700,000 Chinese.

These military victories were supplemented by diplomatic missions and in 139 BC Wudi sent an envoy, Zhang Qian, to seek allies among the states beyond the Xiongnu. Although Zhang Qian failed in his main aim, his extraordinary journeys – the first lasting 12 years – took him as far as Bactria and Ferghana (modern Turkestan), and he returned with valuable information about the states of Central Asia and hearsay about the distant Roman empire. In 104 and 102 BC and again in 42 BC, Chinese armies crossed the Pamirs, reaching Ferghana and the former Greek kingdom of Sogdiana where they defeated a force of Xiongnu and

captive Roman soldiers. Crossing deserts and some of the world's highest mountains Wudi's troops reached places over 2,000 miles (3,000 km) from their capital, thus surpassing the achievements of even the Roman legions.

This expansion had far-reaching consequences, opening the trade routes between China and the West. Traffic along the Silk Roads flourished and the Han capital was flooded with Western travellers and luxuries. The burden of the wars, however, broke the economy and the Western Han never fully recovered. The state coffers were emptied, conscription and heavy taxation ruined agriculture; the gap between wealthy landlords and impoverished peasants widened, with the latter fleeing to the mountains, leaving the land untilled. A swollen administration milked the tax system while merchants profiteered.

The long wars had weakened central control and economic problems were compounded by the rise of powerful families challenging imperial authority. Officials and consorts manoeuvred to influence the succession, favouring minors and weaklings whom they could dominate. The rivalry was so intense that Wudi was unable to nominate an heir. In 91 BC, open war broke out when the powerful Li family attacked Wudi's wife, the empress Wei, and her family, who had dominated court politics for nearly 50 years and were blamed for its extravagance. In a five-day battle, during which Wudi sought refuge in the countryside, almost the entire Wei family were exterminated and the empress committed suicide. When Wudi died four years later, his eight-year-old successor, Zhaodi, had only been named Heir Apparent two days earlier, having been chosen on the grounds that he was motherless and related to neither the Wei nor the Li families.

(*Above*) After Zhang Qian's reports on the spirited horses of Ferghana, their acquisition became of major importance. Ferghana horses like this gilt-bronze model were known as 'flying' or 'heavenly' horses for their speed and prized far above the local short-legged breeds.

(*Below*) This hollow brick, with the White Tiger of the west indicating its alignment, was found among the ruins of buildings at Han Wudi's tomb, Maoling.

WESTERN HAN
87 BC–AD 23

昭 帝 **Zhaodi**
87–74 BC

宣 帝 **Xuandi**
74–49 BC

元 帝 **Yuandi**
49–33 BC

成 帝 **Chengdi**
33–7 BC

哀 帝 **Aidi**
7–1 BC

平 帝 **Pingdi**
1 BC–AD 6

孺 子 **Ruzi**
AD 7–9

王 莽 **Wang Mang**
AD 9–23

WESTERN HAN	
ZHAODI	*Accession*
Born	74 BC
95 BC, as Liu Fuling	*Father*
Accession	Wudi's son and heir
87 BC	apparent, Liu Ju,
Father	who committed
Wudi	suicide in 91 BC
Mother	*Wives*
consort Zhao	(1) empress Xu
Wife	(poisoned by
Name unknown, a	empress Huo 71
daughter of a	BC)
statesman, Shang	(2) empress Huo
Guanan	(3) empress Wang
Children	(died 16 BC)
none	*Children*
Died	At least 1 son
74 BC	*Died*
Temple name	49 BC
Zhaodi ('Shining	*Temple name*
Emperor')	Xuandi ('Proclaimed
	Emperor')
XUANDI	
Born	
91 BC, as Liu Bingyi	

ZHAODI TO RUZI

The imposition of punishment adversely affects the life of the punished. Its purpose should be not more than the prevention of violence and the forestalling of wrongdoings: to punish one person so that all others can live in peace and security. An official is considered just and equitable if the punishment he chooses does not cause the living to complain and the spirit of the dead to resent.

Decree of Xuandi 72 BC

The Western Han never recovered from the burden of Wudi's wars. **Zhaodi** (87–74 BC) died in suspicious circumstances at the age of 22 and was replaced by a grandson of Wudi and the consort Li – a dissolute and uncouth youth called Liu He, who is not recognized in the official list of emperors. Twenty-seven days later Liu He was ousted by the officials for 'lacking the requisite qualities of respect and decorum' and for sexual indulgences. His successor, **Xuandi** (74–49 BC), was a grandson of Wudi and the empress Wei whose life had been saved by a friendly warden during the rising of 91 BC. Brought up as a commoner, he was unable to control the wealthy families. Xuandi's first empress, Xu, mother of his son,

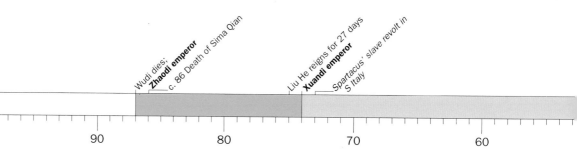

Wudi dies:
Zhaodi emperor
c. 86 Death of Sima Qian

Liu He reigns for 27 days
Xuandi emperor
Spartacus' slave revolt in
S Italy

100   90   80   70   60

Yuandi (49–33 BC), was poisoned by the concubine Huo, who replaced Xu as empress and whose father, Huo Guang, was so wealthy that he was buried in a jade suit.

Zhaodi, Xuandi and Yuandi all adopted what were known as 'reformist' policies aimed at easing public misery by avoiding military ventures, reducing taxes and modifying the harsh penal code. Xuandi remitted taxes and cut official salaries; Yuandi ruthlessly cut the imperial establishments, forbidding banquets, reducing expenditure on hunting lodges and parks and drastically pruning the imperial shrines at which 24,555 meals a day were being provided by a staff of over 42,000

MODERNISTS VS. REFORMISTS

The later Western Han reigns were marked by a power struggle between 'modernists' and 'reformists'. Both groups supported their doctrines by reference to earlier dynasties. The modernists believed in using state resources to strengthen China and drew on Qin legalist ideas, stressing the practical, material aims of government. The reformists extolled the Zhou dynasty, now regarded as an example of moral government. Both accepted that agriculture came first, and trade and commerce second; they differed over the degree of government control and intervention in the economy. Wudi and the modernists believed in maximizing revenue by allowing landowners to exploit unused land and create large estates even when this involved the consequent dispossessing of peasant smallholders. They advocated state control of the means of production and of mines, and established state monopolies of salt and iron. They favoured strict control of prices and markets including active participation with state caravans trading in border regions. The reformists attacked the inequalities which such a system produced, urging a limitation of the size of landholdings, and argued that the aim of government should be to alleviate the lot of the people, not to embark on commercial ventures or foreign trade.

(Below) When a minor provincial official, Chu Yun, attempted to persuade Han Chengdi to remove corrupt officials, the incensed emperor ordered Chu to be removed and executed. Chu hung on to a balustrade which broke but after one of Chengdi's leading generals had offered to die in Chu's place, the emperor relented and ordered that the broken balustrade be left as a reminder of an honest official.

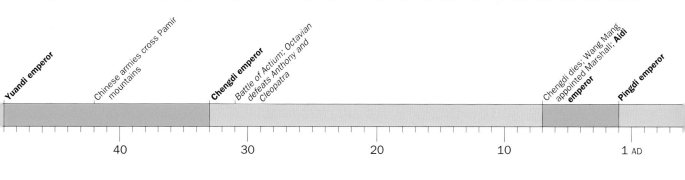

Yuandi emperor

Chinese armies cross Pamir mountains

Chengdi emperor

Battle of Actium; Octavian defeats Anthony and Cleopatra

Chengdi dies; Wang Mang appointed Marshall; **Aidi** emperor

Pingdi emperor

40   30   20   10   1 AD

WESTERN HAN

YUANDI
Born
  75 BC, as Liu Shi
Title before accession
  Heir Apparent (67 BC)
Accession
  49 BC
Father
  Xuandi
Mother
  empress Xu
Wives
  (1) empress Fu
  (2) empress Feng
  (3) empress Wang
Children
  At least 1 son
Died
  33 BC
Temple name
  Yuandi ('Original Emperor')

CHENGDI
Born
  51 BC, as Liu Ao
Title before accession
  Heir Apparent (48 BC)
Accession
  33 BC
Father
  Yuandi
Mother
  empress Wang
Wives
  (1) empress Xu (deposed 18 BC)
  (2) empress Zhao
Major concubines
  (1) consort Pan
  (2) consort Zhao
Children
  2 sons by consorts murdered
Died
  7 BC
Temple name
  Chengdi ('Accomplished Emperor')

AIDI
Born
  26 BC, as Liu Xin
Titles before accession
  King of Dingtao (22 BC); Heir Apparent (8 BC)

Accession
  7 BC
Family connections
  grandson of Yuandi; half-nephew of Chengdi
Father
  Liu Kang
Mother
  Ding
Wives
  (1) empress Ding
  (2) empress Fu
Children
  no sons
Died
  1 BC
Temple name
  Aidi ('Sorrowing Emperor')

PINGDI
Born
  9 BC, as Liu Jizi
Accession
  1 BC
Father
  Liu Xing, the grandson of Yuandi's consort Feng; half-nephew of Chengdi
Mother
  Consort Wei
Wife
  Wang (the daughter of Wang Mang)
Children
  None
Died
  AD 6
Temple name
  Pingdi ('Peaceful Emperor')

RUZI
Born
  AD 5, as Liu Ying
Title before accession
  Heir Apparent (AD 6)
Accession
  AD 7
Family connections
  great-great grandson of Xuandi
Wife
  Wang Mang's granddaughter
Deposed
  AD 9
Temple name
  Ruzi ('Young Ziying')

men, but it was like sweeping shifting sand. The apparatus of central government, expanded by Wudi, had become more than the empire could bear. When a weak ruler ascended the throne, the Western Han were doomed.

Yuandi's son, **Chengdi** (33–7 BC), was an irresponsible youth of 19 who amused himself with incognito trips into the city to watch cock-fighting. Falling in love with a concubine of low birth, Zhao Feiyan ('Flying Swallow'), he deposed his wife, the empress Xu, and had his two sons by other women murdered to safeguard Zhao's position. Political affairs were left to his mother, the dowager-empress Wang, and her family, four of whom became Marshall of State. Chengdi's successor, **Aidi** (7–1 BC), aged 17 on accession, was obsessed by his young lover, Dong Xian, on whom he lavished wealth and titles, appointing him Marshall of State and even giving him the imperial seals, offering to abdicate in his favour. On Aidi's death at 23 the dowager-empress Wang swiftly regained the seals and gave her nephew Wang Mang high office. Wang dominated the remaining years of the Western Han. When his first choice of emperor (chosen from Xuandi's 58 descendants since none of Yuandi's had survived), the eight-year-old **Pingdi** (1 BC–AD 6), died after six years, he picked an even younger candidate, **Ruzi** (AD 7–9), aged two, as successor. The imperial family rose in protest but were swiftly defeated and Wang Mang, supported by the officials, took the throne himself. By popular consent, the Liu family had lost the Mandate of Heaven and Wang Mang was therefore justified in declaring himself emperor with the dynastic title Xin ('New') in AD 9.

WANG MANG

From now on all land belongs to the nation, all slaves are private possessions, and neither land nor slaves are subject to trade.

Decree nationalizing the land which Wang Mang was later forced to revoke c. AD 9

Wang Mang's Xin dynasty received short shrift from the Han historians who wrote after its fall, and **Wang Mang** (AD 9–23) himself was later described as having a 'large mouth, receding chin, bulging eyes and a loud, hoarse voice'. He was in fact an able administrator who chose his ministers well, but his support in the capital never extended to the provinces where lesser members of the Han imperial family still held sway. Wang Mang professed Confucianism and spared the life of the last Western Han infant emperor, Ruzi, who later married Wang's grand-

Pingdi dies
Ruzi emperor
Ruzi deposed; Wang Mang of 'Xin' emperor
Yellow River changes course
Wang Mang's land reforms fail
Tiberius emperor in Rome
Peasant revolts
Red Eyebrows rebellion starts
Wang Mang killed; civil war follows
Guang Wudi of Eastern Han emperor

WANG MANG

Born	*Children*
45 BC, as Wang Mang	at least 1 daughter (who married Pingdi)
Title before accession	*Died*
Marquis of Xindu (16 BC); regent (8 BC)	AD 23
Accession	*Note*
AD 9	Wang Mang founded the Xin ('New') dynasty, but it is not recognized by official histories.
Father	
Wang Wan, the brother of Yuandi's empress Wang	

(*Right*) Wang Mang. Watercolour from an 18th-century album of imperial portraits.

(*Below*) The use of inscribed standard measures and weights introduced by Qin Shihuangdi continued in the Wang Mang period. Bronze inscribed measure, 9 AD.

daughter, but when Wang embarked on an ambitious programme of reform, attacking the privileges of the wealthy and the landowners, he was unable to carry it through and had to repeal his own edicts on the redistribution of land and the ban on sale of slaves. His greatest success was fiscal. By insisting that all gold be exchanged for copper, he cornered the market, and at his death in AD 23 the treasury held some 5 million oz (140,000 kg) of gold (more than the total supply in medieval Europe) and the strain was felt as far afield as Rome where the emperor Tiberius forbade the wearing of silk since it cost gold. Natural disasters – the Yellow River changed course twice in six years – increased popular misery and having alienated the monied classes Wang Mang found himself friendless when a rebellion broke out in AD 23 and he was slain by a common soldier.

EASTERN HAN DYNASTY
25–88

光武帝 Guang Wudi
25–57

明帝 Mingdi
57–75

章帝 Zhangdi
75–88

Woodcut of Guang Wudi from a Ming dynasty encyclopedia, the *Sancai tuhui*, 1607.

GUANG WUDI	
Born	*Died*
5 BC, as Liu Xiu	57
Accession	*Temple name*
AD 25	Guang Wudi
Wives	('Shining Martial
(1) Guo Shengtong	Emperor')
(divorced 41, died	*Note*
52)	All that remains of
(2) Yin Lihua (died	the Eastern Han
64)	tombs are tumuli
Children	near Luoyang,
10 sons, 5 by each	Henan.
wife	

GUANG WUDI

The fall of Wang Mang was followed by a bitter 2-year civil war with competing rebel groups battling for supremacy. The main force, the Red Eyebrows (red paint on their foreheads distinguished them from government troops), were a disorganized and uneducated army of peasants driven to revolt by famine after Yellow River floods in the east. As the rebels moved west, powerful members of the former imperial family used them to regain the throne, but unable to agree on a candidate they fell out among themselves. When **Guang Wudi** (AD 25–57), a typical representative of these provincial landowners, declared himself emperor in 25, he was faced with 11 rival claimants whom it took a decade to subdue. The devastation of this period – during which Chang'an and the Western Han imperial tombs were sacked – was such that the emperor later forbade the word 'war' to be uttered in his presence.

With Chang'an destroyed, Guang Wudi moved the capital east to Luoyang, and his dynasty is therefore referred to as 'Eastern Han'. He was a natural leader, born into a family of wealthy southern landowners descended from the earlier Han emperor, Jingdi (157–141 BC). Like Gaodi before him, his first tasks were consolidation and reconstruction. He

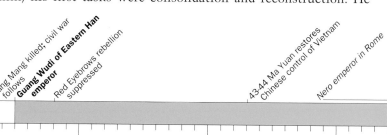

Wang Mang killed; civil war follows

Guang Wudi of Eastern Han emperor

Red Eyebrows rebellion suppressed

43-44 Ma Yuan restores Chinese control of Vietnam

Nero emperor in Rome

10   20   30   40   50

(*Above*) Alcohol played a regular part in Han life and this tomb brick shows a brewer conducting a lively trade from his stall. Brewing was a profitable occupation and from Han Wudi's time onwards periodic attempts were made to establish a government monopoly, but these were always short-lived since they proved impossible to enforce. (Sichuan Provincial Museum,Chengdu).

(*Above*) The inscription on this golden seal, recently discovered in Kyushu in southern Japan, shows that it was given to a Japanese envoy by Guang Wudi in 57 AD. The seal corroborates Chinese texts recording the visits of Japanese envoys bearing tribute in 57 and 107 AD (Tokyo National Museum).

(*Right*) Confucian scholars teaching students the classical texts which were essential for state examinations. Brick relief, Eastern Han period (Sichuan Provincial Museum,Chengdu).

initially strengthened imperial authority by appointing his sons as local kings and princes, reducing their power later when the throne was secure. War had swept away most of the old imperial aristocracy and their bloated bureaucracy, and through economy and skilful management he soon restored imperial finances. He re-established the state monopolies of iron, salt and liquor, and giving agriculture priority, made a land census, reduced the poll tax on peasants and stabilized prices by buying surpluses for relief in times of hardship. A professed Confucian, he practised the ancestral rites and promoted education, establishing over 100 state institutes for training administrative candidates in the classics at government expense. By the end of his reign the majority of lower rank provincial officials were appointed by examination. He was, however, determined to keep real power in his own hands and limited the role of senior officials, relying instead on his own Inner Secretariat ('inner' meaning 'within the palace') which was drawn mainly from consort families.

Here lay the rub. By using political marriages to balance regional factors, Guang Wudi increased the problem of consort interference in politics. The strength of local clans was expressed by the famous general, Ma Yuan, who accepted office with the comment: 'In present times, it is not only the sovereign who selects his subjects. The subjects also select

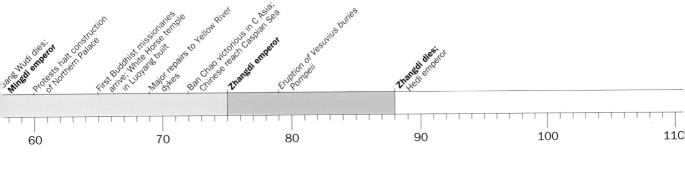

STONE SCULPTURE

Stone was a latecomer in Chinese sculpture, appearing first in the Han dynasty when its qualities of endurance led to an association with immortality. Han Wudi had stone figures of immortals placed in his parks like decoy ducks on a lake to attract beings from the other world. The most famous group of Western Han statuary was placed on the tomb of Wudi's successful general, Huo Qubing (died 117 BC), which was deliberately designed like a 'magical mountain', a possible home of the immortals.

Under the Eastern Han, the use of stonecarving blossomed, invading architecture, public works and above all the tomb. From the 1st century onwards, the practice of erecting 'spirit roads' – formal avenues of stone monuments and figures lining the approach to an important tomb – spread rapidly throughout the empire, eventually crossing into neighbouring Vietnam and Korea. By the end of the Han a classical tradition of stone sculpture had evolved which lasted well into the 20th century.

This tradition, seen in its purest form in the spirit road, was based on ancient beliefs which had nothing to do with aesthetic ideas but which were common to all classes of society. These beliefs were associated with ancestor worship at the tomb and rested on the idea that images contained inherent powers to bring about that which they represented: a stone tiger, for example, would deter grave robbers not because it looked fierce but because the act of creating it brought into existence the powers of a tiger; invisible, these powers were equally efficient in the seen and unseen worlds. Animals, with the ability to fly or change form (a caterpillar turns into a butterfly, a tadpole into a frog) were believed to possess supernatural gifts and could be used to communicate with and seek help from the spirit world.

Statues were therefore made to achieve a result – practical, moral or magical – and their powers were harnessed by the state (already in the 1st century AD the use of tomb statuary was regulated by imperial decree). Subjects were chosen for their symbolism and the sculptor's task was to convey the subject's essential characteristics rather than give an accurate representation.

Today, apart from tumuli and rammed-earth foundations, the only surviving Han monuments are stone sculptures and towers. As well as animals and officials (symbolizing good government) carved in the round, there are large numbers of stone reliefs in tombs illustrating different aspects of daily and official life. The most unusual

(Above) 'Horse trampling a barbarian' — part of the group of statues placed on the tomb of Huo Qubing (d.117 BC), a young general whose cavalry victories secured the Gansu corridor to the west.

(Above) Details of the upper sections of a memorial tower from 190–195 AD at Pingyang, Sichuan. The figure in the half-open door represents the deceased, halfway between this world and the next.

(Right) As well as animals, Han spirit roads included stone officials. Several pairs have survived in Shandong — one, military, bearing a long sword, and the other, a civil official, with hands clasped in front. Stone military official, Confucian Palace, Qufu, Shandong, 2nd century AD.

monuments are, however, pairs of carved stone towers (*que*) marking the start of the spirit road. Built exactly like contemporary wooden towers used to display edicts outside official buildings, they provide valuable evidence of early architectural techniques and their decoration served as a showcase for Confucian propaganda. Designed to influence and educate illiterate viewers, the decoration consisted of linear reliefs like strip cartoons, illustrating well-known legends and historical events chosen for their moral or political value. While the lower sections of the towers show scenes from this world, the upper parts are carved with immortals and legendary heroes who might help the deceased in his new life. The sculptors display a perfect mastery of space, proportion and perspective and although the towers are 20 ft (6 m) tall every detail is visible from the ground.

(Left) The earliest stone figure of a named individual in China, this statue of the great 3rd-century BC engineer, Li Bing, made in 168 AD and found in 1974, shows how statuary was expected to serve practical, memorial and supernatural purposes. One of three statues designed as water gauges for Li Bing's spectacular irrigation system in Sichuan, it was originally placed in a strategic site in the river: if the water level rose above the shoulders, measures should be taken against flood, if it fell below the ankles, against drought. Dujiang Weir, Guanxian, Sichuan.

(Far left) Stone elephant, near the White Horse Temple, Luoyang. Although this elephant is not attached to any particular known tomb, it may have marked the entrance to the Eastern Han imperial burial grounds.

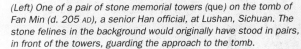

(Left) One of a pair of stone memorial towers (que) on the tomb of Fan Min (d. 205 AD), a senior Han official, at Lushan, Sichuan. The stone felines in the background would originally have stood in pairs, in front of the towers, guarding the approach to the tomb.

(Below) The most popular tomb animals were tigers: as kings of the wild and beasts of prey, they symbolized the ruler and military prowess and were often adorned with wings and horns giving them additional supernatural powers (Guanlinmiao Museum, Luoyang).

INFLATION AND CURRENCY

Pressure on state finances led to a shortage of money and in 175 BC, Wendi allowed private minting of copper coinage. The market was flooded with increasingly worthless money. Rulers with copper mines in their domain became 'richer than the emperor himself'. Wudi re-established a state monopoly, but was unable to check illicit minting; in a vain attempt to control raging inflation he introduced his own 'White Stag Notes' made from the skin of a rare stag in his hunting park, cut into square, fringed pieces, which the princes were obliged to buy for 400,000 copper coins. This short-lived experiment was followed by new imperial 'white coins' of an alloy of silver and tin with arbitrary values of 3,000, 500 and 300 copper cash (cash – small copper coins usually tied on strings – was the common currency), but these coins, and their successors – copper coins with a red border – were soon forged and the problem was only solved by the issue of copper coins worth their intrinsic value.

Bronze moulds for casting copper coins. Wuzhu coins were introduced by Han Wudi in 126 BC and proved so successful that they were still in use in the early Tang dynasty, some 700 years later. (Below) a glazed pottery money-box, decorated with wuzhu coin patterns, c. 2nd century AD.

their sovereign.' To secure northern loyalty, the emperor, a southerner, chose a northern wife, Guo Shengtong, and named her son Heir Apparent. In 41, when no longer dependent on northern support, he bowed to pressure from his southern supporters and deposed Guo in favour of a southerner, Yin Lihua. (Later historians described this episode as sudden romance, but Yin, aged 41, had already borne the emperor five sons.) Chosen for their powerful family backing, such empresses became the focus for political intrigue. The imperial practice of rewarding successful generals, administrators and relatives with huge grants of land and peasants was copied by officials, leading to a steady increase in the number of large landowners and a consequent decline in central revenues. With an unassailable economic position, the landowners consolidated their power by monopolizing the highest posts at court, and although Guang Wudi and his immediate successors kept control, from 88 AD the empire was governed by consort families.

MINGDI AND ZHANGDI

One night in a dream emperor Ming[di] saw a deity flying in front of his palace which had a golden body and emanated sunlight from the neck. The next day he asked his ministers to explain the identity of this deity. One of them, Fu Yi, replied that he had heard of a sage in India called 'the Buddha', who had attained salvation, who was able to fly and whose body was of a golden hue.

From the *Sutra in Forty-two Sections*, probably late Han

Mingdi (57–75) and his successor, **Zhangdi** (75–88), continued Guang Wudi's policies aimed at stability at home and expansion abroad. With the return of prosperity and order, China once more expanded her influence. In 43–44, Ma Yuan had crushed a serious rising in the south, re-establishing Chinese control in central Vietnam. Under Mingdi, the process went further and the brilliant general, Ban Chao, extended the empire's borders further than ever before. Having successfully pacified Mongolia and quelled the Xiongnu, between 73 and 76 Chinese armies regained the entire Tarim Basin. In 91, Ban Chao became protector-general of the Western regions with headquarters at Kucha on the northern rim of the Tarim Basin, and his troops crossed the Pamirs reaching the Caspian Sea. Only Parthia remained between China and Rome: the envoy that Ban Chao sent to look for Da Qin (Rome) turned back on reaching Mesopotamia. The empire was now larger than under Wudi, but once again expansion proved short-lived, and after Ban Chao's death in 102 China's hold on Central Asia weakened.

Mingdi, however, while officially supporting Confucianism, was 'narrow-minded with a penchant for revealing confidential information' and the atmosphere at court was clouded by fear. His officials were frequently victimized by slander and punishments were harsh. Death of suspects in prison was widespread and over half the 500 officials arrested

MINGDI	
Born	childless 79)
AD 28, as Liu Yang	*Major concubine*
Accession	consort Jia
AD 57	*Children*
Father	9 sons
Guang Wudi (eldest	*Died*
son of)	75
Mother	*Temple name*
empress Yin	Mingdi ('Brilliant
Wife	Emperor')
empress Ma (died	

ZHANGDI	
Born	(2) consort Liang
57, as Liu Da	(died 83)
Accession	(3) consort Shen
75	*Children*
Father	8 sons, none by
Mingdi (5th son of)	empresses
Mother	*Died*
consort Jia	88
Wives	*Temple name*
empress Dou (died	Zhangdi
97)	('Methodical
Major concubines	Emperor')
(1) consort Song	
(died 82)	

for suspected complicity in a failed uprising in 71 died from flogging. (Opposition to such severity led in 84 to a ban on flogging during the investigation of criminal cases.) Mingdi's policies of active public works, such as major repairs to the Yellow River dykes and improving the transport system for grain from the east, involved a heavy use of conscript labour and the resulting labour unrest was exacerbated by court extravagance. Although conscript protests had halted construction of the emperor's Northern Palace in 60, his wife and her family continued to build large residences with well-stocked stables and to hold 'lavish banquets by the hundred'. The emperor's attempt to dissociate himself from such extravagance and give an example of economy by refusing to build a mausoleum for himself, preferring to be buried in a side-chamber of his mother's tomb, pleased the Confucians but had little real impact.

Zhangdi's upbringing was a rare example of domestic harmony at court. He was the fifth of Mingdi's nine sons and his mother, the consort Jia, was a cousin of the childless empress Ma. Jia and Ma remained such close friends that Zhangdi's first Heir Apparent, Liu Qing, was the son of a concubine chosen by the empress Ma. Later, however, Zhangdi's wife, the empress Dou, replaced Liu Qing with Zhangdi's fourth son, the later Hedi emperor. Again, unusually, the two princes remained friends.

HAN PALACES

The splendour of Han palaces is described in a poem from c. 208 BC in which the poet tries to tempt the soul back to earth:

O soul, come back! return to your old
    abode.
Hear while I describe for you your quiet
    and reposeful home.
High halls and deep chambers, with
    railings and tiered balconies;
Stepped terraces, storeyed pavilions,
    whose tops look on the high
    mountains;
Lattice doors with scarlet interstices,
    and carving on the square lintels;
Draughtless rooms for winter; galleries
    cool in summer;...
The chambers of polished stone, with
    kingfisher hangings on jasper hooks;
Bedspreads of kingfisher seeded with
    pearls, all dazzling in brightness;
Arras of fine silk covers the walls;
    damask canopies stretch
    overhead....
Bright candles of orchid-perfumed fat
    light up flower-like faces that await
    you;

Twice eight handmaidens to serve your
    bed, alternating each night in duty,
The lovely daughters of noble families,
    far excelling common maidens....
O soul, come back!

Chu Ci, Songs of the South

Such palaces were set in parks and gardens filled with rare plants and animals, and Han Wudi's empress is described as: 'gazing about her from high Orchid Terrace.'

Poetical descriptions of Han palaces inspired many later paintings such as this Song dynasty work, An Imperial Palace of the Han period *by Zhao Bozhu. (National Palace Museum, Taiwan).*

EASTERN HAN DYNASTY
88–220

和 帝 **Hedi**
88–106

殷 帝 **Shangdi**
106

安 帝 **Andi**
106–125

順 帝 **Shundi**
125–144

冲 帝 **Chongdi**
144–145

质 帝 **Zhidi**
145–146

桓 帝 **Huandi**
146–168

灵 帝 **Lingdi**
168–189

献 帝 **Xiandi**
189–220

EASTERN HAN	
HEDI	*Father*
Born	Hedi
79, as Liu Zhao	*Died*
Accession	September 106
88	*Temple name*
Father	Shangdi ('Die-young
Zhangdi	Emperor')
Mother	
consort Liang	**ANDI**
Wives	*Born*
(1) empress Yin	94, as Liu Yu
(divorced 102)	*Accession*
(2) empress Deng	106
(died 121)	*Father*
Children	Liu Qing, the 2nd
2 sons by unknown	son of Zhangdi
mothers	*Wife*
Died	empress Yan (died
106	126)
Temple name	*Major concubine*
Hedi ('Harmonious	consort Li
Emperor')	(poisoned 115)
	Children
SHANGDI	1 son
Born	*Died*
105, as Liu Long	125
Accession	*Temple name*
February 106	Andi ('Peaceful
	Emperor')

HEDI TO HUANDI

After the emperor Zhangdi, the Han dynasty steadily declined under a succession of child-emperors. **Hedi** (88–106), the son of Zhangdi and a consort, was nine years old on accession and the dowager-empress Dou and her powerful general brother, Dou Xian, took control of the country. Hedi's reign was plagued by natural disasters – locusts, droughts and floods between 92 and 100 – and to avoid widespread dispossession, the government intervened actively to help peasant farmers by remitting taxes, giving grain relief and allowing the poor to hunt and fish on state land. In 91, however, Hedi, restless under the dowager-empress Dou's domination, had taken the fateful step of enlisting the eunuchs to rid himself of the Dou clan. The move was temporarily successful but henceforth imperial politics became a three-way struggle. Having called consort families into play against officials, emperors now turned to the eunuchs to protect them against their wives' families. Wooed by clans and emperors alike, the eunuchs became increasingly powerful and, belying their name, were given hereditary titles which could be passed to adopted sons. Consort families now had a vested interest in placing easily dominated minors on the throne and the remaining emperors of

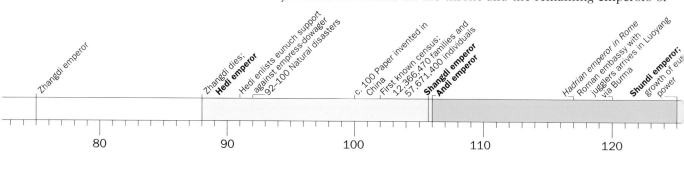

EASTERN HAN

SHUNDI
Born
115, as Liu Bao
Accession
125
Father
Andi
Mother
consort Li
Wife
empress Liang Na
(died 150)
Major concubine
consort Yu
Children
1 son
Died
144
Temple name
Shundi
('Submissive
Emperor')

CHONGDI
Born
143, as Liu Bing
Accession
144
Father
Shundi
Mother
consort Yu
Died
145
Temple name
Chongdi ('Modest
Emperor')

ZHIDI
Born
138, as Liu Zuan
Accession
145
Family background
great-great-
grandson of
Zhangdi
Died
146
Temple name
Zhidi ('Upright
Emperor')

HUANDI
Born
132, as Liu Zhi
Accession
146
Family background
great-grandson of
Zhangdi
Wives
(1) empress Liang
(died 159) younger
sister of dowager-
empress Liang Na
(2) empress Deng
(divorced and died
165)
(3) empress Dou
(died 172)
Children
1 son by Deng
Died
168
Temple name
Huandi ('Martial
Emperor')

the Han dynasty were all children. Neither of Hedi's empresses had sons, and when he died the dowager-empress Deng, bypassing the older of Hedi's two sons by other consorts, chose a three-month-old baby as Heir. Her choice, the emperor **Shangdi** (106), died before he was one year old and was followed by Hedi's nephew, the emperor **Andi** (106–125), aged just 12.

A weak ruler, Andi left politics to his wife's family, the Yan. His reign was beset by continuing natural disasters and frontier problems, particularly in Central Asia. A successful campaign against the warlike Qiang in the northwest in 107 gave some respite, but the cost was ruinous, leading to demands for a general withdrawal from Central Asia. The childless empress Yan had had Andi's son by a concubine, Li, demoted from Heir Apparent, and after Andi's death in 125 her choice, Shaodi (a grandson of Zhangdi), slipped through the role of emperor so swiftly that his date of birth is unknown and he remains unrecognized in the official Chinese list of emperors. Reigning from May to December, he was ousted and killed during a eunuch coup in favour of Andi and Li's son who now became the emperor **Shundi** (125–144), aged 11. When the new emperor made a political marriage with the future empress, Liang Na, power shifted once again to the northern clans.

The empress Liang Na was childless and the reign of minors continued with the choice of **Chongdi** (144–145), Shundi's son with the consort Yu, who after reigning for only five months died at the age of two. Chongdi's eight-year-old successor, **Zhidi** (145–146), a great-great-grandson of Zhangdi, lasted for a mere 16 months, and was followed by **Huandi** (146–168), a great-grandson of Zhangdi who was already 14. There then started the reigns of the 'bad emperors'. The names of Huandi and Lingdi (the emperor who followed Huandi) became synonymous with oppressive government. Natural disasters – a devastating earthquake in 151 followed by a plague of locusts in 153 – led to widespread famine and popular risings throughout the empire. Low morale, lax administration and corruption had totally undermined the relief system and the central government was no longer able to cope with these signs of heavenly displeasure. Huandi withdrew into the isolation of his palace, leaving power in the hands of the eunuchs. Good men now refused official posts, preferring the 'pure life' of the country to the 'impure court'.

Huandi's three empresses, Liang, Deng and Dou, were all without heirs. The first died; the second was divorced for drunkenness and black magic; the third became dowager-empress, choosing another great-great-grandson of Zhangdi as the new emperor, Lingdi.

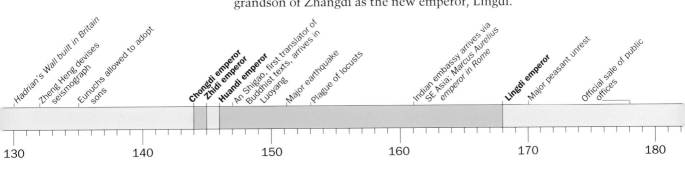

LINGDI	
LINGDI	(died 178)
Born	(2) empress He
156, as Liu Hong	*Major concubine*
Accession	consort Wang
168	(poisoned by
Family background	empress He 181)
great-great-	*Children*
grandson of	2 sons
Zhangdi	*Died*
Father	189
Liu Changdong	*Temple name*
Mother	Lingdi ('Quick-witted
Deng	Emperor')
Wives	
(1) empress Song	

LINGDI

Lingdi's reign (168–189) started and ended with attempts to massacre the eunuchs. On the 12-year-old's accession, the regent Dou Xian enlisted the scholars in a plot to rid the court of eunuch domination, but, with almost unbelievable carelessness, allowed his plans to leak out. The alerted eunuchs woke the emperor and in a dramatic midnight audience forced Dou Xian to kill himself. There followed 20 years of eunuch rule. The senior officials were killed or disgraced and their families forbidden to hold office, posts being filled with eunuchs or their relatives and protégés. The emperor appointed a eunuch commander-in-chief, and to

HAREMS

All the emperors kept harems, referred to as 'side-courts'. Candidates were chosen once a year from virgins aged 13–20 of good families. They were examined by a eunuch counsellor and a physiognomist for their beauty, deportment, complexion, hair and behaviour. In AD 52, for example, the leader of the powerful Ma family, offered three of his daughters aged 15, 14 and 13 for examination and the youngest was accepted for the harem of the Heir Apparent. Successful girls were given a rank and appropriate title. Guang Wudi reduced the ranks from 14 to 3 with the titles honourable lady, beautiful lady and chosen lady, each rank having progressively more members. By the end of the 9th century the harem contained 6,000 ladies, more than twice the number during the Western Han. The position of concubine was highly prized: it could further the family fortunes and the mother of a son might become empress.

Spring Morning in the Han Palace. *Detail from a Ming dynasty handscroll by Qiu Ying (c. 1495–1552).*

Major rebellion by Yellow Turbans

massacre of eunuchs; Luoyang sacked; **Xiandi emperor**

Caracalla grants Roman citizenship to all free men in empire

Xiandi ousted: Cao Pi establishes Wei kingdom; Wei Wendi emperor

Mingdi emperor

190 200 210 220 230

PAPER

The greatest Han invention was paper. Although fragments of pure rag paper have been found from the 2nd century BC; the earliest known hemp paper with writing on it is from around AD 109. Cai Lun, who died in AD 121, developed a method of mass-producing paper from tree bark, hemp and linen. In a land in which scholarship and writing were highly prized, its use spread rapidly. By the 3rd century AD it was in general use, having replaced the earlier bamboo, wood and silk slips. Together with the brush, inkstone and ink, paper became known as one of the scholar's Four Treasures.

The invention spread to Korea and Japan in the 7th century, reaching Europe via Central Asia and the Arabs in the 12th century.

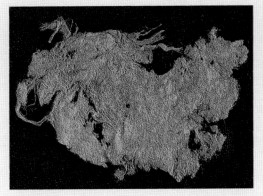

(Left) This hemp paper found in a Western Han tomb near Xi'an in 1957 is the earliest known example of paper in the world.

(Below) Ming dynasty woodcut illustrating the preparation of paper. Pounded bamboo shoots were mixed with lime and boiled for several days to make a soup from which the fibres were extracted using a bamboo screen. Excess water was then pressed out and the sheets of paper dried against a heated wall.

(Above) Fragment of paper from 2nd century AD discovered by Aurel Stein in the Gobi desert (British Library).

(Right) The value of ink, as one of the scholar's Four Treasures, is reflected in the costly decoration of this gilt-bronze ink-slab container inlaid with turquoise stones.

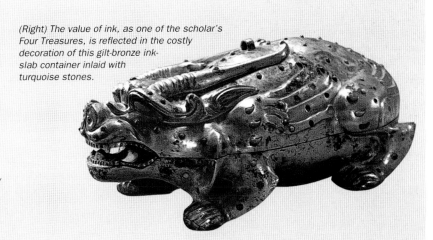

(*Right*) Once convicted or conscripted for forced labour, a peasant's chance of returning home was slight. Row after row of pits at this late 2nd-century cemetery at Xidajiaocun contain youthful labourers, many still shackled. Some were buried with small coins; a few had brick epitaphs like this (*below*) which records that the prisoner had been condemned to four years' hard labour.

supplement the tax revenues, steadily falling through the exactions of corrupt officials, authorized the open sale of posts and titles from a hall in the palace. Ignoring the distinction between the public and private purse the emperor now had all monies paid into his 'Hall of Ten Thousand Gold Pieces'. Slowly the administration disintegrated, unable to cope with a serious and growing agricultural crisis. Without funds the central relief system no longer functioned and each new drought or flood increased the number of landless. This rural unrest culminated in 184 when a major rebellion by the Yellow Turbans (named after their headgear) broke out in the east. Fuelled by refugees from disastrous Yellow River floods, over 360,000 armed men swept west. Shortly afterwards an equally serious revolt took place in the southwest where the Five Pecks of Rice sect (so-called after the tribute members paid to their leader) established a breakaway state in Sichuan. Both movements were led by Daoist religious leaders of faith-healing sects and their popular appeal and rallying cry that the emperor had forfeited the Mantle of Heaven led to imperial claimants springing up in other provinces.

During the long struggle to quell these risings, the political scene was radically altered. Unable to rely on central troops, provincial rulers raised their own and power passed into the hands of the new warlords who now manipulated the emperors as puppets. On Lingdi's death there was the usual battle over succession. The dowager-empress Deng and Lingdi's wife, the empress He, disagreed as to which of his two sons should accede. When the elder boy, the son of the empress He, aged 15, was installed, an able and ruthless warlord from the west, Dong Zhuo, intervened with his troops to crush the eunuchs' power. After occupying and destroying the capital Luoyang, he ordered a massacre in which 2,000 eunuchs were killed. (The burning of the imperial library at Luoyang is reckoned to have caused far greater loss of literary records than the First Emperor's Burning of the Books.) The young emperor, Shundi (whose reign is not recognized as legal by Chinese historians), and his half-brother fled. Seeking refuge in the fields, the present and future Sons of Heaven eventually returned in a commoner's cart. The elder boy was deposed and later killed; his younger half-brother Xiandi became the last Han emperor.

XIANDI	
XIANDI	(1) empress Fu
Born	(2) empress Cao
181, as Liu Xie	(died 260)
Accession	*Abdicated*
189	220
Father	*Died*
Lingdi	234
Mother	*Temple name*
consort Wang	Xiandi ('Dedicating
Wives	Emperor')

Ming dynasty watercolour of Xiandi from an 18th-century album of imperial portraits.

XIANDI

The tale of **Xiandi's** reign (189–220) is like a Shakespearean drama. The eunuchs, having broken the power of the officials, had themselves now been eliminated by the military, leaving the throne in the hands of warlords. Chivvied from Chang'an to Luoyang and then back again, the young ruler with a nominal court became a refugee, seeking shelter where he could find it. As after the fall of the Qin 'the deer was running' and the throne open for capture. Central authority had disappeared and there was now a three-way power struggle between the generals. Cao Cao, the adopted son of a eunuch, had assassinated the warlord Dong Zhuo; controlling the north, he offered the emperor protection. Cao Cao's daughter married Xiandi and on Cao Cao's death in 220, his son, Cao Pi, usurped the throne as emperor of the Wei dynasty and legitimate holder of the Mantle of Heaven. The Han dynasty was thus officially ended. The following year Liu Bei (161–223), a soldier of fortune who had become a powerful warlord in the south, declared himself emperor in Sichuan, taking the dynastic name Han (known as Shu Han after a former state in Sichuan) and in 222 a third general, Sun Quan, founded the Wu dynasty in the south. China had entered the period of the Three Kingdoms.

The macabre events of these years illustrate the peculiar resilience of the Chinese imperial system. An emperor was essential: like the hub of a wheel, he was the centre of the whole system and only he could communicate with heaven. It was not, however, necessary for the emperor to act. Others could do this for him as long as he could be seen, like the hub cap, shining in the centre. The imperial system was more than a form of government; it reflected a particular view of the cosmos and it is noteworthy that among the myriad rebel movements throughout the imperial period, none, until this century, suggested changing the system, only its ruler.

THE SILK ROADS

There were several routes between China and the West. The main Silk Road leading from the Western Han capital Chang'an to Central Asia and beyond split in two, passing from oasis to oasis as it skirted north and south of the Tarim Basin with its dreaded deserts. On the far side the ways joined again at Kashgar before crossing the mighty Pamirs into Central Asia and India, eventually reaching Persia and the eastern Mediterranean. Han Wudi's conquests brought the Euro-Indian oasis settlements of Central Asia into the Chinese sphere and for a short while the whole Tarim Basin was governed by a Chinese protector-general.

Other routes went south, overland to ports in the Hanoi region of North Vietnam or later Canton, and thence by sea via Indonesia and the Malay peninsula to the Indian Ocean from where there was regular sea traffic to the Roman Orient. From the 1st century AD onwards, trade passed along the 'Burma Road' from Yunnan to Burma and India, crossing the Mekong River on a suspension bridge. In AD 122 jugglers from Da Qin (Rome) arrived from the south and were followed in 166 by a group of merchants claiming to be ambassadors from the Roman emperor, Antun (Marcus Aurelius Antoninus). The sea traffic was in the hands of Arab traders whose dhows monopolized maritime commerce in the east.

The most valuable Chinese export was silk. Fragments of Han silk, some with polychrome patterns, have been found in Central Asia, Siberia and the Middle East and Roman silk imports led to such a drain of gold and silver eastwards that they harmed the Roman economy. The Chinese envoy Zhang Qian, whose search for allies in 135 BC led him to the fringes of the Hellenistic world, found bamboo and silk products from Sichuan in Bactria (northern Afghanistan) and Ferghana. The trade was, however, two-way. Zhang Qian brought alfalfa, pomegranates and grapes back with him, and Western jade, pearls, coral, glass, fine linen and wool travelled east along with horses from the rich Central Asian plains. The spirited horses of Ferghana were particularly prized and have been immortalized in the bronze 'flying horse' whose foot rests on a swallow found in a Han tomb in Gansu. Whatever the route, it was a trade in luxuries – each carefully packed bale passing through the hands of many nationalities speaking different languages and using different currencies.

The Silk Roads were, however, more than a conduit for trade. Han Wudi's successes pierced the nomadic barrier in the west, opening a door to the rest of the known world. Hitherto, China's foreign contacts had been with border peoples, mostly nomads whose way of life compared unfavourably with the sophisticated Han empire. Now Zhang Qian's reports and Chinese military victories revealed the existence of distinct civilizations of a comparable standard, leading to a cross-fertilization of technical skills and ideas. With the merchants came craftsmen and monks, and, in the long run, China's greatest import along the Silk Roads was Buddhism, brought by missionaries from India.

(Left) The Han established military garrisons and regular control posts along the Silk Roads. A swift system of communications was maintained between regularly spaced beacon towers by the use of red and blue flags and smoke by day, fire by night. 1st-century beacon tower, Jiaohe in the Turfan depression (modern Xinjiang).

(Above) Speeding through the air, this horse's hoof rests lightly on the back of a passing swallow. Gilt-bronze model of a Ferghana 'heavenly' horse, Gansu.

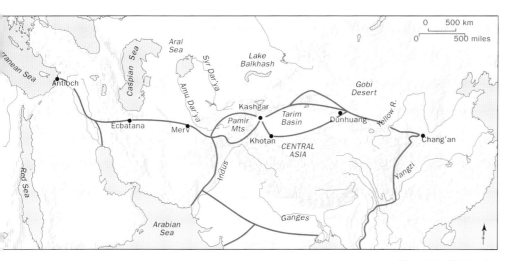

Map of the Silk Roads

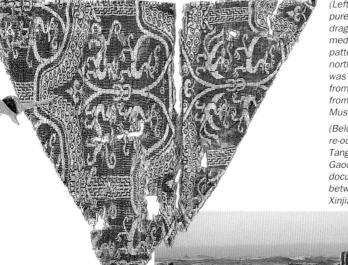

(Left) This fragment of cloth with a purely Chinese design of stylized dragons and phoenixes set in medallion and lozenge-shaped patterns was found in a fort northwest of Dunhuang. The cloth was next to a wooden document from 98 BC and is believed to date from the reign of Han Wudi (British Museum).

(Above) When Buddhism first arrived in China, its images were incorporated in local folklore and early representations of Buddha, such as this on the stone lintel of a tomb in Sichuan, were carved alongside or as pendants to traditional Chinese figures of immortals or auspicious beasts. Mahao, Leshan, Sichuan, Eastern Han period.

(Below) Under Tang Taizong and Gaozong, Chinese armies swept westwards, re-occupying earlier Han dynasty settlements on the Silk Roads to Central Asia. Tang dynasty remains of large Chinese-style walled cities have survived at Gaochang and Jiaohe, (modern Xinjiang), and numerous Tang official and private documents have been found in the ruins, illustrating active cultural exchanges between these regions and China. Ruins of Tang dynasty city at Gaochang, Xinjiang.

TOMB FIGURINES

Figurines from Han tombs give an extraordinarily vivid picture of their times. The importance of recreating a familiar world for the dead meant that the use of terracotta figures, first widely used for underground armies, was expanded to cover almost every aspect of life. Tombs, built like houses underground, were furnished with attendants, ladies of fashion, male and female servants and animals for food. Models of houses give a fascinating glimpse of contemporary building styles, ranging from the multi-storey courtyard houses of the wealthy to simple dwellings on stilts in swampy areas. Made from separate movable pieces, these houses were complete to the smallest detail, with metal pots on the kitchen stove, grain in the granary, a watchdog at the gate and birds on the roof. Han society was predominantly agricultural and there are models of cow and sheep pens, pigsties complete with latrines, rice fields with irrigation dykes, wells, granaries with peasants delivering sacks of grain and farm machinery.

This underground world was a cheerful place with its kitchen stoves with pans, fish and kebabs, and tables laid with cups, wine jars and chopsticks. Men play an early form of Chinese chess, elegant ladies with long flowing sleeves dance to the music of drums and acrobats perform routines which can still be seen today. Finally there are entertainers: like court jesters in the European Middle Ages, these are often dwarfs who exaggerate their deformities as they accompany their half-spoken, half-chanted ballad with a drum or pair of clacking castanets.

The figures, filled with movement, are a triumph of the Chinese sculptural genius for catching the essence of a subject in a simple form. Like the Terracotta Army they were made from moulds and assembled before firing; most were then covered with white slip and painted. Under the Eastern Han, however, lead glazes were introduced: the addition of iron gave a brown colour and copper-oxide gave a brilliant green which degrades into a silvery fluorescence on exposure. Workers found in graves near the kilns show signs of lead poisoning.

(Above) Model stoves were often shown complete with cooking utensils and ingredients such as the fish and kebabs visible here.

(Right) The sheer joy and exuberance of this drummer is typical of Sichuan figurines of popular entertainers.

(Above) This dancing lady is typical of the Western Han modelling style. Her body is out of proportion and merely outlined, but the figure, with its long sleeves swinging as she dances, is instantly recognizable and filled with movement.

(Right) The figures, modelled separately, were arrayed on a platform depicting a real-life musical and acrobatic performance. The spectators, more important and therefore taller than the performers, stand with folded arms at the side while a musician strikes a stone chime hanging from a frame at the back.

(Left) In certain regions, figurines tended to be made in wood, like this group of lacquered servants found in a tomb in Hubei.

(Below) Architectural models range from simple single-storey houses on stilts and high towers to large manor-house complexes like this. Here the roof can be lifted off, revealing the rooms inside. These include a large hall with dishes and musicians awaiting a banquet; the courtyard on the left leads to the kitchen (Henan Provincial Museum, Zhengzhou).

(Above) Agricultural models include farm machinery such as hand-powered winnowing machines and tilt-hammered grain huskers like these.

(Right) Many variations of this board game, called liubo, have been found. Liubo, played with counters on a marked board, was believed to be a favourite pastime of the immortals and Chinese miniature gardens often include a small flat stone which visiting spirits could use as a board.

THE THREE KINGDOMS

WEI
Wendi
220–226
Mingdi
227–239
Shaodi
240–253
Gao Gui Xiang Gong
254–260
Yuandi
260–264

WU
Wudi
222–252
Feidi
252–258
Jingdi
258–264
Modi
264–280

SHU HAN
Xuande
221–223
Hou Zhu
223–263

PERIOD OF DISUNION

WESTERN JIN
Wudi
265–289
Huidi
290–306
Huaidi
307–312
Mindi
313–316

EASTERN JIN
Yuandi
317–322
Mingdi
323–325
Chengdi
326–342
Kangdi
343–344
Mudi
345–361
Aidi
362–365
Hai Xi Gong
366–370
Jian Wendi
371–372
Xiao Wudi
373–396
Andi
397–418
Gongdi
419

LIU SONG
Wudi
420–422
Ying Yang Wang
423
Wendi
424–453
Xiao Wudi
454–464
Mingdi
465–472
Cang Wu Wang
473–476
Shundi
477–479

QI
Gaodi
479–482
Wudi
483–93
Mingdi
494–498
Dong Hunhou
499–500
Hedi
501

LIANG
Wudi
502–549
Jian Wendi
550
Yu Zhang Wang
551
Yuandi
552–554
Jingdi
555–556

CHEN
Wudi
557–559
Wendi
560–566
Lin Hai Wang
567–568
Xuandi
569–582
Hou Zhu
583–589

SUI
Wendi
581–604
Yangdi
604–617
Gongdi
617–618

TANG
Gaozu
618–626
Taizong
626–649
Gaozong
649–683
Zhongzong
684, 705–710
Ruizong
684–690, 710–712
Wu Zetian
690–705
Xuanzong
712–756
Suzong
756–762
Daizong
762–779
Dezong
779–805
Shunzong
805
Xianzong
805–820
Muzong
820–824
Jingzong
824–827
Wenzong
827–840
Wuzong
840–846
Xuanzong
846–859
Yizong
859–873
Xizong
873–888
Zhaozong
888–904
Aidi (Zhaoxuan)
904–907

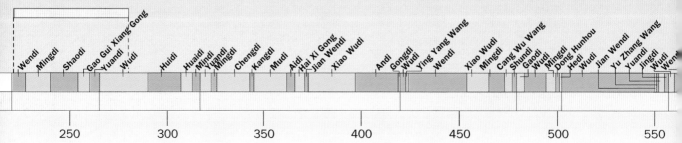

Wei Wendi (220–226)

Chen Hou Zhu (583–589)

Sui Wendi (581–604)

Tang Gaozu (618–626)

CONFUSION, REUNIFICATION AND THE GOLDEN AGE

The Three Kingdoms Period AD 220–280
The Period of Disunion AD 265–589
The Sui and the Tang dynasties AD 581–907

THE FALL OF THE HAN DYNASTY was followed by three and a half centuries of almost incessant warfare and instability. Chinese civilization was threatened by northern barbarians and the foreign religion of Buddhism. Internal dissension had left northern China at the mercy of non-Han steppe nomads, while the irrelevance of Confucianism to contemporary political and economic problems created a spiritual vacuum, opening the door to Buddhism which offered an escape from the problems of this world.

In a vain attempt to restore the Han empire, a series of dynasties sought supremacy, but although the Western Jin briefly reunited the country, the growth of powerful regional landowners made strong central government impossible. From 316 to 589 China was divided between traditional Chinese in the south and non-Han rulers in the north. With land reform the sinicized northerners restored a stable central economy, creating a base for reunification by a northern general, the founder of the Sui dynasty. Strengthened by the infusion of northern military vigour and energy and the incorporation of Buddhism into a Confucian society, the new empire, under the Sui and Tang, surpassed that of the Han and became China's Golden Age.

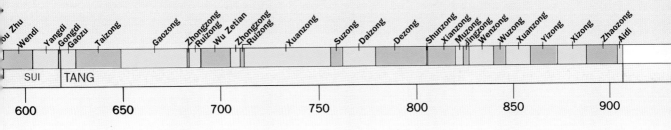

ou Zhu Wendi Yangdi Gongdi Gaozu Taizong Gaozong Zhongzong Ruizong Wu Zetian Zhongzong Ruizong Xuanzong Suzong Daizong Dezong Shunzong Xianzong Muzong Jingzong Wenzong Wuzong Xuanzong Yizong Xizong Zhaozong Aidi

SUI | TANG

600   650   700   750   800   850   900

THE THREE KINGDOMS
220–280

文帝 **Wei**
Wendi
220–226

明帝 **Mingdi**
227–239

少帝 **Shaodi**
240–253

高贵乡公 **Gao Gui Xiang Gong**
254–260

元帝 **Yuandi**
260–264

RIVAL KINGDOMS
Wu
Wudi
222–252
Feidi
252–258
Jingdi
258–264
Modi
264–280
Shu Han
Xuande
221–223
Hou Zhu
223–263

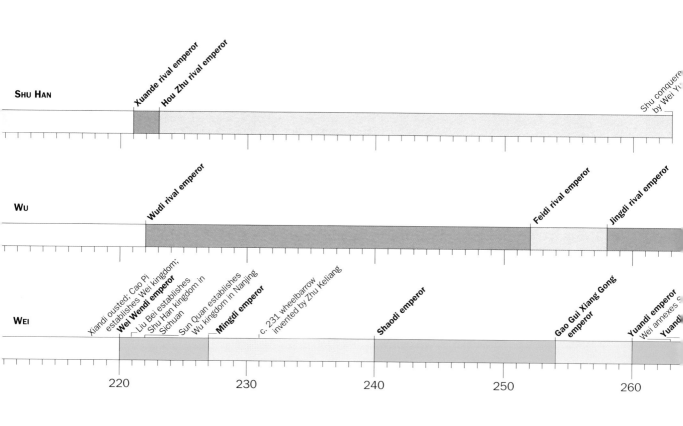

SHU HAN

Xuande rival emperor
Hou Zhu rival emperor
Shu conquered by Wei Yt

WU

Wudi rival emperor
Feidi rival emperor
Jingdi rival emperor

WEI

Xiandi ousted; Cao Pi establishes Wei kingdom; **Wei Wendi emperor**
Liu Bei establishes Shu Han kingdom in Sichuan
Sun Quan establishes Wu kingdom in Nanjing
Mingdi emperor
c. 231 wheelbarrow invented by Zhu Keliang
Shaodi emperor
Gao Gui Xiang Gong emperor
Yuandi emperor
Wei annexes S
Yuandi

220   230   240   250   260

Portraits of Wei Wendi, Liu Bei and Sun Quan from the *Thirteen Emperors* scroll by the Tang court painter, Yan Liben (Museum of Fine Arts, Boston).

WEI	
WENDI	*Died*
Birth name	253
Cao Pi	*Temple name*
Accession	Shaodi ('Young
220	Emperor')
Father	
Cao Cao	GAO GUI XIANG GONG
Died	*Accession*
226	254
Temple name	*Died*
Wendi ('Literary	260
Emperor')	*Temple name*
	Gao Gui Xiang Gong
MINGDI	('Duke of Noble
Accession	Country')
227	
Died	YUANDI
239	*Accession*
Temple name	260
Mingdi ('Brilliant	*Died*
Emperor')	264
	Temple name
SHAODI	Yuandi ('Original
Accession	Emperor')
240	

THE THREE KINGDOMS

All down the ages rings the note of change,
For Fate so rules it; none escapes its sway.
The kingdoms three have vanished as a dream,
The useless misery is ours to grieve.

Excerpt from the *Romance of the Three Kingdoms*

Wei, Wu and Shu Han kingdoms

The Three Kingdoms period which followed the Han dynasty is remembered as the golden age of chivalry and romance. The Wei kingdom in the north was created by Cao Cao and his son Cao Pi, who reigned as **Wei Wendi** (220–226). The Shu Han kingdom was formed in the west by the warlord Liu Bei, who ruled as Shu Han Xuande. In the south, the general Sun Quan set up the Wu kingdom and ruled as Wu Wudi. Much debate has centred around which of these three kingdoms was the legitimate heir to the Han dynasty and hence the Mantle of Heaven. The Wei are now generally recognized by Chinese historians as the official imperial line.

The exploits of the founders of these three kingdoms were later immortalized in the famous novel *Romance of the Three Kingdoms*. Cao Cao is remembered as a cruel tyrant: having slain his host under a misapprehension, he remarked: 'I would sooner betray the whole world

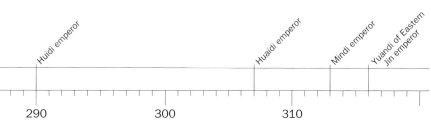

Modi rival emperor

Wu conquered by Wudi of Western Jin

...udi of Western Jin emperor

Huidi emperor

Huaidi emperor

Mindi emperor

Yuandi of Eastern Jin emperor

270   280   290   300   310

(*Right*) Map of China during the Three Kingdoms period.

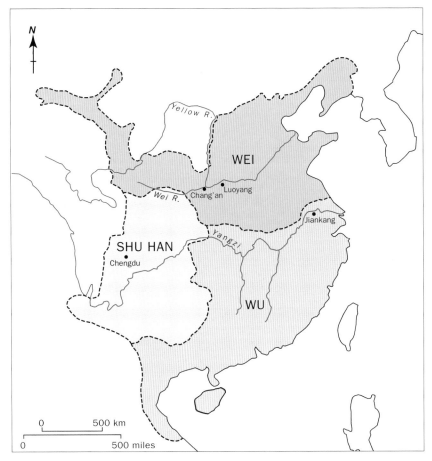

(*Below*) *The Romance of the Three Kingdoms*, compiled by Lo Guanzhong in the 14th century is one of the most popular historical novels in China; its heroes became household names and woodcut prints of famous scenes were hung up at the Chinese New Year. Qing dynasty coloured woodcut.

(*Right*) Guan Yu, the faithful associate of Liu Bei (Zhaolie), founder of the Shu Han kingdom, became one of the most famous heroes of the wars of the Three Kingdoms and from the Ming dynasty onwards was known as Guandi, God of War. Temples to Guandi sprang up throughout the empire and numerous figures and portraits were painted of the hero who was seen as the defender of the weak and oppressed against the strong.

So Wu was subdued and ceased to exist as a state; its four provinces, 83 districts, 310 departments, 523,000 families, 32,000 military officers, 213,000 soldiers, 2,300,000 inhabitants, its stores of grain and over 5,000 shops, all fell booty to the victorious Chin [Jin] dynasty. In the women's quarters of the palace were found more than 5,000 persons.

Luo Guan Zhong *Romance of the Three Kingdoms*

than let the world betray me.' The tall, aquiline Liu Bei and his trusty companions Guan Yu and Zhang Fei are identified with loyalty, and his minister Zhuge Liang became a byword for successful cunning and diplomacy. Sun Quan's bravery was such that when the first Ming emperor was building his tomb at Nanjing, he allowed Sun Quan's tomb mound to remain as a guard although it blocked the direct approach to the new mausoleum.

Each ruler tried to re-establish unity and claimed a legitimate right to the Mantle of Heaven, but none were able to control the regional factions. Wei Wendi attempted to restore central finances through state agricultural settlements, and emphasized his Confucianism by erecting stone tablets inscribed with the classics in the capital. Wendi was followed by a series of weak rulers. **Mingdi** (227–239) was faced with a serious revolt by eight local chieftains and his reign, like those of his successors – **Shaodi** (240–253) and **Gao Gui Xiang Gong** (254–260) – was dominated by frequent attacks from northern tribes. In 263, however, the last Wei emperor, **Yuandi** (260–264), conquered the Shu Han kingdom, now under Liu Bei's dissolute son, Hou Zhu. Two years later, however, Yuandi's throne was usurped by one of Wei Wendi's generals, Sima Yuan, founder of the Western Jin dynasty, who ruled as Wudi. In 280, Wudi easily defeated the remaining kingdom, Wu, whose emperor Modi, Sun Quan's grandson, was a cruel drunkard famed for his harem of 5,000 concubines. China was once again united.

**THE PERIOD OF
DISUNION**
(265–589)

Western Jin

武 帝 Wudi
265–289

惠 帝 Huidi
290–306

怀 帝 Huaidi
307–312

愍 帝 Mindi
313–316

Eastern Jin

元 帝 Yuandi
317–322

明 帝 Mingdi
323–325

成 帝 Chengdi
326–342

康 帝 Kangdi
343–344

穆 帝 Mudi
345–361

哀 帝 Aidi
362–365

海 西 Hai Xi Gong
366–370

簡 文 帝 Jian Wendi
371–372

孝 武 帝 Xiao Wudi
373–396

安 帝 Andi
397–418

恭 帝 Gongdi
419

Liu Song

武 帝 Wudi
420–422

营 阳 王 Ying Yang Wang
423

文 帝 Wendi
424–453

WESTERN JIN	
WUDI	HUIDI
Accession	*Accession*
265	290
Died	*Died*
289	306
Temple name	*Temple name*
Wudi ('Martial Emperor')	Huidi ('Beneficial Emperor')

The Western Jin

*At this time in Chang'an there were not more than one hundred
families. Weeds and thorns grew thickly as if in a forest. Only four carts
could be found in the city. The officials had neither robes of ceremony
nor seals.*

Contemporary observer after the sack of Chang'an in 316 during Jin
Mindi's reign

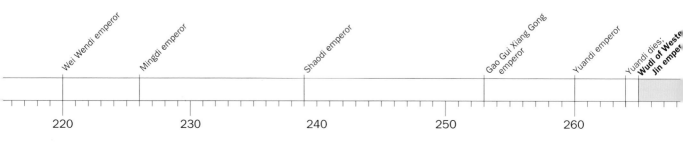

Wei Wendi emperor

Mingdi emperor

Shaodi emperor

Gao Gui Xiang Gong emperor

Yuandi emperor

Yuandi dies; **Wudi of Western Jin emperor**

220   230   240   250   260

孝武帝 Xiao Wudi
454–464

明帝 Mingdi
465–472

苍梧王 Cang Wu Wang
473–476

顺帝 Shundi
477–479

Liang

武帝 Wudi
502–549

简文帝 Jian Wendi
550

豫章王 Yu Zhang Wang
551

元帝 Yuandi
552–554

敬帝 Jingdi
555–556

Qi

高帝 Gaodi
479–482

武帝 Wudi
483–493

明帝 Mingdi
494–498

东昏侯 Dong Hunhou
499–500

和帝 Hedi
501

Chen

武帝 Wudi
557–559

文帝 Wendi
560–566

临海王 Lin Hai Wang
567–568

宣帝 Xuandi
569–582

后主 Hou Zhu
583–589

WESTERN JIN	
HUAIDI	MINDI
Accession	*Accession*
307	313
Died	*Died*
312	316
Temple name	*Temple name*
Huaidi ('Cherished Emperor')	Mindi ('Compassionate Emperor')

Jin Wudi (265–289) was strong and efficient. He improved communications by building a pontoon bridge over the Yellow River and cleared the western trade routes. In Luoyang he collected an imperial library of over 30,000 volumes and appointed as Minister of Works, Pei Xiu, the first cartographer to use a grid-system, drawing maps on a scale of 125 miles to 1 inch. Despite disbanding his troops and settling them on the land as taxpaying peasants he was, however, unable refill the treasury. The

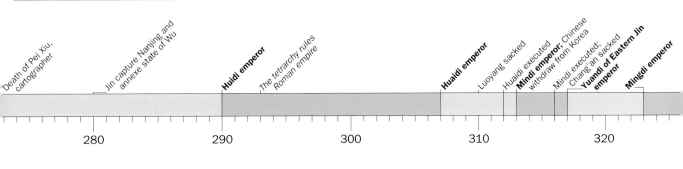

habit of rewarding loyalty with gifts of huge estates and vast numbers of peasants had undermined the imperial tax system (based on peasant poll taxes and corvée labour) by withdrawing land and manpower from the central registers. Economic power had shifted to the regions where local manor houses now replaced the imperial administration. Peasants, driven from their fields by natural disasters, civil war and northern invasions, fled as rebels or exchanged independence for security as serfs on the great estates, often being recruited into private armies. Economically unassailable, occupying most of the higher offices of state, the great landowners now had the military force to challenge the throne.

Wudi had given each of his 25 sons a principality and on his death unity was shattered by sibling rivalry. Two princes sought help from northern tribes and Wudi's heir, the weak and witless **Huidi** (290–306), was driven helplessly from one capital to another in a situation of utter chaos. His brother and successor, **Huaidi** (307–312), having invited Xiongnu support, found himself their prisoner and his capital destroyed. His successor, Wudi's grandson **Mindi** (313–316), was captured in 316 and killed while Chang'an was sacked.

The northerners now held the central plains and the Chinese were forced south to the Yangzi Valley where a minor prince, gathering the remnants of the court, declared himself as the emperor Yuandi of the Eastern Jin dynasty. Thus started the 'Period of Disunion' in which China was divided into the 'Northern Dynasties' under non-Han rulers and the 'Southern Dynasties', guardians of Chinese civilization with their capital at Nanjing.

The Eastern Jin

For just over a century the Eastern Jin provided relative stability. Their rulers were unremarkable men, weak and at the mercy of the great landowner-generals – only five of the 11 emperors reigned for more than six years. They employed good officials, however, and benefited from the general longing for peace. As guardians of the imperial tradition they maintained Confucian rites, reviving the importance of ancestor worship and the use of tomb statuary which had been banned by the Wei on grounds of expense.

The court at Nanjing became a refuge from northern 'barbarians' and the centre of Chinese civilization. It was a luxurious court, adopting Han customs, and the streets of Nanjing bustled with merchants and missionaries arriving along the southern trade routes through Burma. Scholars, poets and artists gathered in the new metropolis and there was an extra-

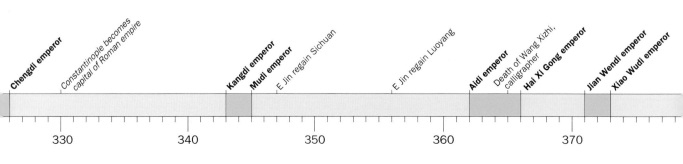

Chengdi emperor

Constantinople becomes capital of Roman empire

Kangdi emperor

Mudi emperor

E Jin regain Sichuan

E Jin regain Luoyang

Aidi emperor

Death of Wang Xizhi, calligrapher

Hai Xi Gong emperor

Jian Wendi emperor

Xiao Wudi emperor

330   340   350   360   370

EASTERN JIN

YUANDI	*Temple name*
Accession	Aidi ('Sorrowing
317	Emperor')
Died	
322	**HAI XI GONG**
Temple name	*Accession*
Yuandi ('Original	366
Emperor')	*Died*
	370
MINGDI	*Temple name*
Accession	Hai Xi Gong ('King
323	of the Western
Died	Ocean')
325	
Temple name	**JIAN WENDI**
Mingdi ('Brilliant	*Accession*
Emperor')	371
	Died
CHENGDI	372
Accession	*Temple name*
326	Jian Wendi
Died	('Refined Literati
342	Emperor')
Temple name	
Chengdi	**XIAO WUDI**
('Accomplished	*Accession*
Emperor')	373
	Died
KANGDI	396
Accession	*Temple name*
343	Xiao Wudi ('Filial
Died	Martial Emperor')
344	
Temple name	**ANDI**
Kangdi ('Healthy	*Accession*
Emperor')	397
	Died
MUDI	418
Accession	*Temple name*
345	Andi ('Peaceful
Died	Emperor')
361	
Temple name	**GONGDI**
Mudi ('Reverent	*Accession*
Emperor')	419
	Died
AIDI	419
Accession	*Temple name*
362	Gongdi ('Respectful
Died	Emperor')
365	

ordinary flowering of the arts. Political disunity brought cultural fermentation in which classical art was fertilized by Daoism and foreign Buddhist influences . The transition from the harsh central plains to the luxuriant southern landscape was a revelation which gave new meaning to Daoist interest in man's role in nature. In this friendly world of wooded hills and fertile well-watered valleys the Daoist call for meditation and self-expression was stronger than Confucian appeals to social duty. Scholars turned from public life, becoming hermits, or, like the famous group of Daoists, the Seven Sages in a Bamboo Grove, reacted against the formal Confucianism of their official life and deliberately flouted convention, seeking to escape political turmoil in philosophical discussions, writing poetry and drinking. One of the group, Liu Ling – who was always accompanied by a servant carrying a bottle of wine and a spade with which to dig his grave – summed up their attitude, declaring that to a drunken man the 'affairs of this world appear as so much duckweed in a river.' Wang Xizhi (306–365) developed the beautiful flowing grass script, raising calligraphy to the highest of all arts: his characters, 'light as a floating cloud, vigorous as a startled dragon', were very different from those of the square clearly defined Han Confucian script. The unaccustomed beauty shaped the newly emerging landscape painting – the word for landscape is 'mountain-water' and Gu Kaizhi and others laid the foundation of Chinese figure painting.

At the same time Buddhism provided an inspiration to architects, painters and sculptors, attracting patrons from the court downwards. Buddhism, which arrived in China in the 1st century, was now the official religion of the northern emperors. The southern state was founded on Confucianism but the Buddhist offer of salvation and escape from the pains and chaos of this world attracted intellectuals and populace alike. Xiao Wudi became a Buddhist in 381 and filled his palace with monks; in 399 the

(Right) Example of Wang Xizhi's calligraphy from an Eastern Jin handscroll *Kuaixue Shiqing*.

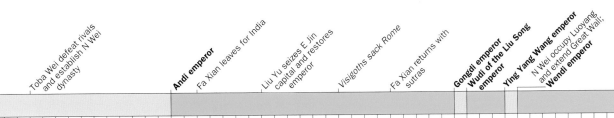

Toba Wei defeat rivals and establish N Wei dynasty

Andi emperor

Fa Xian leaves for India

Liu Yu seizes E Jin capital and restores emperor

Visigoths sack Rome

Fa Xian returns with sutras

Gongdi emperor
Wudi of the Liu Song emperor

Ying Yang Wang emperor

N Wei occupy Luoyang and extend Great Wall; **Wendi emperor**

390 400 410 420 430

Detail from the scroll *The Admonitions of the Instructress* showing the emperor with one of his concubines, by Gu Kaizhi (c.344-406). Gu Kaizhi became famous at the Eastern Jin court at Nanjing for his portrait and figure painting; his subjects are portrayed with an expressiveness and individualism that were new in Chinese portraiture. Although none of his original paintings has survived, the Chinese have always had a tradition of copying great works of art faithfully and this is one of two copies, probably made in the Tang dynasty (British Museum).

monk Fa Xian left for India, settling in Nanjing on his return in 414 to translate the Buddhist texts he brought back. Buddhism was fashionable and money and artistic energy poured into religious buildings and the creation of countless icons. The very few examples of southern Buddhist art which have survived show a lightness and elegance that was new in Chinese art.

At first, Jin stability was helped by northern weakness. The north, under the Sixteen Kingdoms, was riven by nomadic tribes of Mongol, Turkic, Tungu and Tibetan origin. Hordes of refugees fled south, among them many large landowning families. With their thousands of dependents, these families quickly established positions of strength around Nanjing, urging military ventures to regain their lost homelands. Their pressure, resisted by **Yuandi** (317–322), dominated the remainder of the dynasty, with perpetual friction between the peace and war groups. **Mingdi** (323–325) was weak and his reign too short to have much influence. **Chengdi** (326–342) was unable to restrain the revanchists, who provoked a series of minor, usually unsuccessful, engagements. **Kangdi** (343–344) only lasted a year, but under **Mudi** (345–361) the tide appeared to turn. In 347, he regained Sichuan and in 356 recaptured Luoyang, but the city was captured again by northerners during the reign of **Aidi** (362–365) nine years later. Little is known of Aidi's successors, **Hai Xi**

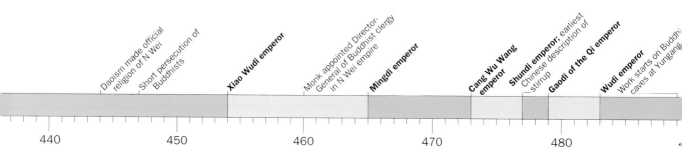

Daoism made official religion of N Wei

Short persecution of Buddhists

Xiao Wudi emperor

Monk appointed Director-General of Buddhist clergy in N Wei empire

Mingdi emperor

Cang Wu Wang emperor

Shundi emperor: earliest Chinese description of stirrup

Gaodi of the Qi emperor

Wudi emperor

Work starts on Buddhist caves at Yungang

440   450   460   470   480

LIU SONG

WUDI	*Accession*
Born	454
355, as Liu Yu	*Father*
Accession	Wendi
420	*Wife*
Wife	empress Wang
empress Cang (died	(died 464)
408)	*Major concubine*
Major concubine	consort Ji (died
consort Hu Jiechao	462)
Died	*Died*
422	464
Tomb	*Temple name*
Chuningling,	Xiao Wudi ('Filial
Qilinpu, Nanjing,	Martial Emperor')
Jiangsu	
Temple name	**MINGDI**
Wudi ('Martial	*Born*
Emperor')	449, as Liu Yu
	Accession
YING YANG WANG	465
Born	*Father*
c. 404, as Liu Yifu	Wendi (11th son of)
Accession	*Abdicated*
423	472
Father	*Died*
Wudi	477
Died	*Temple name*
423	Mingdi ('Brilliant
Temple name	Emperor')
Ying Yang Wang	
('Sun King of Ying');	**CANG WU WANG**
also known as	*Born*
Shaodi	471, as Liu Ye
	Accession
WENDI	473
Born	*Family background*
406, as Liu Yilong	adopted son of
Accession	Mingdi
424	*Died*
Father	476
Wudi	*Temple name*
Mother	Cang Wu Wang
consort Hu Jiechao	('King of Cangwu');
Died	also known as Feidi
453	
Tomb	**SHUNDI**
Changningling,	*Born*
Nanjing, Jiangsu,	464, as Liu Jun
south of	*Accession*
Ganjiaxiang (earlier	477
known as tomb of	*Father*
Chen Wendi)	Mingdi (3rd son of)
Temple name	*Died*
Wendi ('Literary	Murdered 479
Emperor')	*Temple name*
	Shundi
XIAO WUDI	('Submissive
Born	Emperor')
448, as Liu Jun	

Gong (366–370) and **Jian Wendi** (371–372), who ruled only five years in total. **Xiao Wudi** (373–396) started well. In 383, Jin forces repulsed a major attack from the north, but three years later, the situation was transformed by the emergence of a single power in the north – the Toba (or Northern) Wei dynasty, against whose forces the Jin armies were powerless. The Jin were meanwhile facing rural unrest, with widespread peasant movements in the west and pirate bands, known as 'The Immortals', in the east. Both were crushed but left misery and famine in their wake, and the continual fighting increased the power of the generals at the expense of the emperor. In the Jin's dynastic twilight, **Andi** (397–418) welcomed the great Buddhist pilgrim, Fa Xian, home from his travels in 414, and Fa Xian settled in Nanjing to translate the documents that he had brought back from India. When the Toba Wei attacked, the last emperor, **Gongdi** (419), a younger son of Xiao Wudi, was forced to abdicate within a year of accession in favour of general Liu Yu, the founder of the Liu Song dynasty.

The Liu Song

With **Song Wudi** (420–422), the emperors came back on stage. Born a poor woodcutter and fisherman, he turned to soldiering during the unrest in 399 and quickly rose to the rank of general. He supported the failing Jin until 420 when, convinced of the Jin's inability to rule, he usurped the throne. His dynasty, the third of the six 'Southern Dynasties' based in Nanjing, was called Liu Song to distinguish it from the great Song dynasty five centuries later.

Under Wudi and his son Wendi, the southern empire reached its peak, but the aura of legitimacy which had protected the Jin was gone and the throne was once again open game. The power of the great families was unbroken; the throne was seldom inherited by direct succession and the next 160 years are a dismal story of changing dynasties against a background of constant, usually unsuccessful wars against the 'barbarian' north. The founders of these dynasties were soldiers of fortune, often of low birth, whose descendants, lacking prestige and education, were easy prey for the next usurper.

Song Wudi re-established internal order and, rebuffing northern invaders, enlarged the frontiers. After his death, a disastrous successor, his unruly 19-year-old son, **Ying Yang Wang** (423), was swiftly replaced by an older half-brother, the emperor **Wendi** (424–453), under whom the realm prospered for 30 years. As a Confucianist, Wendi revived the Han ideal of a civil service based on scholarship. He tried to attract scholars

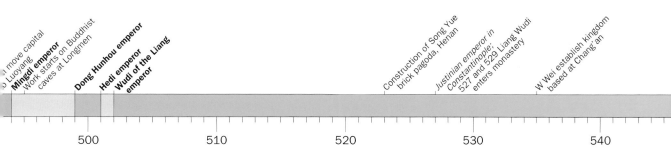

Southern Dynasties tomb statuary around Nanjing and Danyang, Jiangsu, includes some of the finest animal statuary ever carved in China. Huge stone fabulous beasts, up to 4m high, with horns and elaborate wing patterns, guarded imperial tombs; equally large creatures without horns but with a large outstretched tongue, symbol of communication with heaven, were placed on royal tombs. Fabulous *bixie*, tomb of Xiao Jing (d. 523), a cousin of Liang Wudi, Nanjing.

back into public life, fostering the teaching of the classics, and attempted to check the growing power of religious establishments which were causing a serious drain on state resources. Buddhist and Daoist monastic lands fell outside the land register and their monks and nuns were exempt from taxation and corvée labour. These privileges encouraged the wealthy to place their estates under monastic title while encouraging the poor to enrol as monks, and by the early 5th century the wealthy Buddhist church was becoming a state within a state, economically independent of central authority. In 435, Wendi ordered an enquiry into the morals of monks and nuns; those not strictly obeying monastic rules were expelled. All temple building and the casting of images without official licence were banned.

The perennial struggle with the north continued. In 424, the Northern Wei had captured Luoyang and in 450, having camped on the outskirts of Nanjing, proposed a peaceful alliance to be cemented by two royal marriages. The southern war party persuaded Wendi to refuse, and the Wei, in unaccustomed terrain and weakened by supply problems were driven north, leaving a trail of desolation behind them. When, however, the southerners attacked the north the following year they were soundly beaten.

Xiao Wudi (454–464) started well but according to the historians ended as a drunkard and miser. His successors are marked by a total lack of ability and propriety. The 16-year-old Liu Ye was so wild and irresponsible that he was killed within a year by one of his own officers and is not included in the imperial list. His successor and uncle, **Mingdi** (465–472) – Wendi's 11th son – nicknamed 'the Pig' for his fatness, patronized Buddhism, built a magnificent pagoda and poisoned his wife, brother-in-law, three brothers and 28 nephews. **Cang Wu Wang** (473–476), also known as Feidi, was a juvenile delinquent whose downfall was caused by shooting blunt arrows at a target he had painted on a sleeping minister's belly. The minister retaliated by having him murdered and replaced by his 13-year-old half-brother, **Shundi** (477–479). This last Song emperor was deposed within two years by an elder member of the powerful Xiao family, Xiao Daocheng, the emperor Gaodi of the Qi dynasty.

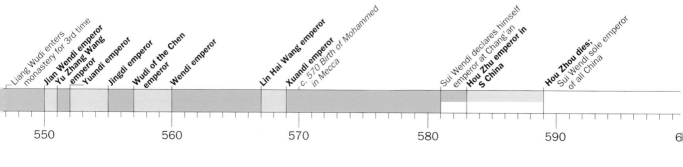

Liang Wudi enters monastery for 3rd time
Jian Wendi emperor
Yu Zhang Wang
Yuandi emperor
Jingdi emperor
Wudi of the Chen emperor
Wendi emperor
Lin Hai Wang emperor
Xuandi emperor
c. 570 Birth of Mohammed in Mecca
Sui Wendi declares himself emperor at Chang'an
Hou Zhu emperor in S China
Hou Zhou dies; Sui Wendi sole emperor of all China

550   560   570   580   590

6

QI	
GAODI	Accession
Born	494
423, as Xiao Daocheng	*Family connection*
	nephew of Gaodi
Accession	*Father*
479	Jingdi (posthumous
Father	title)
Xiao Cheng (died	*Died*
447) given	498
posthumous title Qi	*Tomb*
Xuandi	Xinganling,
Wife	Danyang, Jiangsu
empress Lu (died	*Temple name*
475)	Mingdi ('Brilliant
Died	Emperor')
482	
Tomb	DONG HUNHOU
Danyang, Jiangsu	*Born*
Temple name	582?, as Xiao Bao
Gaodi ('High	Chuan
Emperor')	*Accession*
	499
WUDI	*Father*
Born	Mingdi
439, as Xiao Ze	*Died*
Accession	500
483	*Temple name*
Father	Dong Hunhou
Gaodi	('Marquis of
Wife	Eastern
empress Pei (died	Fatuousness')
481)	
Died	HEDI
493	*Born*
Tomb	486
Jinganling,	*Accession*
Danyang, Jiangsu	501
Temple name	*Father*
Wudi ('Martial	Mingdi
Emperor')	*Died*
	501
MINGDI	*Temple name*
Born	Hedi ('Harmonious
447, as Xiao Luan	Emperor')

The Qi

Qi Gaodi (479–482), an ardent Buddhist who filled the palace with monks, traced his lineage back 600 years to one of Han Gaodi's commanders, but his dynasty was short-lived. His son, **Wudi** (483–493) was able, peaceful but extravagant and on his death things took the customary downturn. Two young princes were enthroned in quick succession, Yulin, aged 21, and Hailing, aged 15, but both were murdered by their uncle who became the emperor **Mingdi** (494–498). Mingdi's son, **Dong Hunhou** (499–500), aged 19, was killed to make way for his 15-year-old half-brother, **Hedi** (501). Nicknamed 'the idiot eastern marquis', Hedi hated study, had his tutors and six brothers killed and finally slew his best adviser, the brother of the regent Xiao Yan. The latter retaliated by attacking Nanjing and after a long siege in which 80,000 people died from hunger and sickness, Xiao Yan took the throne in the name of the Liang dynasty as Liang Wudi. Hedi was executed by his own guard who sent the head, preserved in wax, to Xiao Yan.

The Liang

Liang Wudi (502–549) has been described as 'almost the only personality of interest to occupy the throne in the Southern Dynasties' and his reign was the longest and most stable of the period. From a powerful, aristocratic family linked to the imperial Qi, he held many senior posts before becoming regent to Qi Hedi. He combined the best of Confucian and Buddhist virtues. Recognizing that Confucian ethics were essential for good government, he founded five new institutes and made it compulsory for the sons of nobles and imperial princes to attend academies teaching the classics. He was a first-class scholar, composed his own edicts, wrote poetry and patronized the arts, his court becoming a centre for writers and painters. His career illustrates the Chinese ability to embrace different philosophical and religious beliefs. Confucian through his office, and interested in Daoism as a youth, he became one of the most devoted Buddhists ever to sit on the Chinese throne. He was genuinely attracted by the Buddhist ideals of boundless compassion, meditation and personal salvation and sent an envoy, Song Yuan, to India to collect new texts. Passionate, strong-willed and ambitious, Wudi concentrated on spiritual rather than martial aims. In the end this created a gulf between himself and the people. Hating to take life (only with the greatest reluctance would he authorize an execution), he banned the sacrifice of animals in the ancestral rites, ordering that they be replaced by pastry imitations, and he forbade the weaving of cloth with representations of immortals, men or animals which might be cut when the material was used. In 527, and again in 529 and 547, he laid aside the throne to enter the Dong Dai monastery as a monk, only returning to public life when his ministers paid a huge ransom.

Meanwhile the Toba Wei, who had moved their capital south to Luoyang in 494, continued their attacks. In 502 and 505, Wei armies swept into southern China, but after the Wei split into two kingdoms in

LIANG	
WUDI	**YU ZHANG WANG**
Born	*Accession*
463, as Xiao Yan	551
Accession	*Father*
502	Wudi
Father	*Died*
a cousin of Qi	551; murdered by
Gaodi (died 494),	brother Xiao Yi
posthumously given	*Temple name*
title Liang Wendi	Yu Zhang Wang
Wife	('King of Yuzhang')
empress Xi (died	
499)	**YUANDI**
Died	*Born*
549	507, as Xiao Yi
Tomb	*Accession*
Xiling, Danyang,	552
Jiangsu	*Father*
Temple name	Wudi (7th son of)
Wudi ('Martial	*Died*
Emperor')	554
	Temple name
JIAN WENDI	Yuandi ('Original
Born	Emperor')
501, as Xiao Gang	
Accession	**JINGDI**
550	*Born*
Father	542, as Xiao
Wudi (3rd son of)	Fangzhi
Wife	*Accession*
empress Wang	555
(died 549)	*Father*
Died	Yuandi (9th son of)
550	*Abdicated*
Tomb	556
Zhuangling,	*Died*
Danyang, Jiangsu	558
Temple name	*Temple name*
Jian Wendi	Jingdi ('Esteemed
('Refined Literati	Emperor')
Emperor')	

(Right) Liang Wudi's deep Buddhist convictions led him to renounce the throne three times and enter a monastery. In this Ming woodcut of Wudi in a temple *(above)*, worshippers offer obeisance to the emperor rather than to the Buddha behind the altar.

534 the southerners were encouraged to try a new offensive. While Wudi was in the monastery in 547, the southerners attacked only to be soundly beaten, losing 23 provinces. In reaction against his father's Buddhism, the future **Jian Wendi** (550) now rebelled against his father, urged on by a wily northern rebel, Hou Jing. Once again, Nanjing was besieged and when the rebels broke into the palace, only one tenth of the garrison were still alive. Wudi, pale and emaciated but true to his principles, greeted the gloating victor with the words 'You have campaigned long. You must be tired'. Hou Jing spared his life, becoming regent for Jian Wendi.

Liang Wudi had numerous brothers and sons whose memorials have survived around Nanjing. His eldest son, Xiao Tong, compiled China's most famous anthology, the *Wen Xuan* ('Literary Selections'), but unfortunately he died before his father. The younger sons were of a different ilk and within eight years

THE DEVELOPMENT OF DAOISM

The collapse of Han Confucian government revived intellectual interest in Daoism. Commentaries on the classic *Dao de Jing* were followed by the *Zhuangzi*, the second great Daoist set of texts. 'Purity-debates' contrasted intellectual probity with political turpitude and the Seven Sages in a Bamboo Grove set the fashion by rejecting official life and deliberately following a life of hedonism, encouraging eccentricity as a protest against Confucian convention. Other Daoists revived the search for alchemy as a source of immortality. The earliest Chinese medical works date from the 2nd and 3rd centuries AD and Daoist investigation into the properties of elements and plants produced a vast pharmacopoeia. One school preached salvation through Inner Hygiene with a rigid diet – no alcohol, meat or grain – and breathing exercises and meditation to rid the body of the 'three worms' – disease, old age and death.

The most striking developments, however, were the growth of a popular Daoist religion and the adoption of institutional practices such as the establishment of organized monasteries and convents similar to those of the Buddhists. They mobilized the force of peasant uprisings, such as the 'Yellow Turbans' revolt, at mass-meetings in which the participants were encouraged to confess their sins and believe in faith healing. The promise of immortality inspired believers to overcome their fear of death and attack armed militia and regular soldiers with primitive weapons such as sticks and stones. Daoist sects gained a privileged position similar to that of the

(Above) Qing dynasty painting of the Seven Sages of the Bamboo Grove (British Museum).

(Right) Song dynasty statue of Laozi, carved from the living rock at the foot of Mt. Qingyuan, Fujian.

Buddhists and vied with the latter in mass-producing texts and painted and sculptural icons. They developed an enormous pantheon, headed at first by a triad of deities and then by a supreme deity, Lord Huanlao, an amalgam of the mythical Yellow Emperor and Laozi, reputed father of Daoism. Beneath him was a hierarchy of immortals and historical persons, cult heroes raised to semi-divinity for their good works on earth. This celestial bureaucracy was matched by the officialdom of hell; both were based on the contemporary administrative system and judges of hell are always portrayed in the robes of worldly officials.

The Daoist hierarchy was never as rigid or cohesive as the Buddhist. The crushing of the 'Yellow Turban' movement prevented the creation of a central organization and it remained essentially a collection of local sects with their own priests and cults. Their association with magic and popular superstition endeared them to the populace but lowered their general reputation, and neither their moral nor intellectual standards reached those of the Buddhists.

(*Above left*) Proof of Liang Wudi's proselytizing influence can be seen as far afield as Sichuan where, in 529, Buddhist figures in niches were carved on his orders over the original Han dynasty reliefs on this monumental tower from the end of the 1st century AD. Pingyang *que*, Mianyang, Sichuan.

(*Above right*) The column, originally one of a pair, carries an inscription tablet recording that this is the spirit road to the tomb of Liang Wendi, father of Wudi, founder of the Liang dynasty. The statuary was erected in 502. Danyang, Jiangsu.

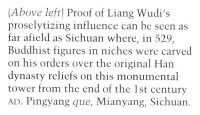

Figurines of typical thickset and bearded Northern Wei warriors found in Northern Dynasties tombs (British Museum).

the Liang dynasty ended. Jian Wendi was killed by his former ally, Hou Jing, who, after a short interlude under **Yu Zhang Wang** (551), fell under an attack by Wudi's seventh son, **Yuandi** (552–554). The horrors of the Nanjing siege had been compounded by drought and locusts leading to widespread famine and the hated Hou Jing was literally cut into pieces and thrown to the starving mob.

Yuandi combined a love of literature and collecting with extreme cruelty, eliminating rivals and starving their offspring to death in prison. He favoured Daoism and believed that his collection of precious Daoist texts had magical powers of protection. When defeated by northern troops under a grandson of Liang Wudi who had fled north for safety, he deliberately burned his library of over 200,000 books for failing him. Leaving the burning hall in a white robe of mourning he abdicated in favour of his ninth son, **Jingdi** (555–556), who was killed at 16 by Chen Baxian, the new usurper of the throne, who took the name Chen Wudi.

The Chen

The last of the Southern Dynasties never had a chance. The devastation of the later Liang years had disorganized the administration, which was corrupt and inefficient. None of the Chen emperors was able or strong enough to halt the decline. The founding Chen emperor,

CHEN	
WUDI	*Dethroned*
Born	568
500, as Chen	*Died*
Baxian	570; murdered
Accession	*Temple name*
557	Lin Hai Wang ('King
Wife	of Linhai')
empress Zhang	
(died 570)	**XUANDI**
Died	*Born*
559	516, as Chen Xu
Tomb	*Accession*
Wananling, Nanjing	569
Jiangsu	*Family connection*
Temple name	brother of Wendi
Wudi ('Martial	*Died*
Emperor')	582
	Temple name
WENDI	Xuandi ('Proclaimed
Born	Emperor')
504, as Chen Qian	
Accession	**HOU ZHU**
560	*Born*
Died	552, as Chen
566	Shubao
Temple name	*Accession*
Wendi ('Literary	583
Emperor')	*Father*
	Xuandi (eldest son
LIN HAI WANG	of)
Born	*Died*
551, as Chen	589
Bozong	*Temple name*
Accession	Hou Zhu ('Later
567	Master')

Wudi (557–559), was a clever, mild and deeply religious man who became a monk a year after his succession. His nephew, **Wendi** (560–566), was industrious, but ruled for too short a time to have a lasting influence. His young and inexperienced 16-year-old son, **Lin Hai Wang** (567–568), was deposed within two years by his uncle, **Xuandi** (569–582). Wendi had originally wished to leave the throne to Xuandi, but had been prevented by powerful government ministers who feared that Xuandi might prove too independent. Xuandi was an active military leader who recovered some territory in the north in 573, but later suffered a severe defeat by the Northern Zhou who had reunified all northern China in 581. The last Chen emperor, **Hou Zhu** (583–589), was described by Chinese historians as 'drunk, dissolute, neglectful of the Great Spirits of Heaven and his ancestors, addicted to foolish superstitions and surrounded by worthless companions.' His self-indulgence and extravagance were notorious. State affairs were left to the eunuchs while he remained in his luxurious palace enjoying 'frivolous' music. The new ruler of the north, Yang Jian, founder of the Sui dynasty, preceded his attack on the Chen by distributing 300,000 copies of a memorandum listing Hou Zhu's faults, thus convincing the population that their emperor had lost the Mandate of Heaven. When northern troops entered the palace, Hou Zhu, tying himself together with two concubines, tried to hide in a well but was discovered. Yang Jian spared him and his family in the interests of the now reunited empire.

Portraits of Chen Hou Zhu (*above*) and Chen Xuandi (*right*) from the *Thirteen Emperors* scroll, by Yan Liben, second half of the 7th century (Museum of Fine Arts, Boston).

BUDDHISM

The original Buddha, the prince Gautama, was born in southern Nepal in the 5th century BC. Abandoning court life and family ties, Gautama found salvation through meditation and preached that man could only earn release from worldly misery by the gradual accumulation of merit through a long series of reincarnations leading to the blessed state of *nirvana* or non-existence. Merit was earned by obeying the sacred rules – not to kill, steal, commit adultery, tell lies or drink alcohol – and by renouncing all worldly pleasures including family life.

In the 1st century AD, however, an alternative, milder version developed in which salvation could be attained through an instant moment of enlightenment opening the doors to a Western Paradise filled with happy beings free from worldly suffering. It was this Mahayana Buddhism which arrived in China during the Han dynasty. The earliest Buddhist settlement, the White Horse Temple at Luoyang, was founded by a Parthian missionary, An Shigao, who arrived with Indian texts in AD 148. Initially, Buddhists gained popularity by allying themselves with the Daoists, only emerging as an independent, strong church under the patronage of the non-Chinese northern rulers in the 3rd and 4th centuries AD.

The cliff shrines at Yungang, near the Northern Wei capital, Datong, are the earliest stone carved caves in China; most of the 51,000 surviving stone figures date from between 453 and 494. This colossal Buddha typifies the early Indian-influenced style; the alien deity is the epitome of authority and its whole sculptural treatment expresses the idea of an all-powerful being withdrawn from the petty problems of this world.

The northern emperors' decision to adopt Buddhism as an official religion was partly a political attempt to maintain their identity. In 335, a tribal ruler made this clear: 'We were born out of the marches and though We are unworthy, We have complied with our appointed destiny and govern the Chinese as their prince....Buddha being a barbarian god is the very one we should worship.' They feared that Confucian advisers would soon outwit them; Buddhist monks, on the other hand, were mostly foreign and entirely dependent on their rulers' pleasure. To become acceptable, however, the Buddhists had to modify certain doctrines such as Buddha's injunction to sever all family ties, and to accept a modicum of ancestor worship. Translators of Buddhist scriptures modified doctrine to suit local prejudices and 'Husband supports wife' and 'Wife comforts husband', for example, reappeared as the Confucian precepts 'Husband controls wife' and 'Wife reveres husband'.

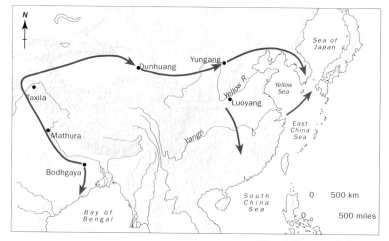

(Above) The spread of Buddhism.

(Below) The Buddhists adopted the Chinese habit of erecting stone tablets (stelae) carved with images and texts. Dedicatory stele from the Six Dynasties period, 529 AD.

The Northern Wei rulers made full use of the Chinese habit of using sculpture to spread official doctrines. The magnificent imperial cliff shrines – Yungang (main period, 460–494) in the north and Longmen (495–535) near Luoyang – carved near their capitals were in part their answer to the imperial tombs of the south with their impressive stone animal guardians. These sculptures were not only expressions of belief but symbols of legitimacy. Primarily designed to glorify Buddha, they reflected both the wealth and power of the northern emperors and the Chinese need to placate the ancestors. A typical inscription at Yungang is: 'We respectfully make and present this holy image in honour of the Buddhas, Bodhisattvas, and pray that all living creatures may attain salvation, and particularly that the souls of our ancestors and relatives [names given] may find repose and release.'

(Above) The shrine cave walls at Yungang were carved with tightly packed figures against an architectural background with tile-roofed buildings, elaborate portals and balustrades.

(Left) Exterior of the Yungang caves near Datong.

(Below) Lotus cave, Longmen (carved 512–528).

THE NORTHERN DYNASTIES

And, Sir, the last Emperor – so they say – fled from Saragh [Luoyang] because of the famine, and his palace and walled city were set on fire.... So Saragh is no more, Ngap [the great city of Yeh, further north] no more!'

A Sogdian merchant writing to his partner in Samarkand about the destruction of Luoyang in 311 by the northern Xiongnu tribe

Political instability in the north was even greater than that in the south. From 304 to 439, a period known by the Chinese as 'the Sixteen Kingdoms', a succession of northern tribal rulers fought for control and the political landscape resembled a kaleidoscope of short-lived warring states. In the late 4th century, however, a nomadic people of Turkic origin – the Xian Bei or Toba Wei – acquired dominance, and in 386 they defeated their last rival, unifying northern China under what was now known as the Northern Wei empire, the first of the five 'Northern Dynasties.

Although the emperors of the Northern Dynasties were never recognized as legitimate by Chinese historians, events in the north had a decisive influence on Chinese history. Behind the military confrontation lay a clash of ideas and ideals which was eventually solved by an incorporation of northern elements into Chinese civilization. Despite political division and economic stagnation – large areas returned to a system of bartering – this was a time of intellectual ferment, with a continual cross-fertilization from the refugees flowing north and south. The greatest common influence was, however, Buddhism, which entered China both through Central Asia along the Silk Roads and from the south. With its universal offer of salvation, regardless of nationality and rank, Buddhism cut across political frontiers, and with its missionaries came merchants and travellers bringing Western inventions and art motifs, further enriching intellectual and artistic life.

Slowly the northerners became sinicized. Although historians speak of 'hordes', the northerners were always heavily outnumbered by the local population and intermarriage was common. More important, having no written language, the northerners were obliged to use Chinese script. Despite the political division, China thus remained a cultural unity. In 494, when the Northern Wei moved their capital south from Datong to Luoyang, the Northern Wei emperor Xiao Wendi ('Filial Cultured

Northern Wei friezes showing the arrival at the shrine of the emperor and empress with their followers give an excellent picture of the degree of sinicization at the northern court. The figures are entirely Chinese and the treatment of the subjects reflects southern advances in figure painting. The court ladies following the empress are alive, one turning to talk to another and there is a depth to the scene lacking in earlier Han dynasty reliefs. Friezes similar to this example from Longmen are still in situ at a Northern Wei cave site at Gongxian, Henan (Nelson-Atkins Gallery, Kansas City).

THE NORTHERN WEI (386–534)

THE SIXTEEN KINGDOMS (304–439)

THE NORTHERN DYNASTIES

The most striking architectural innovation brought by the Buddhists from India was the pagoda, based on the Indian stupa. Built to house religious relics or valuable texts, pagodas were usually placed singly in the courtyard of a temple built on traditional Chinese lines. This pagoda at Dengfeng, Song Yue monastery, Henan, built in 523, is the oldest complete brick building in China.

Emperor') imposed a drastic policy of sinicization at court. Northerners were obliged to speak Chinese, wear Chinese dress, take Chinese surnames and, deprived of their tribal titles, were reclassified like Chinese families of standing.

The wealth of the north came from land reform. Inheriting the same financial system as the south, in which land taxes were light and the main tax burden borne by free peasants (in poll tax and corvée labour), the northerners suffered the same problem of dwindling central revenues. The great landowners and Buddhist establishments (estimated in 554 at 30,000 with 2 million monks and nuns), took so much money and manpower out of the system that strong central government was impossible. In 485, Xiao Wendi introduced a radical land reform known as the Equal Fields system designed to maintain or increase the number of independent peasants. All state land was nationalized and every peasant family allotted an equal share of about 19 acres (7.5 ha). Of this a small proportion could be held permanently for long-term crops such as mulberry trees for silk, but the main part returned to the state on death for redistribution. Although these measures could not regain land already in private hands they prevented further erosion and stabilized central finances, creating a sound economic basis which made the future reunification possible.

In 535, military revolts against the sinicization at court had split the Wei into rival Eastern and Western Wei kingdoms, followed respectively by the Northern Qi and Northern Zhou dynasties, and there was a partial return to northern styles with an emphasis on the military and the foreign nature of Buddhism. This reverse was brief. In 581, four years after the Zhou had defeated the Qi and reimposed northern unity, a Zhou general, Yang Jian, usurped the throne. This was the man who so easily overcame the effete Southern Chen in Nanjing, and founded the Sui dynasty as emperor Wendi, ruler of all China.

E. WEI(534–550) | N. QI (550–577)

SUI (581–618)

W. WEI (535–557) | N. ZHOU (557–581)

CHINA REUNIFIED

500

600

SUI DYNASTY
581–618

文帝 **Wendi**
581–604

炀帝 **Yangdi**
604–617

恭帝 **Gongdi**
617–618

Portrait of Sui Wendi from the *Thirteen Emperors* scroll by Yan Liben (Museum of Fine Arts, Boston).

WENDI	
Born 541, as Yang Jian	*Children* 5 sons, 1 daughter (who married the Heir Apparent of the Northern Zhou emperor)
Title before accession regent for Northern Zhou child-emperor (580)	
Accession 581	*Died* 604
Father Yang Zhong	*Tomb* Tailing, Fufeng county, Shaanxi
Wife empress Wenxian (died 602)	*Temple name* Wendi ('Literary Emperor')

Like the overture to a great opera, the Sui heralded the revival of imperial glory. Although the 'empire' had survived in name during the Period of Disunion, its rulers had been mostly military usurpers, governing only a few provinces, and failing to attract the elusive aura of legitimacy. In 40 years the Sui introduced the elements needed for genuine imperial rule – a strongly centralized military and civil administration with a sound financial base. They created an effective canal system linking north and south and, while using Buddhism as a unifying force, revived Confucianism as a source of good administration and legitimacy.

WENDI

With the armed might of a Cakravartin king [model Indian Buddhist king], We spread the ideals of the Ultimately Enlightened One. With a hundred victories in a hundred battles, We promote the practice of the ten Buddhist virtues. Therefore We regard the weapons of war as having become like the offerings of incense and flowers presented to Buddha, and the fields of this world as becoming forever identical with the Buddha-land.

Imperial edict of 581

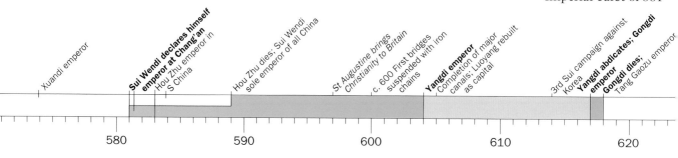

Yang Jian, the emperor **Wendi** (581–604), was a typical member of the new northern aristocracy created through intermarriage between northern chieftains and the old Chinese aristocrats. His family had served the northern rulers for over two centuries and were connected to the Northern Zhou imperial family. Born a Buddhist, he later received a typical nobleman's education in the military arts and held military and civilian posts from the age of 14 onwards. His daughter married the heir apparent of the Northern Zhou and when the emperor died unexpectedly in 578, the throne passed rapidly through her husband to his six-year-old son. In the ensuing confusion Yang Jian, as regent, seized the throne. His abilities and experience gained widespread support and he soon turned his attention southwards, easily overcoming the last Chen emperor, Hou Zhu. After three centuries of division, China was at last reunited.

Wendi's administrative experience coupled with a strong sense of duty made him an extremely able ruler. His palace and capital, Chang'an, were based on classical cosmological plans as visible symbols of imperial power. Expert engineers and architects designed exquisite novelties for the imperial palace, such as a pavilion for several hundred guests which could be rotated swiftly by a mechanism underneath. 'It seems like the work of a god; the barbarians who saw it were struck with awe, and the emperor was delighted.'

His most urgent task was to ensure internal peace by removing the private armies which had flourished during the Period of Disunion. He ordered complete disarmament, settling disbanded soldiers on the land as peasant farmers and reorganizing the imperial army under strict central control. The Great Wall was repaired, and, by establishing agricultural colonies in border regions and extending the canal system linking the rich rice-growing south to the northern border regions, Wendi made it possible to maintain large frontier forces.

Wendi appointed excellent ministers and reformed the administration, replacing the northern system – strongly influenced by lineage and aristocracy – with an impartial system of selection giving southerners their due (at his accession, 65 per cent of officials were northerners). A glutton for work, he presided over the dawn audiences, dealt with mountains of paperwork, personally reviewed judicial decisions and examined official candidates. Building on earlier Northern Dynasties land reforms, he carried through a major redistribution of land, doubling the taxable population from four million households in 589 to nearly nine million in 606. Above all, he insisted on the strict and uniform application of the law, refusing to exempt one of his sons who had stolen money from the treasury from punishment although the young prince was dying.

Wendi was an austere man. Short-legged and long-waisted, he had a reserved manner. He was suspicious of possible rivals, including his sons, and liable to violent rages, even beating an official to death; he was, however, faithful and generous to old friends. By nature parsimonious, he eschewed luxury at court and rationed the cosmetics for court ladies. His wife, a member of the powerful northern Dugu family, insisted on

THE GRAND CANAL

The emperor caused to be built dragon-boats, phoenix vessels, war boats of the 'Yellow Dragon' style, red battle cruisers, multi-decked transports, lesser vessels of bamboo slats. Boatmen hired from all the waterways...pulled the vessels by ropes of green silk...The boats followed one another poop to prow for more than 200 leagues [60 miles]. Requisitioning was relentless; the morning's order had to be carried out by the evening...the birds and beasts were almost extinguished and prices leapt up, the tail of a pheasant costing ten rolls of fine silk.

Thus wrote the historians of the Sui dynasty about the Dragon Fleet which Yangdi commissioned to sail with his court on the newly constructed Grand Canal. The emperor's boat had four decks with private apartments, a throne room and 120 exquisitely decorated rooms for concubines. His entourage included the imperial family, ministers and court officials, priests and ambassadors, followed by eunuchs, palace attendants and servants. It took 80,000 men to pull the fleet, which was accompanied by musicians and a mounted guard on both banks, which were shaded by willow trees.

The 1,250-mile-long (2,000-km-long) Sui canal system led from Hangzhou in the southeast to the southern capital Yangzhou on the Yangzi; then northwest to Luoyang, connecting with the Huai and Yellow Rivers *en route*; from there it proceeded northeast to the northern Beijing region. The most dramatic improvement in communications since the First Emperor's highway system, it provided the first effective transport link between the southern 'rice-bowl' and the arid northern plains.

Sections of the Sui Grand Canal, and a beautiful marble bridge admired by Marco Polo in the 12th century, are still in use in the Hangzhou region.

(Right) The Grand Canal at Suzhou.

(Below) Water transport was supplemented by a road-building programme to improve access to the northern frontier. The Anyi bridge, built between 605 and 616, is made from over 1,000 stones weighing a ton each. This is the earliest spandrel bridge in the world; the open arches lightened the weight, thus increasing the possible length and it spans 37.4m.

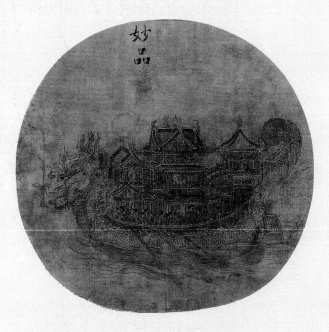

(Above) By giving the boat the form of a dragon, the Chinese relied on the mythical powers of the dragon to control water spirits and preserve them from disaster. The tradition of dragon boats has survived in popular dragon-boat festivals in southern China. Yuan dynasty painting (Museum of Fine Arts, Boston).

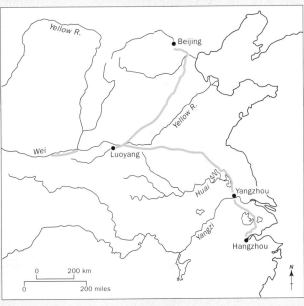

Route of the Sui and Tang Grand Canal.

(*Above*) Buddha on a lotus throne in his paradise beneath a bodhi tree, 593 AD (Museum of Fine Arts, Boston).

(*Right*) The late 6th century saw a new sculptural style in which expressions of serenity were combined with increasingly realistic bodies (Nelson-Atkins Gallery, Kansas City).

monogamy; he had no sons by other consorts and when he fell in love, she had the girl murdered. Later the grieving emperor, riding alone in the mountains, lamented: 'I may be honoured as the Son of Heaven but I have no freedom.'

Wendi remained true to his early Buddhist upbringing. Although he accepted Confucianism officially, reviving the state cult of ancestor worship, he never sympathized with Confucian scholars, shouting 'You bookworm' at an official who urged him not to kill the last surviving Zhou princes. He realized that Buddhism, with its offer of salvation to all regardless of nationality and rank, was a powerful force for reunification and he actively sponsored the spread of the Buddhist church. Buddhist services were held nightly at court and imperial funds poured into repairing the damage done during the brief Northern Zhou persecution of religious bodies in 574. Four thousand temples were built, over 100,000 new images made and one and a half million images restored in gold, bronze, sandalwood, ivory and stone.

YANGDI	
Born	empress Wenxian
569, as Yang	(died 602)
Guang	*Wife*
Title before accession	empress Xiao (from
Heir Apparent (600)	Liang family)
Accession	*Died*
604	617
Father	*Temple name*
Wendi (2nd son of)	Yangdi ('Arbitrary
Mother	Emperor')

GONGDI	
Born	*Died*
c. 611, as Yang Yu	618
Accession	*Temple name*
617	Gongdi ('Respectful
Family connection	Emperor')
grandson of Yangdi	

(*Above*) Portrait of the emperor Sui Yangdi from the *Thirteen Emperors* scroll by Yan Liben (Museum of Fine Arts, Boston).

(*Opposite page, top*) Pagodas came in all sizes and forms – brick or stone, round, square or many-sided, single or multi-storied – and in taller examples, the traditional Chinese construction methods developed for early palace and city towers were used. Pagodas like this, the earliest surviving stone pagoda in China, are common in stone reliefs from the early Buddhist period. Pagoda at Shentong temple, Shandong 611 AD.

YANGDI AND GONGDI

Yangdi (604–617), Wendi's second son, inherited his father's vision of a great empire but lacked the judgment and ability to carry it through. Unlike Wendi, he was a southerner at heart, serving in the south when young and marrying a gifted member of the leading southern Liang family. A devout Buddhist, he absorbed southern interest in Daoism and art; a poet and scholar, he supported Confucian studies, commissioning an anthology of over 70,000 entries and collecting vast imperial libraries at Chang'an and Luoyang.

Within a few years, however, the *folie de grandeur* and love of luxury which were to cause his downfall became apparent. Overriding official protests, Yangdi ordered the rebuilding of the second capital, Luoyang. Although nothing remains of this city, contemporary critics of his extravagance have left a vivid picture of its splendour. Two million corvée labourers were employed on its palaces and huge artificial lakes with pavilion-studded islands. The pleasure park covered 60 sq miles (155 sq km) and when he rode there in winter the bare branches were decked with silk flowers and leaves. Work on the canal system imposed an even greater burden. Yangdi continued Wendi's canal works but on a much larger scale. By 618, 1,250 miles (2,000 km) of canals linked the entire country, except Sichuan, and provided an effective system of transport across Central China and from the southern Yangzi Valley to the northern Beijing area. A powerful, unifying factor of inestimable military and economic value, its cost was exorbitant. Every man between 15 and 50 was liable to mobilization and over five million people, including women and children providing food, were involved. The inevitable popular discontent was fanned by the construction of a personal, luxurious 'Dragon Fleet' in which the emperor sailed with his court on inspection trips.

Yangdi's downfall, however, was triggered by foreign ventures. Wendi had tried in vain to subdue Korea. Undaunted, Yangdi resumed the task with disastrous results. Despite crippling losses of life and money, three major campaigns failed to defeat the Koreans, and their king reneged his promise to pay homage (whereupon his ambassador was killed, cooked and given to the troops to eat). Conscription and corvée demands had drained the countryside of labour, leaving the remaining peasants with increasingly heavy tax burdens. Preoccupied with Korea, Yangdi ignored the mounting unrest at home and when the Yellow River flooded, peasant uprisings swept the country. Ruthless attempts to crush opposition could not stem the tide and in 617, a northern military figure, Li Yuan, captured Chang'an. Yangdi abdicated and fled south where he was strangled by the son of a minister whom he had disgraced; in Chang'an, his grandson, **Gongdi** (617–618), was placed on the throne and Li Yuan became regent. In the following year, Li Yuan captured the Sui eastern capital, Luoyang. Deposing the puppet emperor Gongdi, Li Yuan declared himself founding emperor of the Tang dynasty whilst guaranteeing the lives of the Sui imperial family.

TANG DYNASTY
618–649

高祖 Gaozu
618–626

太宗 Taizong
626–649

The emperor Gaozu, Ming watercolour.

GAOZU	
Born	*Wife*
566, as Li Yuan	empress Dou
Title before accession	*Children*
Duke of Tang (572)	22 sons (also
Accession	daughters)
618	*Abdicated*
Father	626
Li Bing, the son of	*Died*
Li Hu who helped to	635
found Northern	*Tomb*
Zhou dynasty	Xianling, San Yuan
Mother	county, Shaanxi
a member of the	*Temple name*
northern Dugu	Gaozu ('High
family, sister to Sui	Progenitor')
Wendi's wife	

GAOZU

You may use copper as a mirror for the person; you may use the past as a mirror for politics; and you may use man as a mirror to guide the judgment in ordinary affairs. These three mirrors I have always cherished; but now that Wei Zheng is gone, I have lost one of them.

Tang Gaozu on the loss of his trusted minister Wei Zheng

Li Yuan, like Sui Wendi, came from a northern aristocratic family with a long tradition of government service and like Wendi usurped the throne from a minor to restore social order. As the emperor **Gaozu** (618–626), he named his dynasty Tang after the region where he had formerly served.

The empire was split between rival factions and for six years, helped by his 17-year-old son, Li Shimin, Gaozu fought to restore peace. Li Shimin (who became the emperor Taizong) later edited the official histories, taking credit for Gaozu's achievements, and painting him as a mediocre ruler with a weakness for musical entertainments and girls. In reality, Gaozu was an able ruler with shrewd judgment who successfully established political, economic and military institutions which lasted for the entire Tang period. His excellent policy of pacification, sparing

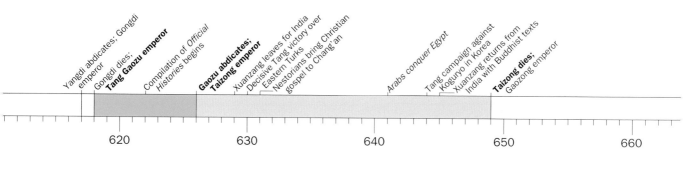

Yangdi abdicates; Gongdi emperor
Gongdi dies;
Tang Gaozu emperor
Compilation of Official Histories begins
Gaozu abdicates; Taizong emperor
Xuanzang leaves for India
Decisive Tang victory over Eastern Turks
Nestorians bring Christian gospel to Chang'an
Arabs conquer Egypt
Tang campaign against Koguryo in Korea
Xuanzang returns from India with Buddhist texts
Taizong dies;
Gaozong emperor

620   630   640   650   660

TAIZONG	
Born	*Wife*
599, as Li Shimin	empress Wende
Titles before	(died 636)
accession	*Children*
Prince of Qin (618),	14 sons
Heir Apparent (626)	*Died*
Accession	649
626	*Tomb*
Father	Zhaoling, Li Quan
Gaozu (2nd son of)	county, Shaanxi
Mother	*Temple name*
empress Dou	Taizong ('Supreme
	Ancestor')

the Sui imperial family, granting an amnesty and then appointing and rewarding former Sui officials, healed civil war divisions and laid the groundwork for his son's brilliant reign.

Gaozu had 22 sons. In 626, a failed palace plot led to the death of the heir apparent and Li Shimin, second son of the empress Dou, persuaded Gaozu to abdicate in his favour.

TAIZONG

The ruler depends on the state, and the state depends on its people. Oppressing the people to make them serve the ruler is like someone cutting off his own flesh to fill his stomach. The stomach is filled but the body is injured: the ruler is wealthy but the state is destroyed.

The emperor Taizong

Taizong (626–649) was one of the great Chinese emperors. Even allowing for the partiality of his own historians, he emerges from the pages as a man of exceptional character with a keen rational intelligence, towering above his contemporaries. His military successes under Gaozu had established his reputation – on one occasion he had entered Chang'an in triumph, clad in golden armour, followed by two rebel 'emperors' and their courts and accompanied by 10,000 heavily armed cavalry. In Chinese eyes, however, he is more highly esteemed for his scholarly and administrative qualities. Educated in the classics, an excellent scholar and calligrapher, he attracted able ministers, established close relations with his advisers, accepted criticism and lived frugally, and his early reign is praised as an example of ideal Confucian rule. He attracted artists and scholars to his court and had a keen interest in natural history. On one occasion, the court painter, Yan Liben, complained bitterly to his son that the emperor had summoned him from his meal to draw an unusual bird which had just alighted on the lake.

(*Above*) An example of Taizong's poetry, in his own writing, found at Dunhuang. Such texts were copied by skilled carvers who could reproduce accurately the fine calligraphy (Bibliothèque Nationale de France, Paris).

(*Right*) The Tang general, Guo Ziyi, won the support of the Uighur tribes who had sacked Luoyang in the 7th century through personal bravery and diplomacy. Here he is seen unarmed and alone, receiving homage from the warlike Uighur leaders (National Palace Museum, Taiwan).

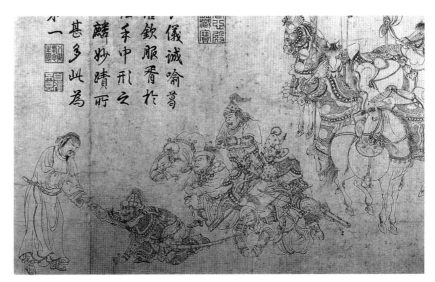

(*Left*) Portrait of Taizong, Qing dynasty painting (National Palace Museum, Taiwan).

(*Right*) Painted stucco figure of a foreign soldier wearing a helmet and scale armour and a stucco shield. From Mingai, Xinjiang province, 6th or 7th century AD.

(*Left*) The court painter, Yan Liben, recorded the arrival of the Tibetan envoy who was sent to fetch his royal master's bride, Taizong's adopted daughter, the Tang princess Wencheng. Taizong, surrounded by court ladies, is seated on the sedan to the right; the Tibetan, in brightly patterned clothing, is the figure on the far left (Palace Museum, Peking).

Taizong had a phenomenal capacity for work; officials worked in shifts to keep pace and unfinished documents were pasted on his bedroom walls to read at night. Solicitous for his subjects' welfare, he limited public works with their burden of taxes and corvée labour. This moral approach gave the Tang a prestige which remained unchallenged for generations and far surpassed that enjoyed by the Han. A rationalist, Taizong's approach to politics was eminently pragmatic and he used Daoism and Buddhism to supplement Confucianism whenever it was useful. Since Confucianism encouraged stability and provided good officials, he sponsored state academies with scholarships, improved the examination system and used ancestor worship at the tomb to strengthen the legitimacy of the ruling family. Recognizing the importance of the written word, he placed the keeping of records and compilation of history, previously written by independent scholars, under an official Bureau of Historiography, within the reach of imperial influence.

Under Taizong, China regained her position as a great world power. With a brilliant combination of military force and diplomacy, using one tribe to destroy another, he altered the whole balance of power in northern Asia, utterly destroying the Eastern Turks and

gaining control of the Ordos and Inner Mongolian regions. Chinese troops swept through Central Asia: the Tarim Basin was brought under direct Chinese civil administration and garrisons were established in the great trading centres of Kucha, Khotan, Yarkand, Kashgar, Kushar, Tukmak and Karashahr. In Tibet, a Tang princess was sent in marriage to the powerful new king under a peace treaty which lasted 20 years. Only Korea remained recalcitrant. A disastrous defeat for the Chinese in 645 was followed by an indecisive campaign two years later; Taizong died while preparing a third.

Military expansion brought trade. The way to the West was now wide open, and in the early 7th century Chang'an was the largest and most cosmopolitan city in the world. Its streets were thronged with foreigners from India, Central Asia and Japan – travellers, merchants and missionaries lured by tales of China's fabulous wealth. It was a time of confidence, vitality and openness to new ideas, of religious toleration (as well as Buddhist temples, there were Muslim mosques, Jewish synagogues

(*Above*) Numerous tomb figurines reflect the presence of foreigners in Chang'an. The narrow-sleeved jacket with lapels worn by this Persian became a fashion among nobles at the Tang court (Royal Ontario Museum).

(*Above right*) As northerners, the Tang were accustomed to travel and in early Tang tombs, the ox-cart, a valuable means of transport, often formed the centrepiece of figurine processions placed in the tomb (Seattle Art Museum).

(*Right*) Pavilion in the Great Mosque, founded in 742 in the Muslim quarter of Chang'an. The mosque is built like a Chinese courtyard temple but with an east-west, rather than the customary Chinese north-south axis. The buildings, rebuilt in 1392 by the Ming, have been thoroughly restored during this century.

and Nestorian Christian churches) and the upper classes revelled in foreign goods and adopted foreign customs, playing polo from Persia and wearing Western-style clothing with narrow sleeves and turned-back collars. Literary descriptions, surviving paintings and sculptures, particularly from tombs, give some idea of the extraordinary flowering of the arts and the sophisticated luxury of court life.

Taizong's later period was tarnished with the usual effects of unlimited power. After 630, he became increasingly arrogant and extravagant, neglecting state affairs for long and costly hunting trips. Against his officials' advice he embarked on grandiose public works and palace building, capriciously having a palace which had taken two million man-days of labour destroyed on completion because the site was too hot and the style ostentatious. After the death of his beloved wife, the empress Wende, in 636, he was plagued by the succession question. His heir, Li Cheng Qian – the eldest of 14 sons, an intelligent, lame homosexual – became obsessed by his Tartar ancestry and adopted Turkic habits. Wearing Turkish clothes, he spoke only Turkish and lived in a felt tent, stealing sheep and cooking them in nomad fashion over a camp fire. Officials who remonstrated were killed, and when he became involved in a plot against Taizong's favourite son, the prince Tai, both sons were disgraced and the empress Wende's youngest son, Li Zhi (Gaozong), was made Heir.

(*Above*) In 1625, workmen in Chang'an found a large stone tablet with texts in Chinese and an unknown script. A Chinese Christian convert took a rubbing of the latter text which was later identified as Syriac and translated by a Jesuit, Father Semedo, at the court of Ming Wanli. The text refers to Alopen, a monk who had arrived in Chang'an around 625 from Syria and describes the arrival of Nestorian Christianity in China (Lateran Museum, Rome).

(*Right*) The Tang were famous for their love of entertainments and this large stone lion with a small headless attendant, found on Taizong's tomb, represents the lion dance, still performed today. The huge, not altogether serious lion, is dominated by a man, who was probably a foreigner. Virtually all stone statues of foreigners in the Chang'an region lost their heads in some early wave of xenophobia.

HORSES

The horse symbolized status and military power. As northerners, the Tang were aware of the military value of a skilful cavalry and horses enjoyed a special position at court. When the Tang took power, there were only 5,000 horses in the pastures in Gansu; within 50 years 706,000 horses grazed in eight great pasturelands north of the River Wei. Gifts of up to 50,000 horses were received as tribute; each new horse was assigned to a herd of 120 kept in pastoral 'Inspectorates' of 50,000 horses, and branded with the character 'official' and its origin, quality ('flying', 'dragon', 'wind'), class of work (war, post, royal mount) and the name of its inspectorate. Numbers were strictly controlled with heavy penalties for the loss of an animal. When disease killed 180,000 horses, the Tang histories bewailed: 'Horses are the military preparedness of the state; if heaven takes this away, the state will totter to a fall.' Taizong had his six favourite war steeds commemorated in verse, painted by the court painter Yan Liben and carved in stone for his tomb. Gaozong and later Tang emperors placed a colossal pair of winged horses at the start of the spirit roads leading to their mausolea.

Riding was a preserve of the nobility at court, forbidden to artisans and merchants by an edict of 667. Northern women had always enjoyed greater freedom of movement than those in the south and male and female courtiers rode for pleasure and hunting. Dancing horses performed at court. At a banquet for a Tibetan delegation in the early 8th century, horses danced 'caparisoned with silk thread, pigmented in the five colours, with garnishings of gold. Unicorn heads and phoenix wings had been applied to the tops of their saddles. When the music was played, each of the horses followed it, fluently responsive, and when they came to the middlemost stanza, the performers of the music gave them wine to drink, at which they took the cups in their mouths; then they lay down, and got up again. The Tibetans were greatly astonished.'

This contemporary account was confirmed by the discovery in the 1970s of a silver gilt flask in a Tang tomb on which a dancing horse holds a cup in its mouth (*opposite, below left*).

The dancing horses of the famous Tang emperor Xuanzong (712–756) were even more celebrated. On his birthday, 100 of the finest tribute horses, arrayed in rich embroideries fringed with gold and silver, their manes studded with precious stones, danced intricate manoeuvres in two troops, their heads tossing and tails beating to the music of young musicians clad in yellow shirts and jade-embossed belts. They also danced on three-tier benches, standing stock still while these were lifted into the air by athletes. The display was accompanied by a battalion of guards in golden armour, a ceremonial orchestra and other entertainments such as foreign acrobats, performing elephants and richly clad palace girls playing the 'thunder drums'.

(Below) One of six stone panels with carvings of Taizong's favourite war steeds. The reliefs were placed three-a-side in a covered corridor on the tomb. The first pair are stationary or walking, the second, trotting and the third galloping, thus creating a moving picture.

(Right) The Tang imperial spirit road began with a pair of colossal stone winged horses, ready to transport the deceased to the land of the immortals. The heavenly nature of this horse on Tang Suzong's tomb, Jianling, Shaanxi, is emphasized by a relief of clouds between the legs.

(Left) The nobility revelled in the new game of polo, introduced from Persia and numerous figurines of polo players have been found. This mural, showing a game of polo, was found in the tomb of Gaozong and Wu Zetian's son, Li Xian.

(Opposite page, centre) All the Tang love of horses was expressed in their three-colour (sancai) glazed pottery tomb horses. Saddled or unsaddled, they are shown in every conceivable position: grazing, galloping, heads raised or turned to scratch a leg. Sancai glazes were used almost exclusively for tombwares. Polo player (Idenutsu Museum of Arts, Tokyo).

(Right) Tang women rode, played polo and hunted, often wearing western clothing. A contemporary historian noted that 'palace ladies who rode behind the carriages all wore Central Asian hats exposing their faces, without a veil. When they broke into a gallop, their hair was suddenly exposed.' Treatise on Carriages and Dress in the official Tang Histories (Shaanxi Provincial Museum).

(Above) This silver-gilt flask shows a dancing horse drinking from a wine-cup. The influx of westerners had a strong influence on metal-workers who adopted western techniques such as the use of repoussé gilt on silver, the two colours giving a three-dimensional effect. The flask is based on the leather drinking bottles used by nomads in the north (Shaanxi Historical Museum, Xi'an).

TANG DYNASTY
649–712

高宗 **Gaozong**
649–683

中宗 **Zhongzong**
684; 705–710

睿宗 **Ruizong**
684–690; 710–712

武后 **Wu Zetian**
690–705

Woodcut of Wu Zetian from the Ming encyclopedia *Sancai tuhui*, 1607.

GAOZONG	
Born	*Major concubines*
628, as Li Zhi	(1) consort Wu
Accession	Zhao (Zetian)
649	(2) consort Xiao
Father	*Children*
Taizong (9th son of)	8 sons
Mother	*Died*
empress Wende	683
Wife	*Tomb*
empress Wang	Qianling, Qian
(demoted, then	county, Shaanxi
murdered by	*Temple name*
Wu Zetian in 655)	Gaozong ('High
	Ancestor')

GAOZONG

Young and inexperienced, aged 21 on accession, **Gaozong** (649–683), was physically weak, suffering frequent incapacitating attacks of dizziness. Well-meaning but indecisive, he quickly fell under the spell of his captivating and ambitious consort, Wu Zhao (later known as Wu Zetian), formerly his father's concubine. Wu ousted Gaozong's wife, Wang, by suffocating her own newborn daughter and then accusing the empress of the crime. Once installed as empress herself, Wu Zetian began to act in her husband's name, installing her own supporters in office and brutally exterminating opponents; when Gaozong was left half-blind and paralysed by a stroke in 660, her position became impregnable. For half a century, until her death in 705, this extraordinary woman dominated the empire.

Gaozong had inherited a contented populace with rising standards of living and a well-run administration, and for most of his long reign there was peace at home. Abroad, Wu Zetian conducted an active policy of expansion, carrying Chinese dominion to its furthest point ever. In Central Asia, the Chinese made contact with the Arabs who had conquered the Sassanid kingdom (the first Arab ambassador arrived in

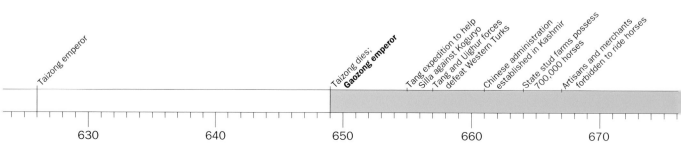

Taizong emperor

Taizong dies;
Gaozong emperor

Tang expedition to help
Silla against Koguryo

Tang and Uighur forces
defeat Western Turks

Chinese administration
established in Kashmir

State stud farms possess
700,000 horses

Artisans and merchants
forbidden to ride horses

630   640   650   660   670

China in 651) and between 660 and 668 they finally defeated Korea. Later, however, the cost of military trouble with Tibet and on the north-west border forced a certain retrenchment.

Determined to retain power after her husband's death, Wu Zetian manipulated the succession. She had the popular crown prince, Li Hong, poisoned and other princes exiled, finally getting her third son, Li Zhe, declared Heir Apparent. Gaozong's will reinforced her position, specifying that the heir should ascend the throne without delay, even before his father was encoffined, and that he was to refer to the empress Wu in all matters of civil and military importance.

ZHONGZONG AND RUIZONG

The first reign of Li Zhe, the emperor **Zhongzong**, lasted for just six weeks in 684. Weak and untrained, he was totally dominated by his wife, the empress Wei, and on accession appointed her father chief

ZHONGZONG	
Born 656, as Li Zhe	*Wife* empress Wei (died 710)
Titles before accession Prince of Ying, Heir Apparent (680)	*Children* 4 sons
Accession 684 (first reign, ousted after a 6-week reign); 705 (second reign)	*Died* 710; probably poisoned by Wei
Father Gaozong (7th son of)	*Tomb* Dingling, Fuping county, Shaanxi
Mother empress Wu Zetian	*Temple name* Zhongzong ('Moderate Ancestor')

Foreign contacts led to a keen interest in other lands. When the great Buddhist monk, Xuanzang, returned from India in 645, Gaozong welcomed him as much for the knowledge he brought back from his journeys as for his Buddhism. Xuanzang settled down in the Temple of Great Goodwill to translate the 75 Buddhist sutras he had brought back with him. There, the Great Goose pagoda was built to house his documents. Yet another pagoda (*far right*) was built at the Xingjiao temple to house Xuanzang's own remains.

(*Right*) The exotic aura surrounding Xuanzang's travels is well illustrated in this silk portrait found in Dunhuang. The monk, whose very features seem to have been westernized, wears foreign clothing and is accompanied by a tiger (Musée Guimet, Paris).

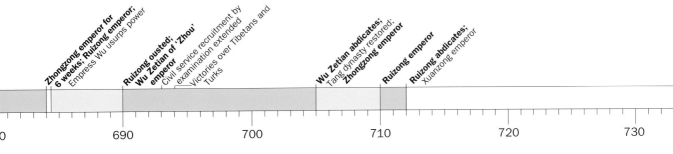

Zhongzong emperor for 6 weeks; Ruizong emperor; Empress Wu usurps power

Ruizong ousted; Wu Zetian of 'Zhou' emperor

Civil service recruitment by examination extended

Victories over Tibetans and Turks

Wu Zetian abdicates; Tang dynasty restored; Zhongzong emperor

Ruizong emperor

Ruizong abdicates; Xuanzong emperor

690   700   710   720   730

(*Right*) It was a time of intense diplomatic activity. In this mural foreign ambassadors are being received at court. The two elegantly clad figures on the right are from Korea; the bare-headed, large-nosed figure in the centre is an envoy from the west. Mural from Li Xian's tomb, Qianling, Shaanxi, 706.

RUIZONG	
Born	*Abdicated*
662, as Li Dan	712
Accession	*Died*
684 (first reign,	716
ousted in 690);	*Tomb*
710 (second reign)	Qiaoling, Pucheng
Father	county, Shaanxi
Gaozong (8th son of)	*Temple name*
Mother	Ruizong ('Far-
empress Wu Zetian	Sighted Ancestor')
Children	
6 sons	

Watercolour of Wu Zetian from an 18th-century album of imperial portraits.

minister. When another minister remonstrated, Zhongzong retorted: 'What is to stop Us from handing over to him the entire empire? And of what concern to Us is your wretched opinion?'

Charging Zhongzong with treason, Wu Zetian had him replaced by his younger brother **Ruizong** (684–690). Ruizong's puppet status was abundantly clear; he never inhabited the imperial apartments, did not appear at state functions and was kept a virtual prisoner in the Inner Palace. Wu Zetian openly took power, receiving ministers in person instead of 'behind the curtain'. In 690, she took the final step: Ruizong abdicated and after the customary triple refusal, she accepted the throne, the only woman ever to become emperor of China.

WU ZETIAN

A Sage Mother shall come to Rule Mankind; and her Imperium shall bring Eternal Prosperity.

An inscription on a stone found in Lo River in 688, probably fabricated by the empress' nephew, Wu Chengsi, in order to create an imperial aura around Wu Zetian

Wu Zetian (690–705) was an extraordinary woman, attractive, exceptionally gifted, politically astute and an excellent judge of men. With single-minded determination, she overcame the opposition of the Confucian establishment through her own efforts, unique among palace women in not using her family.

Her rise to power was steeped in blood. Fearing rivalry in the palace, she had the arms and legs of Gaozong's wife, the ex-empress Wang, and his beautiful concubine Xiao amputated and then threw what remained of them into a wine vat to die. Their supporters were killed or exiled and

Taizong's ministers removed. Within a few years: 'The power of the empire all devolved on the empress. Promotion and demotion, life or death, were settled by her word. The emperor sat with folded hands.'

An attempt to remove Wu Zetian in 684 was ruthlessly quelled: 12 collateral branches of the imperial family were exterminated and members of the old aristocracy replaced by officials loyal to herself. Her secret service ran a reign of terror, their victims supplied by informers who were offered free passage to the capital to denounce possible opponents. In 697 this culminated in a wholesale purge of scholars and high families who were disgraced, killed or exiled and their sons banned from office.

Under Gaozong, Wu Zetian had participated in state services previously the exclusive preserve of the ruler, and in 666 she had led a procession of women in the most sacred of all rites on Mount Tai. Intensely superstitious, she persuaded Gaozong to take new auspicious titles which she could share, becoming 'Heavenly Empress', and matched his patronage of scholars by founding her own institute to make a 'Collection of Biographies of Famous Women'. After Gaozong's death, she increasingly usurped imperial privileges, establishing temples to her ancestors and posthumously raising her mother to 'dowager-empress' with a tomb of imperial grandeur.

(*Below*) To further her imperial ambitions, Wu Zetian actively sought support from the Buddhist church which, unlike the Confucians, recognized the importance of women. In 673 she commissioned and contributed 20,000 cash for this monumental statue of Maitreya, the Buddha of the Future, at Longmen; the statue's features and expressions, which vary according to the angle of viewing, are said to be based on the empress herself. At the same time Wu founded numerous monasteries dedicated to a newly-found text provided by a monk supporter, Xue Huaiyi, in which it was predicted that a woman would be born of such merit that she would become the universal leader.

WU ZETIAN

Born c. 625, as Wu Zhao	*Mother* Lady Yang (died 670)
Position before accession concubine of Taizong, then of Gaozong, becoming empress in 655, regent for Ruizong (684)	*Husband* Gaozong
	Children several with Gaozong
	Abdicated 705
Accession 690	*Died* 705
Father Wu Shihou, a supporter of Tang Gaozu	*Tomb* Qianling, Qian county, Shaanxi

Wu Zetian succeeded because her principal policies – extension of Chinese power abroad, strengthening imperial authority and satisfying popular needs – provided a more successful government than the imperial family could offer. The oppression of powerful officials was counterbalanced by generosity to lower ranks and the widening of recruitment to include commoners and gentry. Her decrees and Acts of Grace combined practical relief measures with popular promotions and salary increases. Finally, she used all the arts of Daoist and Buddhist propaganda to bring her image before the people as a deity. Taking the title

(*Right*) Wu Zetian, possibly mistrusting the Confucian scholars who wrote the texts, asked for a memorial stele without characters, saying that her deeds would speak for themselves. Later dynasties ignored her wishes, however, and her tablet carries 13 inscriptions, mostly from 10th to 12th centuries. One text is in both Han script and Nuchen, a script which has since become extinct. Qianling, joint tomb of Gaozong and Wu Zetian.

'Sage Mother', she ordered statues of the original 'Sage Mother' of Laozi, founder of Daoism, to be placed in all Daoist temples. Her hijacking of Buddhism was more spectacular. In 685, she made her lover, Xue Huaiyi – an unruly pedlar of aphrodisiacs and cosmetics – abbot of the prestigious White Horse temple and he rewarded her by finding the 'Great Cloud' sutra, a spurious text prophesying the imminent reincarnation of Maitreya, the Future Buddha, as a female deity under whom: 'Harvests will be bountiful, joy without limit. The people will flourish, free of desolation and illness…The rulers of neighbouring lands will all come and offer allegiance.'

State-sponsored temples preaching this doctrine were established in every prefecture, and – taking the title 'Maitreya the Peerless' – Wu commissioned a gigantic stone Maitreya Buddha to be carved at Longmen whose features were said to resemble her own.

In 690, a series of auspicious omens were accompanied by splendid pageants and when she took the final step, declaring herself 'Holy and Divine Emperor' of a new Zhou dynasty there was no opposition.

With age, Wu Zetian lost her judgment. In 697, she took two young Zhang brothers as lovers, indulging their every whim. They ruled the court with flagrant immorality – bullying, drinking, gambling and flouting all conventions with 'money poured out like sand'. Bribery and corruption were rampant and the empress lost public sympathy. When courtiers finally assassinated the two brothers in 705, the dishevelled empress, roused by the noise, tried vainly to save them and then returned helplessly to bed. The next day she abdicated and the Tang dynasty resumed its course with a sorry replay of the reigns of Zhongzong and Ruizong.

ZHONGZONG AND RUIZONG

Twenty-one years in seclusion had not improved **Zhongzong's** (705–710) ability to rule and there was a bitter power struggle between the factions of the two ex-emperors. The empress Wei and her lover, Wu Sansi (a nephew of Wu Zetian), ran the court with open corruption, seizing land, taking child slaves and selling Buddhist monkhoods for 30,000 cash and positions at court for 300,000. Wei is believed to have poisoned Zhongzong in 710, keeping his death secret until she had installed her relatives in key posts and placed his last surviving son, Chong Mao, aged 15, on the throne. Chong Mao is not included in the imperial list, and within two weeks, the rival faction, led by Wu Zetian's daughter, the princess Taiping, had dragged the young emperor from the throne, summoning her younger brother, **Ruizong** (710–712), to replace him. With probably genuine reluctance, Ruizong complied, but when the princess tried to dislodge his designated heir, the future Xuanzong, Ruizong abdicated in favour of his gifted son.

Military official on Qiaoling, tomb of the emperor Ruizong.

TANG MAUSOLEA

Taizong chose a mountain 3,900 ft (1,200 m) tall for his tomb mound, thus setting the pattern for some of the world's greatest tombs. The underground palace with the coffin was tunnelled into the mountainside and around the entrance, a tomb city was built, based on the capital, Chang'an, with triple-walled enclosures and corner and gate towers. Within the city were sacrificial halls and temples and dwellings for tomb attendants, including the dowager-empress and her court. The 'spirit road' was 0.6 miles (1 km) long and lined with a minimum of 68 stone statues averaging 13 ft (4 m) high.

The scale was truly vast. When the first five mausolea were restored in the 8th century, 378 halls were rebuilt in each tomb; Taizong's tomb, Zhaoling, had an outer wall 40 miles (60 km) long; another covered 70 sq miles (182 sq km).

These tombs, designed to reflect the might and glory of the empire, provided the setting for political gatherings. Captive foreign chieftains were brought to offer homage to the imperial ancestors (thus recognizing Tang legitimacy) before being pardoned, fêted and set free. Loyalty and outstanding service were rewarded by an 'accompanying burial' – a tomb within the imperial burial grounds – and over 200 such minor tombs have been found at Zhaoling.

The Tang tombs were systematically destroyed after the fall of the dynasty and the official in charge, Wen Dao, noted: 'of these [tombs], Zhaoling was stronger than the others…From the road which led to the mountain [Wen Dao] saw that the buildings and mansions were grand and beautiful, both in regard to architecture and size, but they did not differ in style from human dwellings.'

Today, apart from a few remnants of the rammed-earth foundations of walls and towers, only the site itself and the

(Above) The stone ostriches on Gaozong's tomb (and on all later Tang mausolea) were designed to impress viewers with the emperors' contacts with distant lands.

(Right) Spirit road at Qianling, joint tomb of Gaozong and Wu Zetian.

(Right) On Gaozong and Wu Zetian's tomb, the basic spirit road is supplemented by 61 stone foreigners, placed in two groups inside the inner enclosure. Originally each figure had an inscription on its back, giving the subject's name, rank and place of origin. These have long since been illegible but the recent discovery of two Song dynasty rubbings of these inscriptions has made it possible to identify about half the figures. They include 16 leaders of Western Turk, Uighur and other border nations who held honorary rank under the Tang emperor.

spectacular statuary give an idea of the tombs' vanished splendour.

Several royal tombs attached to Gaozong's and Wu Zetian's joint tomb, Qianling, have been excavated, revealing exquisite wall paintings of court life. In the princess Yongtai's tomb (she was popularly believed to have been murdered by Wu Zetian), elegant court ladies play shuttlecock, their maids bearing fruit, fans and musical instruments while hoopoes fly among the fruit trees. A prince's tomb contains scenes of polo and hunting with hounds, cheetahs and falcons, high palace walls and turrets bedecked with flags, and a reception for foreign, large-nosed ambassadors.

(Left) Distant view of Qianling.

(Above) A group of palace ladies walk in the gardens while a hoopoe flies by. Mural, tomb of Gaozong's 6th son, Li Xian, Qianling, Shaanxi, 706.

(Left) Twenty seven painted tombs of high officials and royalty have been excavated in the Chang'an area from the early 7th–late 9th centuries, including three imperial tombs. These belonged to the princes Yide and Zhanghuai and the princess Yongtai, who had all been persecuted to death by the empress Wu Zetian and were only given formal burials in 706 by the emperor Zhongzong. Details of a palace maid, mural from Zhanghuai's tomb, Qianling, Shaanxi, 706.

TANG DYNASTY
712–756

 # Xuanzong
712–756

Woodcut of Xuanzong from *Sancai tuhui*, 1607.

XUANZONG	
Born	(3) consort Yang
685, as Li Longji	Guifei
Titles before	(4) consort Wu
accession	*Children*
Prince of Chu (687),	30 sons, 29
Heir Apparent (710)	daughters
Accession	*Abdicated*
712	756
Father	*Died*
Ruizong (3rd son of)	762
Mother	*Tomb*
secondary consort	Tailing, Pucheng
Dou	county, Shaanxi
Wife	*Temple name*
empress Wang	Xuanzong
(demoted and died	('Profound
724)	Ancestor'), also
Major concubines	known as Ming
(1) consort Zhao	Huan
(2) consort Hua	

XUANZONG

The emperor could not save her. He could only cover his face.
And later when he turned to look, the place of blood and tears
Was hidden in a yellow dust blown by cold wind …
Earth endures, heaven endures; sometime both shall end,
While this unending sorrow goes on for ever.

Bai Juyi *A Song of Unending Sorrow*, describing the death of the consort Yang Guifei

Xuanzong (712–756), whose popular name, Ming Huan, means 'Brilliant Emperor', is the most popular of all Chinese emperors and the story of his love for the beautiful concubine, Yang Guifei, has been commemorated in countless poems and ballads. Creating the most brilliant court in Chinese history, he raised the empire to new heights of civilization and splendour, only to lose it all in old age for the love of a woman.

The son of Ruizong and a secondary consort, the lady Dou, Xuanzong's childhood was overshadowed by Wu Zetian, who had his mother murdered and kept his father's family virtual prisoners in the palace. On accession, after years of bitter political intrigue, Xuanzong swept the court clean, executing or exiling all former ministers.

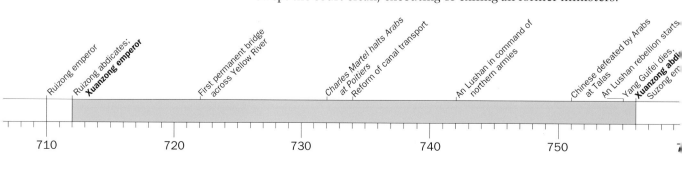

Ruizong emperor | Ruizong abdicates; **Xuanzong emperor** | First permanent bridge across Yellow River | Charles Martel halts Arabs at Poitiers | Reform of canal transport | An Lushan in command of northern armies | Chinese defeated by Arabs at Talas | An Lushan rebellion starts | Yang Guifei dies; **Xuanzong abdi** | Suzong em

710   720   730   740   750

PORCELAIN

Porcelain techniques were perfected around AD 700. Such 'hard porcelain', made only from natural ingredients – the body from clay and feldspathic stone (petuntse) fusible above 1,400°C (2,550 °F) and the glaze of a 10:1 mixture of petuntse and ash – can be scratched by quartz but not with a knife.

The 'three-colour glaze' wares (sancai) were almost exclusively used for tomb goods. Models of white clay were covered with a translucent glaze to which pigments were added: copper for green, cobalt for deep blue and iron for shades ranging from rich amber to soft yellow. The colours were applied by dripping, spotting, or with 'wax resist' – whereby parts were protected from the glaze; when fired, they produced a deliberate blurring and fusion of colours.

The most highly prized Tang wares, however, were white porcelains, mainly produced in the Xingzhou and Ding kilns, Hebei. An Arab traveller noted: 'They have in China a very fine clay with which they make various vases which are as transparent as glass; water can be seen through them. These vases are made of clay.'

The Tang poet Du Fu describes such wares in terms of texture, resonance and translucency, similar to those applied to jade:

The porcelain ... is light yet strong.
It rings with a low jade note and is
  famed throughout the city.
The fine white bowls surpass
  hoarfrost and snow.

Cups were referred to as 'disks of thinnest ice' or 'tilted leaves floating down a stream'; sets of 10 white bowls from Xingzhou struck with little ebony rods were used as chimes.

This harsh beginning left him remarkably unscarred and his reign is famed for its return to humane government. Inheriting a demoralized, corrupt and bloated administration, he streamlined the government and firmly restored the personal authority of the ruler. He appointed few, but excellent, ministers, chosen on merit not family, and brought the provinces back under central control by rotating officials between the capital and provinces. The laws were re-codified and applied humanely and impartially, restoring public confidence after years of terror. The unifying influence of the civil service examination system, which offered commoners a chance of high office and provided highly intelligent officials with a common intellectual background, was extended. A shift in the tax burden from population to land ownership and the easing of currency problems by establishing units of equal value for principal commodities – whereby 1,000 cash, 1 oz (28 g) of silver, 1 bushel of grain, 1 bolt of silk and 1 'weight' of silk floss were roughly equal for revenue purposes – gave a powerful boost to commerce and foreign trade. Transport improved as canals were cleared and the first permanent bridge over the Yellow River was built. The growing power of religious establishments was checked: temple building halted, 'merit cloisters', whereby the rich gave land nominally to the church to escape taxation, banned, and 30,000 monks and nuns returned to lay life. After a successful campaign against the Tibetans who had broken a peace treaty, the frontiers remained largely peaceful and border regions were placed under military governors who were also responsible for civil administration.

Like the Renaissance 'perfect gentleman', Xuanzong was a man of many parts – poet, good calligrapher, talented musician and patron of the arts. He founded the Imperial Academy of Letters (older by a millennium than any European academy) and the atmosphere at court – an harmonious blend of Confucian rationalism, Daoist individualism and an

(*Right*) Stele on Mt. Tai, Shandong, including an inscription written by Xuanzong.

CHANG'AN

Hundreds of houses, thousands of houses – like a great chessboard.
The twelve streets like a huge field planted with rows of cabbages.
In the distance I see faint and small the torches of riders to Court,
Like a single row of stars lying to the west of the Five Gates.

Bai Juyi *Climbing the Terraces of Guanyin and Looking at the City of Chang'an* 827

Chinese cities with their inflammable wooden-framed buildings were easy to destroy but easy to rebuild. Although the rammed-earth foundations of outer walls were sometimes re-used, a capital was usually rebuilt from scratch, according to plan; streets were on a grid pattern and different sections clearly separated within the outer walls. Built on a north–south axis, the entire layout was designed to reflect the emperor's position at the centre of worldly power.

Tang Chang'an, the largest city in the world at that time, was rectangular, 5.5 by 5 miles (9 by 8 km), covering nearly 30 sq miles (80 sq km); its walls contained one million people, and nearly another million lived in the countryside around. Nine large thoroughfares linked the 12 gates (three on each wall); the central road, 498 ft (152 m) wide, led from the southern gate to the imperial palace and city in the north, cutting the city in two: members of the imperial family and officials in the east, merchants, foreign traders and the populace in the west. Behind the city lay the vast imperial park and yet another palace. The entire city was divided into 112 blocks, mostly 650-by-350 pace rectangles, each forming an administrative unit, closing at night within its own walls. There were two large government markets, east and west, the latter, where the foreign merchants congregated, being much the most lively. Records show that some 4,000 families from Central and western Asia (including Persia and Mesopotamia) lived here; contemporary Roman and Arab coins have been found in this section.

An Arab traveller, Ibn Wahhab, in 815 told of the strict segregation between east and west: 'The city was very large and extremely populous; that it was divided into two great parts by a very long and very broad street; that the Emperor, his chief ministers, the soldiers, the Supreme Judge, the eunuchs, and all belonging to the imperial household, lived in that part of the city which is on the right hand eastward; that the people had no manner of communication with them [those in the east]; and that they were not admitted into places watered by canals from different rivers, whose borders were planted with trees, and adorned with magnificent dwellings. The part on the lefthand westward is inhabited by the people and the merchants, where are also great squares and markets for all the necessaries of life. At break of day you see the Officers of the King's Household, with the inferior servants...who come...into that division of the city, where are the public markets, and the habitations of the merchants; where they buy whatever they want, and return not again to the same place till the next day.'

12th-century Arabic manuscript *Akhbar ul Sin wal Hind* ('Observations on China and India')

The Linde Hall, built in 664, where the emperor received officials and held important Buddhist ceremonies. Its 3 main buildings—the front, middle and rear halls—were known as the Three Halls of Religion.

(Right) Early 8th century murals in Prince Yide's tomb give an idea of the magnificence of Chang'an's city walls with their towering gate and corner towers.

(Left) Plan of Tang Chang'an showing the imperial park and Daming Palace north of the city walls.

Daming Palace · Park · N · E. market · Imperial City · W. market · Serpentine Lake · 0 2000 m

(*Above*) Xuanzong spent his winters with Yang Guifei at a beautiful Summer Palace near the Huaqing Hot springs about 30km from Xi'an.

(*Above*) Wall paintings with portraits of high-standing Uighurs have survived in cave-temples at Bezeklik. The foremost figure has been identified from a cartouche above his head as the 'Tutuq Bugra [from the house of Sali]' — a family which had flourished in the region for a long while.

openness to new ideas – attracted scholars, painters, poets and musicians. Xuanzong was a warm, genuinely affectionate man, deeply attached to his brothers and family, who made close friends with artists and ministers alike.

Personally familiar with the results of court intrigue, Xuanzong kept the eunuchs and consort families out of politics. Even in the harem, Tang women enjoyed considerable contact with the outside world through their families, eunuchs and Buddhist and Daoist clergy, but Xuanzong kept his wife's family out of office and held his prolific offspring in check by prohibiting princes and consorts' relations from holding positions in the imperial guard, appointing them instead to short-term provincial posts. Enforcing economy, he forbade the wearing of pearls and jade ornaments at court; brocades and embroidered clothes were banned and the state brocade factory closed. He was, however, unable to stem the drain on imperial finances resulting from the nobles' entitlement to revenue from their own estates. Xuanzong had 59 children (30 sons and 29 daughters); his fourth son had 55 children, his sixth, 58, and it has been reckoned that their estates accounted for 8 per cent of adult taxpayers and brought in more tax silk than the court treasury.

In his fifties, Xuanzong began to tire of political life. The court, which had earlier been moved to Luoyang where food provisioning was easier, moved permanently back to Chang'an in 735 under a new chief minister, Li Linfu (736–752), whose championship of the old aristocrats at the expense of the newer exam-selected ministers caused friction. Although Xuanzong continued to hold daily audiences until he was 70, he became increasingly absorbed in Daoism and the esoteric Buddhist sect of Tantrism, both heavily involved with magic, spells and contemplation. The Tang imperial family had always supported their right to rule by claiming descent from Laozi, the founder of Daoism, whose family name was also 'Li'. Xuanzong now used this to bolster the imperial position, placing Daoists above Buddhists and demoting the latter to the Court for Diplomatic Relations as foreigners.

Xuanzong never replaced his first wife, the empress Wang, who had been demoted to commoner for being barren, but concubine consorts gained increasing influence. In the early 740s he became infatuated with one of his sons' wives, Yang Guifei, and she, leaving her husband, entered the palace as a Daoist priestess. Hailing from a Sichuan family renowned for its beauties, Yang was witty and accomplished, sharing the

TANG POETRY

*The King's armies have grown grey
  and old
Fighting ten thousand leagues away
  from home.
The Huns have no trade but battle and
  carnage;
They have no fields or ploughlands,
But only wastes where white bones lie
  on yellow sands....
Men die in the field, slashing sword to
  sword;
The horses of the conquered neigh
  piteously to Heaven.
Crows and hawks peck for human
  guts,
Carry them in their beaks and hang
  them on the branches of withered
  trees.
Captains and soldiers are
  smeared on the bushes and
  grass;
The general schemed in vain.
Know therefore that the
  sword is a cursed thing
Which the wise man uses
  only if he must.*

Li Bai *Fighting South of the
  Ramparts*

This was the golden age of poetry. Virtually all China's great poets are from the Tang period, and nearly 3,000 are known by name. The examination system drew intellectuals into the official system and poet-officials were an important element in court life. The three best-known poets in the West all held office. Li Bai (701–762) became a friend of Xuanzong who offered him a sinecure at court on the basis of his poetry. There he formed a group of 'Eight Immortals of the Wine Cup', which included a member of the imperial family, an historian, a famous calligrapher and a drinking Buddhist. Li Bai's closest friend, Du Fu (713–768), held minor posts and Bai Juyi (772–846) spent almost his entire life in government service, becoming governor of Henan province with a residence at Luoyang. The latter's *The Everlasting Wrong*, a romantic epic of the tale of Xuanzong and Yang Guifei, was so well known that even the dancing girls knew it by heart.

Unlike the Han prose poems describing official splendour, Tang poets dealt with personal experience – the beauty of a fleeting moment or single blossom – and social comment – witty characterizations or bitter reflections on the contrast between rich and poor. War was a subject for lament, never patriotic fervour, for war indicated a failure of government and lack of virtue. In a society in which marriages were arranged and contacts between men and women strictly limited, the most intimate and binding relationship outside the family was friendship and the pain of sudden parting takes the place of love in Western poetry. As officials, poets were subject to frequent, often final separations when posted to distant provinces.

(Left) Ming woodcut of the poet Bai Juyi (772-846).

(Right) Ming woodcut of the poet Li Bai (701-62).

(Right) Xuanzong died in a section of the Daming palace which had been his chief residence. Built outside the city wall in the northeast, the site had been chosen in 634 by Taizong for his father Gaozu, who died before it was completed.

THE IRON OXEN OF PUJIN BRIDGE

The rediscovery of four Tang iron oxen in 1989 give a vivid confirmation of the wealth and technical and artistic standards of Xuanzong's China. Until 722, the main route from the north to the central plains and south depended on a pontoon bridge over the Yellow River in southwest Shanxi which was washed away each year in the spring floods. Unwilling to accept this annual break in communications, Xuanzong ordered the construction of a permanent bridge with iron chains held by iron anchors in the form of oxen (oxen were believed to possess the power to quell water). It was a major imperial project, using one third of the total annual production of iron: skilled foundry and metal workers were mobilized from all over the empire and each region had to send its quota of iron-ore blocks. On each bank, four oxen (averaging 10 ft (3 m) long and 5 ft (1.5 m) high) each with a herder were cast solid in one piece with foundations 13 ft (4 m) deep; the largest ox weighs 70 tons (71,000 kg).

The statues embody all that is finest in Tang sculpture. Combining accurate representation with intense vitality, they give the impression of infinite reserves of energy.

(Above) Iron ox, Pujin bridge, Shanxi.

emperor's love of music and dance. The 60-year-old Xuanzong was soon completely under her sway. Economy was forgotten; 700 weavers were employed making the finest damasks and patterned gauzes for Yang Guifei. By 752 her family dominated the political scene and her cousin, the scheming Yang Guozhong, military governor of Sichuan, was strong enough to challenge chief minister Li Linfu. Within the palace, Yang's close friendship with a fat, coarse general of Turkish origin, An Lushan, caused scandalous rumours. Shrewd, cunning and uncouth, the general enjoyed the freedom of the palace and in 751 Yang adopted him as her son.

An's rise coincided with a serious deterioration in China's military situation, caused by the development of powerful border states in Manchuria and Yunnan. Throughout the 740s China was relatively successful in containing both them and traditional enemies such as the Tibetans and Uighurs (who had succeeded the Turks in the northwest), but the rise of Islam changed the whole balance of power. Border defeats in 750 were followed by a decisive Arab victory over Chinese armies in Central Asia at Talas in 751; China's route to India and the West was now permanently cut. Henceforth the Muslims replaced China as the dominant influence in the oasis settlements in the Tarim Basin and along the Silk Roads. These events gave the military governors on the borders increasing power and independence from the centre, and in 755 An Lushan, secure in favour at court – Xuanzong refused to heed warnings about his lover's favourite – rose, declaring himself emperor of the Greater Yan dynasty (a dynasty not officially recognized in the historical records).

With his crack troops, An swept southwards, massacring the population at Kaifeng, capturing Luoyang and eventually Chang'an. The emperor, with Yang Guifei and his immediate family, fled at night for Sichuan; when their route was blocked by Tibetans, his escort mutinied, killing Yang Guozhong and demanding Yang Guifei's death. Weeping, the helpless emperor ordered his chief eunuch to strangle her with a silk cord in the village pagoda, and, after what one of China's leading poets called 'this everlasting wrong', continued his journey west. His son, the Heir Apparent, Suzong, took the throne and a year later Xuanzong returned to Chang'an, which had been recovered from An's control, dying in the palace as 'Retired Emperor' at the age of 77.

BUDDHIST ART AND ARCHITECTURE

A wave of cultural imperialism, expressed in new cliff shrines, swept westwards along the Silk Roads – at the famous Buddhist centre, Dunhuang (in northwest Gansu), which had been flourishing since the Northern Wei, two thirds of the grottoes date from the Sui and Tang – and new sites were opened in provincial regions like Sichuan and Yunnan. A stream of merchants, travellers and missionaries kept contact with India alive, and the return in 645 of the great Chinese monk, Xuanzong, after 16 years of travelling in India and Central Asia, with new texts and seven icons for copying, led to an outburst of sculptural activity. The Great Goose pagoda in Xi'an was built in 652 to house the relics and texts that Xuanzong brought back from India.

Tang imperial support for Buddhism was on the whole based on practical advantages rather than belief. In return for tax exemptions and other privileges, the Buddhist church supported the imperial family, provided useful welfare, and kept the people content with their colourful processions and displays of fabulous treasures.

Commissioning temples and religious paintings and statuary became the vogue, conferring status as well as spiritual merit and giving useful opportunities for conspicuous consumption – whether in the form of vast public works like the 57-ft-high (17.4-m) Maitreya Buddha commissioned by Wu Zetian in 673 at Longmen, or in small icons, such as the exquisitely modelled and bejewelled gilt figure on a lotus base from 871 found in the late 1980s at Famen temple, near Xi'an. Tang realism and their worldly approach to religion transformed the aspect of cliff shrines from small, mystical, dark chapels to large, open stages on which Buddha and his attendants stand as if at court. There is an increasingly close contact between the divine and worldly figures. A scholar monk, Dao Xuan, complained in the late 7th century that: 'Sculptors of the day made images like dancing girls, so that every court lady came to imagine that she resembled a Bodhisattva.'

A rare example of temple sculpture has survived at Nan Chan temple in the Wu Tai Mountains, Shanxi, where the 17 original figures stand on a rectangular platform. Cliff carvings, particularly in Sichuan, and murals preserved in Tang temples on Silk Road sites give vivid pictures of court life; in scenes of the Western Paradise, Buddha sits on a magnificent throne like a Chinese emperor in his palace, while the believers, portrayed as courtiers, gaze from balconies and loggias in delighted wonder at the sumptuous scene below.

(Right) Silk scroll from Dunhuang depicting the return of the monk Xuanzong from India bearing Buddhist sutras. Officials, priests and worshippers lined the road to greet the procession with its packhorses bearing the sacred scripts (Fujita Art Museum, Osaka).

It was an age of conspicuous consumption: the value of a Buddhist icon was almost directly related to its material worth. Recent excavations at the Famen Temple near Xi'an uncovered a large quantity of Tang precious offerings, including many donated by the empress Wu Zetian. All show a very high degree of metal-working techniques with exquisitely engraved objects in silver and gold, often, like this silver-gilt figure on a lotus base, covered with jewels.

(Above) The Bodhisattva Guanyin suffered a sex-change on arrival in China. The male Bodhisattva in India was gradually transformed into a woman by the Chinese; Guanyin was associated with mercy and Chinese sculptors used her form to express their ideal of female beauty. Guanyin was so popular that she was also accepted by the Daoists, partly as a patron of motherhood. This painting of Guanyin from 983 from the Dunhuang caves bears an inscription, in which the donors shown in the two lower rows pray 'that children and grandchildren may abound, that for ten thousand years, and a thousand seasons there may be riches, dignity and prosperity'.

(Above) The largest Buddha in China, carved between 713 and 804, overlooks the confluence of two important rivers at Leshan in Sichuan.

(Left) The Great Goose Pagoda was built on the monk Xuanzong's request, to provide a fire-proof place to house the Buddhist texts that he had brought back from India.

TANG DYNASTY
756–907

肅 宗	**Suzong** 756–762	
代 宗	**Daizong** 762–779	
德 宗	**Dezong** 779–805	
順 宗	**Shunzong** 805	
宪 宗	**Xianzong** 805–820	
穆 宗	**Muzong** 820–824	
敬 宗	**Jingzong** 824–827	

文 宗	**Wenzong** 827–840
武 宗	**Wuzong** 840–846
宣 宗	**Xuanzong** 846–859
懿 宗	**Yizong** 859–873
僖 宗	**Xizong** 873–888
昭 宗	**Zhaozong** 888–904
哀 帝	**Aidi (Zhaoxuan)** 904–907

SUZONG	
Born 711, as Li Yu *Titles before* *accession* Prince Zhong, Heir Apparent (738) *Accession* 756 *Father* Xuanzong (3rd son of)	*Mother* consort Yang Guifei *Children* 14 sons *Died* 762 *Tomb* Jianling, Li Quan county, Shaanxi *Temple name* Suzong ('Respectful Ancestor')

SUZONG AND DAIZONG

The reign of **Suzong** (756–762) and that of his eldest son, **Daizong** (762–779), were dominated by the An Lushan rebellion which lasted until 763, and the records of that decade are biased and incomplete. Both emperors followed a policy of clemency towards the rebels, leaving local leaders in power, thus increasing provincial fragmentation. The population census fell from nearly 53 million in 754 to 17 million in 764 and the Tang dynasty never recovered from the devastation. As the battle swept to and fro across central China (Chang'an was recovered in 757, Luoyang recovered and lost again), the Tibetans entered the fray, sacking Chang'an in 763. Although Daizong returned to the city in 764, the Tibetans remained within striking distance, attacking the capital regularly until 777 and occupying the western horse pastures.

Daizong was never able to control events. Suspicious and indecisive,

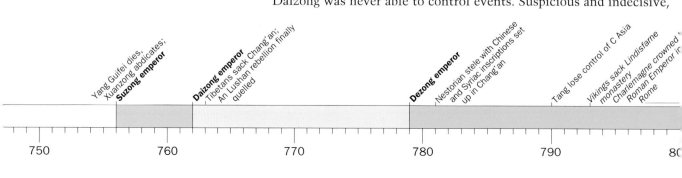

DAIZONG	
Born	*Died*
727, as Li Yu	779
Accession	*Tomb*
762	Yuanling, Fuping
Father	county, Shaanxi
Suzong	*Temple name*
(eldest son of)	Daizong ('Dai
Children	Ancestor')
20 sons	

TANG	
DEZONG	*Died*
Born	806
742, as Li Shi	*Tomb*
Accession	Fengling, Fuping
779	county, Shaanxi
Father	*Temple name*
Daizong	Shunzong
(eldest son of)	('Submissive
Children	Ancestor')
11 sons	
Died	XIANZONG
805	*Born*
Tomb	778, as Li Chun
Chongling, Jingyang	*Title before accession*
county, Shaanxi	Prince of Guangling
Temple name	*Accession*
Dezong ('Virtuous	805
Ancestor')	*Father*
	Shunzong (eldest
SHUNZONG	son of)
Born	*Children*
761, as Li Song	20 sons
Accession	*Died*
805	820; murdered by
Father	two dissatisfied
Dezong	eunuchs
(eldest son of)	*Tomb*
Children	Jingling, Pucheng
23 sons	county, Shaanxi
Abdicated	*Temple name*
805	Xianzong
	('Constitutional
	Ancestor')

Woodcut of Dezong.

he failed to inspire the troops and attached eunuch advisers to provincial military establishments to report on them. Susceptible to mystical Buddhism, he soon allowed affairs of state to drift. Despite the peace, by the end of his reign, at least six border provinces were out of central control, their military governors behaving like independent barbarian chieftains.

DEZONG TO AIDI

From the restoration of peace in 766 to the outbreak of open civil war a century later, there was relative stability and prosperity. The Tang dynasty had, however, lost its dynamism and slowly its energy was drained by two perennial problems: invasions by border states, particularly Tibet and Nanchao (Yunnan), and an inability to control regional governors. The power of the throne was eroded by lack of money, eunuch interference, short reigns – only 2 of the 12 emperors from 779–907 sat on the throne for more than 15 years – and an increasing imperial tendency to rely on mysticism and religious advisers.

Dezong (779–805), Daizong's eldest son, an intelligent and vigorous man of 40, made valiant attempts to reassert imperial authority, but his reforming drive was defeated by an inability to subdue rebellions between 781 and 786 by regional governors claiming hereditary privileges for their sons. Uncertain of military support, Dezong placed the palace army under eunuch commanders, reckoning that their dependence on the throne would guarantee loyalty. The eunuchs abused their position, tyrannizing and plundering citizens and merchants, influencing appointments, taking bribes and adopting sons to perpetuate their own power. Within 20 years their numbers rose to nearly 5,000 and their influence was decisive in questions of succession.

Dezong's eldest son, **Shunzong** (805), was disabled, a stroke leaving

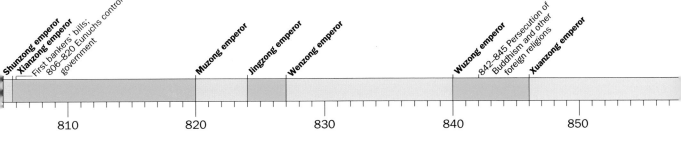

Shunzong emperor
Xianzong emperor
First bankers' bills;
806–820 Eunuchs control government

Muzong emperor

Jingzong emperor

Wenzong emperor

Wuzong emperor
842–845 Persecution of Buddhism and other foreign religions

Xuanzong emperor

810   820   830   840   850

TOMB FIGURINES

The development of three-colour (*sancai*) glazing gave clay figures a new prestige. The finest examples, over 3 ft (1 m) tall, with brilliant colours (blue cobalt, imported from the Middle East, was more valuable than gold) were reserved for the highest ranks. Modelled with extraordinary realism, they combine the Han feeling for movement with perfect anatomical proportions.

The ceramic figurines were used above all to provide the deceased with status, and the subject matter – predominantly human beings – gives a vivid picture of the wealth and leisure of the upper classes. Under the protection of a pair of powerful guardians or 'heavenly kings', the figurines portray a peaceful world in which women, excluded from the stone statuary above ground, hold their own. Seductive female courtiers in daring decollété and elaborate hairstyles are served by graceful serving girls (always pretty) and beautiful dancers and musicians, slender-waisted and supple with 'butterfly eyebrows'. In the 8th century, Xuanzong's favourite consort, Yang Guifei, inspired the so-called 'fat ladies' with full figures and loose flowing robes. Many still carry traces of

make-up: painted red lips, foreheads coloured yellow with powdered lead or arsenic and painted Indian-style flower-patterns between the eyes or on the cheeks.

The Tang love of horses runs through this underground world. A saddled horse formed the centrepiece of funeral processions of troops and musicians; men and women play polo at full gallop (the latter in men's clothing for comfort, hair protected by a wimple), and male and female musicians play on horseback. Hunters ride with falcon at wrist, dogs on their lap and game slung across the saddle. The sculptors knew their

models: saddled or unsaddled, grazing, galloping, heads tossing and hoofs pawing the ground or at rest with head turned as if to scratch a hind leg, these are living creatures with real muscles and breath dilating their nostrils.

The cosmopolitan aspect of Tang life is reflected in numerous models of foreigners – bearded traders with sacks of produce, camels bearing entire troupes of foreign musicians and young, curly-haired dancing boys from Central Asia, bejewelled with anklets, bracelets and occasionally gold leaf necklaces.

The figures were displayed on a cart during the funeral procession, then placed in the tomb around the coffin in order of importance. Their number and size were regulated according to the rank of the deceased. *Sancai*

(Above) 'Fat lady' inspired by Xuanzong's great love, Yang Guifei.

(Right) The Tang nobility were extremely fashion-conscious and tomb models illustrate the frequent changes in style.

(Far right) Guardians, the tallest and hence the most important figures in the tomb, were usually placed facing the tomb chamber entrance or around the coffin.

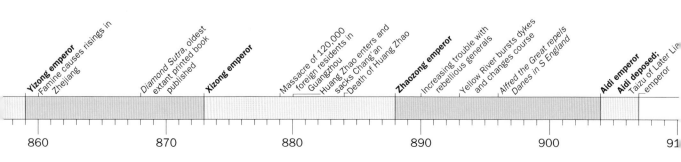

Yizong emperor
Famine causes risings in Zhejiang

Diamond Sutra, oldest extant printed book published

Xizong emperor

Massacre of 120,000 foreign residents in Guangzhou
Huang Zhao enters and sacks Chang'an
Death of Huang Zhao

Zhaozong emperor

Increasing trouble with rebellious generals

Yellow River bursts dykes and changes course

Alfred the Great repels Danes in S England

Aidi emperor
Aidi deposed;
Taizu of Later Lia emperor

860   870   880   890   900   91

SUZONG TO AIDI 115

production lasted from the end of the 7th to the mid-8th centuries; after this, production – which was concentrated in a few kilns in central China – virtually ceased, possibly because the kilns had been destroyed during the An Lushan rebellion.

him nearly mute, and he abdicated within a year. His son, **Xianzong** (805–820), was the last Tang imperial reformer. He won authority by personally leading successful campaigns against rebel provinces (814–819), and his economic and administrative reforms gave the dynasty another half-century of efficient empire-wide administration. Murdered by two discontented eunuchs, Xianzong was succeeded by his son, **Muzong** (820–824), a sybarite who died four years later after a polo accident. His son, **Jingzong** (824–827), a reckless teenager who filled the court with religious quacks and alchemists and shot scented paper darts at his favourite concubines, was murdered by exasperated eunuchs. His half-brother, **Wenzong** (827–840), was studious and well meaning, reviving daily audiences, but inexperienced; a failed attempt to crush the eunuchs left him completely in their power. On his death, at 30, the eunuchs chose his younger brother, **Wuzong** (840–846), slaying two rival candidates and their mothers.

Wuzong's reign was marked by a major persecution of religious orders in 845, targeted primarily at the Buddhists, whose economic independence threatened to create a state within a state. An ardent Daoist, cultivating the family link with Laozi, Wuzong was fatally attracted by immortality potions which affected his sanity and killed him at 33. Wuzong's sons being too young to rule, the eunuchs placed **Xuanzong**

(*Right*) A group of eunuchs. Mural from the tomb of the prince Zhanghuai, 706, Qianling, Shaanxi.

TANG	
MUZONG	**Tomb**
Born	Zhangling, Fuping
795, as Li Heng	county, Shaanxi
Accession	*Temple name*
820	Wenzong ('Literary
Father	Ancestor')
Xianzong (3rd son	
of)	**WUZONG**
Children	*Born*
5 sons	814, as Li Yan
Died	*Title before accession*
824; after a polo	Prince of Ying
accident	*Accession*
Tomb	840
Guangling, Pucheng	*Father*
county	Muzong (5th son of)
Temple name	*Children*
Muzong ('Reverent	5 sons
Ancestor')	*Died*
	846; killed by a
JINGZONG	poisonous Daoist
Born	elixir
809, as Li Zhan	*Tomb*
Accession	Duanling, San Yuan
824	county, Shaanxi
Father	*Temple name*
Muzong (eldest son	Wuzong ('Martial
of)	Ancestor')
Children	
5 sons	**XUANZONG**
Died	*Born*
827; murdered by	810, as Li Chen
exasperated	*Accession*
eunuchs	846
Tomb	*Father*
Zhuangling, San	Xianzong (13th son
Yuan county,	of)
Shaanxi	*Wife*
Temple name	Zhao (not made an
Jingzong	empress)
('Esteemed	*Children*
Ancestor')	12 sons, some
	daughters
WENZONG	*Died*
Born	859; after taking a
809, as Li Ang	Daoist elixir
Accession	*Tomb*
827	Zhenling, Jingyang
Father	county, Shaanxi
Muzong (2nd son	*Temple name*
of)	Xuanzong
Children	('Proclaimed
2 sons	Ancestor')
Died	
840	

(846–859), Xianzong's 13th son, on the throne. Xuanzong (not to be confused with the earlier great Tang emperor of the same name) reversed the anti-Buddhist measures, reviving Buddhist services and allowing limited rebuilding of temples. A prickly eccentric, indulgent to his family but fond of humiliating officials, his 13-year rule was reasonably prosperous, with efficient, just administration, and when the Tibetan royal line died out in 849, he regained territory in the west. He was, however, another convinced Daoist, the fourth emperor in four decades to die from elixirs.

Xuanzong's son, **Yizong** (859–873), was unstable, cruel, inexperienced and capricious, appointing ministers on whim (he tried to make his favourite musician a general), and neglecting the provinces. He favoured the eunuchs, allowed large-scale Buddhist ordinations and lavished gifts on Buddhist temples, encouraging extravagant displays. At his daughter's funeral procession, during a time of hardship, 800 lengths of cloth laid along the funeral way were covered with pearls and jade which had fallen from the dancers' hair, and after cremation, the family sieved the ashes for jewels.

The last three Tang emperors were puppets of the chief eunuch, Tian Lingzi. **Xizong** (873–888), acceding at the age of 12, regarded Tian as a foster-father. Hostility between the eunuch 'Inner Court' and the officials paralysed the administration and the relief system collapsed. Taxes, traditionally lowered in hard times, remained high despite widespread famine which drove peasants off the land and forced them to sell their children as slaves. The machinery of government, distorted by the steady growth of military regionalism and an increasing gulf between

(*Right*) Daoist immortal carrying a dragon-headed staff and emblems of immortality — a gourd with the elixir of immortality and a crane, symbol of longevity, within the peach of eternal life.

(*Far right*) Rare fungi were believed to prolong life and the decoration on this vase symbolizes the life-prolonging effect of sexual intercourse.

wealthy landlords and impoverished peasants, no longer worked and there was a complete breakdown of society. The people rose against the officials and brigands terrorized the peasants. Imperial control was openly challenged by popular risings and powerful regional warlords. In 879, rebels sacked Guangzhou (Canton), massacring 120,000 of the 200,000 foreign residents (southeast Asians, Indians, Persians and Arabs). In 880, rebels took Chang'an, forcing the emperor to flee to Sichuan. Their leader, Huang Zhao, entered the city in a golden carriage, his soldiers decked in brocade with hair tied in red silk ribbons, but the carnage was appalling – 'a tale of arson, pillage, rape and cannibalism, of rustics masquerading as ministers and aristocratic bodies sunk in mud and blood.'

Xizong's flight to Sichuan marked the real end of the Tang dynasty and the remaining years are a tale of flight. Attempts to rally imperial forces were thwarted by bitter rivalry between eunuchs and officials and jealousy between generals. Twice Xizong returned to Chang'an where 'thorns and brambles filled the city, foxes and hares ran everywhere', only to be chased out again, and he died in 888 aged just 27. His successors were alternately fugitives or captives and neither was buried in an imperial tomb. At one time, **Zhaozong** (888–904) was held by a local prefect; in 900 he was deposed by eunuchs, then freed and restored only to be murdered in 904 by a military governor, Zhu Wen. Zhu made Zhaozong's ninth son, **Aidi** (904–907) – also known as Zhaoxuan – emperor, but in 907 usurped the throne himself as the founder of the Later Liang dynasty, thus bringing the long Tang reign to an end.

TANG	
YIZONG	ZHAOZONG
Born	*Born*
833, as Li Wen	867, as Li Jie
Title before accession	*Accession*
Prince of Yun	888
Accession	*Father*
859	Yizong (7th son of)
Father	*Children*
Xuanzong (eldest	10 sons
son of)	*Died*
Mother	904; assassinated
Zhao	*Tomb*
Children	none
8 sons	*Temple name*
Died	Zhaozong ('Shining
873	Ancestor')
Tomb	
Jianling, Fuping	AIDI
county, Shaanxi	*Born*
Temple name	892, as Li Zhu
Yizong ('Exemplary	*Accession*
Ancestor')	904
	Father
XIZONG	Zhaozong (9th son
Born	of)
862, as Li Yan	*Deposed*
Accession	907
873	*Died*
Father	908
Yizong (5th son of)	*Tomb*
Children	none
2 sons	*Temple name*
Died	Aidi ('Sorrowing
888	Emperor'), also
Tomb	known as Zhaoxuan
Jingling, Qian	
county, Shaanxi	
Temple name	
Xizong ('Contented	
Ancestor')	

PERSECUTION OF BUDDHISM

The decrees of 845 ordering the destruction of temples, monasteries and icons, were directed against the economic powers of the Buddhist church which were draining revenues through tax exemptions and withdrawing manpower from the state. There was no Western-style religious persecution of belief; monks and nuns were returned to the tax registers and active life, and millions of acres of arable land recovered for state use. The Buddhist church survived the blow, but never recovered its political and economic position, and the artistic loss was immeasurable. As well as the loss of buildings, bronze statuary was melted down for coinage, iron for agricultural implements while gold, silver and other precious metals were taken by the treasury; only clay, wooden and stone images which had no reuse value were left untouched.

The earliest known Tang temple, Nan Chan in the Wu Tai mountains, was built in 782 and survived the persecution only because of its isolated position.

FIVE DYNASTIES	**NORTHERN SONG**	**SOUTHERN SONG**	**YUAN**
Later Liang	Taizu	Gaozong	Khubilai
Taizu	960–976	1127–1162	(Shizu)
907–910	Taizong	Xiaozong	1279–1294
Modi	976–997	1163–1190	Temur Oljeitu
911–923	Zhenzong	Guangzong	(Chengzong)
	998–1022	1190–1194	1294–1307
Later Tang	Renzong	Ningzong	Khaishan
Zhuangzong	1022–1063	1195–1224	(Wuzong)
923–926	Yingzong	Lizong	1308–1311
Mingzong	1064–1067	1225–1264	Ayurbarwada
926–934	Shenzong	Duzong	(Renzong)
Feidi	1068–1085	1265–1274	1311–1320
934–935	Zhezong	Gongzong	Shidebala
	1086–1101	1275	(Yingzong)
Later Jin	Huizong	Duanzong	1321–1323
Gaozu	1101–1125	1276–1278	Yesun Temur
936–944	Qinzong	Bing Di	(Taiding)
Chudi	1126	1279	1323–1328
944–947			Tugh Temur
			(Wenzong)
Later Han			1328–1329; 1329–1332
Gaozu			Khoshila
947–948			(Mingzong)
Yindi			1329
948–951			Toghon Temur
			(Shundi)
Later Zhou			1333–1368
Taizu			
951–954			
Shizong			
954–960			

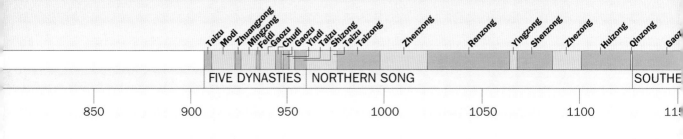

FIVE DYNASTIES NORTHERN SONG SOUTHE

850   900   950   1000   1050   1100   11

Taizu (960–976)

Renzong (1022–1063)

Gaozong (1127–1162)

Khubilai (1279–1294)

CHAOS, DIPLOMACY AND INVASION
Five Dynasties AD 907–960
Northern and Southern Song AD 960–1279
Yuan AD 1279–1368

AFTER 50 YEARS of strife during the Five Dynasties period which followed the fall of the Tang, the Song re-established unity and for three centuries China enjoyed peace. This was a period of intense intellectual, artistic and technical innovation in which painting, literature and philosophy reached new heights and the emergence of an educated, wealthy middle class stimulated the production of fine artifacts.

Militarily weak, threatened by powerful neighbours, the Song survived through successful diplomacy. They bought peace by paying tribute and offering equality (an unprecedented concession), but in 1127 the newly-founded Jurchen Jin dynasty invaded, sweeping through northern China and capturing the capital, Kaifeng. The Song retreated south to Hangzhou where the 'Southern Song' emperors ruled for another one and a half centuries before being defeated by the Mongols.

For nearly a century from 1279 China was under alien rule. Unlike previous invaders, the Mongols never became sinicized and treated the Chinese as inferiors. They adopted multi-national policies, importing non-Chinese advisers and technicians from Central Asia and further west and encouraged foreign religions. Under Khubilai Khan's inferior successors (7 in 74 years), Mongol control weakened and the foreigners were finally driven out by a popular Chinese uprising under Zhu Yuanzhang, the founder of the Ming dynasty.

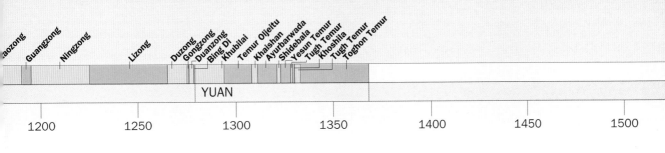

YUAN

1200   1250   1300   1350   1400   1450   1500

FIVE DYNASTIES
907–960

Later Liang

太 祖 **Taizu**
907–910

末 帝 **Modi**
911–923

Later Tang

壯 宗 **Zhuangzong**
923–926

明 宗 **Mingzong**
926–934

废 帝 **Feidi**
934–935

Later Jin

高 祖 **Gaozu**
936–944

出 帝 **Chudi**
944–947

Later Han

高 祖 **Gaozu**
947–948

隐 帝 **Yindi**
948–951

Later Zhou

太 祖 **Taizu**
951–954

世 宗 **Shizong**
954–960

LATER LIANG	
TAIZU	MODI
Born	*Accession*
852, as Zhu Wen	911
Accession	*Died*
907	923
Died	*Temple name*
910	Modi ('Final
Temple name	Emperor')
Taizu ('Supreme	
Progenitor')	

No wonder that Ouyang Xiu should habitually begin his historical essays with the word 'Alas', for the picture of facts and conditions of life of his time would move anyone to pity or terror. The military governors and powerful magistrates had made themselves 'princes', 'kings' or even 'emperors' over great or small pieces of territory, and ruled as licentious tyrants. Organized bandits counted into the millions ran over the country, pillaging, burning, killing, sacking cities and indulging in all forms of cruelty and extortion.

Wang Yitong

Thus commented a modern Chinese historian, Wang Yitong, on one of the darkest periods in Chinese history – 'the Five Dynasties and Ten

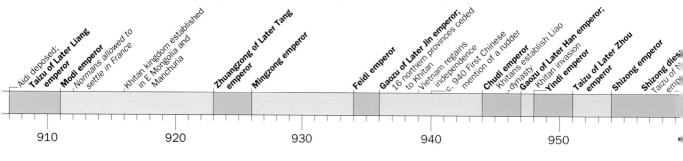

Map showing the Five Dynasties.

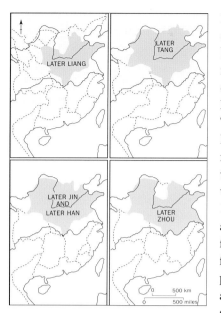

LATER TANG	
ZHUANGZONG *Accession* 923 *Died* 926 *Temple name* Zhuangzong ('Robust Ancestor') MINGZONG *Accession* 926 *Died* 934	*Temple name* Mingzong ('Brilliant Ancestor') FEIDI *Accession* 934 *Died* 935 *Temple name* Feidi ('Yielding Emperor')

LATER JIN	
GAOZU *Accession* 936 *Died* 944 *Temple name* Gaozu ('High Progenitor')	CHUDI *Accession* 944 *Died* 947 *Temple name* Chudi ('Exceeding Emperor')

LATER HAN	
GAOZU *Accession* 947 *Died* 948 *Temple name* Gaozu ('High Progenitor')	YINDI *Accession* 948 *Died* 948 *Temple name* Yindi ('Seclusive Emperor')

LATER ZHOU	
TAIZU *Accession* 951 *Died* 954 *Temple name* Taizu ('Supreme Progenitor')	SHIZONG *Accession* 954 *Died* 960 *Temple name* Shizong ('Genesis Ancestor')

(Right) The semi-nomadic Khitan peoples had close links with the Chinese and shared the Tang pleasures of riding and falconry. There was a brisk trade between the Chinese and Khitan and Khitan nobles wore Chinese silks.

Kingdoms'. The collapse of Tang central government was followed by half a century of chaos. In the north, five dynasties followed in quick succession. The Five Dynasties – the Later Liang, Later Tang, Later Jin, Later Han and Later Zhou – were all founded by military usurpers supported by their soldiers. These dynasties were short-lived, lasting only 16, 12, 11, 4 and 9 years respectively, and little is known of the imperial families. In each case a strong founding emperor was succeeded, peacefully or through usurpation and murder, by his son who was swiftly overthrown by a military rival founding his own dynasty (only the Later Tang achieved three emperors, the last one ruling for barely a year).

The first emperor of the Five Dynasties period, **Liang Taizu** (907–910), was murdered by his son, **Modi** (911–923), who was himself overcome by **Tang Zhuangzong** (923–926), the son of a Turkish general. With three emperors in 13 years – Zhuangzong was followed by **Mingzong** (926–934) and **Feidi** (934–935) – the Later Tang reunited all northern and western China before losing to another Turkish adventurer, **Gaozu** (936–944) of the Later Jin who gave the Beijing region of northern China to his allies, the Khitan. Eleven years later, Gaozu's son, **Chudi** (944–947), was ousted by another Turkish general, **Gaozu** (947–948) of the Later Han; he and his son, **Yindi** (948–951), ruled four years between them until replaced by **Taizu** (951–954) of the Later Zhou. In 960, the *rocade* ended when Zhao Kuangyin, a leading general of Chinese origin, seized the throne from the second Later Zhou emperor, **Shizong** (954–960), and established the Song dynasty (960–1279). Imperial unity was once again restored.

The 10 regional kingdoms in the south were more stable and in Sichuan, protected by its mountains, Chengdu, the capital of the Shu kingdom, became a haven for Tang exiles – officials, poets and artists – who kept Tang civilization alive. The tomb of Wang Jian (907–918), excavated in 1942, contained sculptures and grave goods of the highest quality.

NORTHERN SONG
960–1126

太 祖 Taizu
960–976

太 宗 Taizong
976–997

真 宗 Zhenzong
998–1022

仁 宗 Renzong
1022–1063

英 宗 Yingzong
1064–1067

神 宗 Shenzong
1068–1085

哲 宗 Zhezong
1086–1101

徽 宗 Huizong
1101–1125

钦 宗 Qinzong
1126

TAIZU	
Born	(2) empress Wang
927, as Zhao	(3) empress Song
Kuangyin	*Children*
Accession	2 or more sons
960	*Died*
Father	976
Zhao Hongyin	*Tomb*
(eldest son of)	Yong Anling,
Mother	Gongxian, Henan
Du (died 961)	*Temple name*
Wives	Taizu ('Supreme
(1) empress He	Progenitor')

TAIZU

Taizu (first emperor of the Song) wrote an inscription on stone, which he kept in a secure place in the palace. He instructed that every one of his successors, on being enthroned, was to kneel before this stone and read the inscription, which contained three admonitions: (1) the family and posterity of the House of Chai [family of the later Zhou dynasty] were to be protected. (2) Officials and scholars must not be executed. (3) Agrarian taxes must not be increased … Civil servants did not indulge in any sword-fighting during the Song.

Wang Fuzhi *The Song Dynasty*

Zhao Kuangyin, the emperor **Taizu** (960–976), had the throne thrust on him by mutinous officers at midnight. The last of the Later Zhou emperors, Shizong, had been succeeded by an infant son and the army, distrusting the influence of the dowager-empress, urged Zhao to take control. Forcing him to don a yellow robe, the symbol of imperial authority, the officers presented Zhao to the troops as the new emperor, Taizu. He only accepted the elevation after they promised unconditional obedience. When he entered the capital, he forbade the troops to plunder

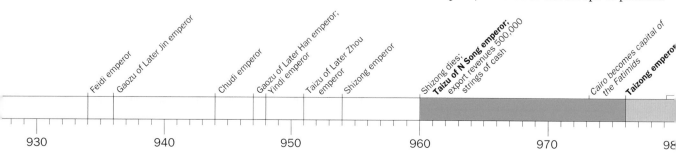

Feidi emperor

Gaozu of Later Jin emperor

Chudi emperor

Gaozu of Later Han emperor;
Yindi emperor

Taizu of Later Zhou
emperor

Shizong emperor

Shizong dies;
Taizu of N Song emperor;
export revenues 500,000
strings of cash

Cairo becomes capital of
the Fātimids

Taizong emperor

930   940   950   960   970   98

(*Above*) Portrait of Song Taizu.

(*Right*) Statuary like this temple guardian, which would previously have been made in bronze (an alloy of copper and tin), was now made in iron. Trade expansion led to such a demand for coinage that the copper needed for bronze was no longer available, and improvements in smelting techniques now made it easier to produce iron of a reliable quality. Iron guardian figure, Temple of the Central Peak (Zhong Yuemiao), 1064, Dengfeng, Song Mountains, Henan.

or harm the citizens and allowed the Later Zhou imperial family to retire peacefully. He then invited his generals to a banquet and when all were wined and dined, persuaded them to retire voluntarily with ample pensions to avoid the risk of future military coups. With this brilliant stroke, Taizu ended two centuries of regional warlordism and for the remainder of the dynasty there was relative internal peace.

With Taizu – eldest son of a Northern Zhou general, Zhao Hongyin – a remarkable family came to power. The Song emperors, descended from a northern family of officials in the Beijing area, were among the most enlightened ever to rule China. Five unusually able rulers with long reigns gave the empire a stability and prosperity which enabled it to survive the devastating loss of half its territory and still achieve a higher standard of living and artistic and technical production than any yet known. Humane, tolerant, artistic and intellectual, remarkably free from the usual imperial sins of extravagance, cruelty, arrogance and unbridled sexuality, the Song emperors inaugurated an era in which the scholar's brush replaced the warrior's steed. Whereas the Tang aristocracy revelled in military arts and competitive sports such as hunting and polo, the Song turned to painting, calligraphy and philosophy. They presided over the final transition from medieval to later imperial China which had begun under the later Tang, and adapted the political system to take account of the shift of power from the old hereditary families to the new middle classes. Under their aegis, genuine political parties emerged and a new philosophy, known as neo-Confucianism, was developed which dominated Chinese political thought until this century. Both Taizu and his successor, Taizong, showed extraordinary administrative ability; although less able, their successors were equally conscientious, deferring to ministers' opinions, lenient and generous

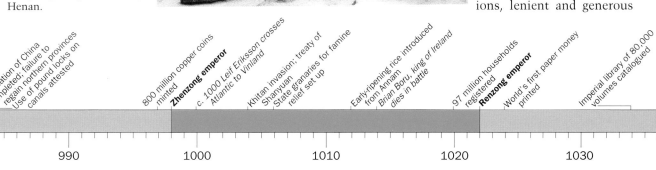

ication of China completed, failure to regain northern provinces · Use of pound locks on canals attested

800 million copper coins minted

Zhenzong emperor

c. 1000 Leif Eriksson crosses Atlantic to Vinland

Khitan invasion; treaty of Shanyuan · State granaries for famine relief set up

Early-ripening rice introduced from Annam · Brian Boru, king of Ireland dies in battle

97 million households registered

Renzong emperor

World's first paper money printed

Imperial library of 80,000 volumes catalogued

990 · 1000 · 1010 · 1020 · 1030

A stone spirit road with mythical beasts and tall officials was erected in front of Confucius' tomb, and the Confucian Temple and family mansion in Qufu were restored.

to officers, officials and subordinates and living modestly, in accordance with Confucian precepts.

Taizu's reunification policy combined strength with leniency. Re-organizing the army, calling the best units to the capital and gradually replacing military governors with civilians, he reimposed central authority over all but two kingdoms and the extreme north. The defeated states were well treated, their officials pardoned and often re-employed, thus attracting loyalty to the central government.

The emperor's foreign policy concentrated on maintaining a precarious peace. Unlike the Han and Tang, the Song remained militarily weak and on the defensive. Powerful neighbours threatened their borders – Vietnam and Dali (Yunnan) in the south and semi-sinicized kingdoms, such as Tibet and Khitan in the west and north – and survival depended on avoiding war.

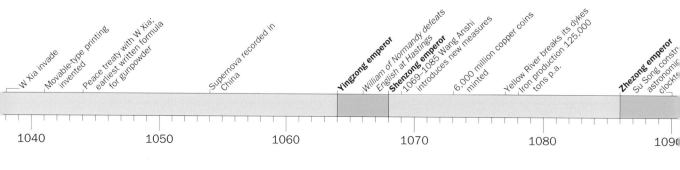

W Xia invade

Movable-type printing invented

Peace treaty with W Xia; earliest written formula for gunpowder

Supernova recorded in China

Yingzong emperor

William of Normandy defeats English at Hastings

Shenzong emperor
1069–1085 Wang Anshi introduces new measures

6,000 million copper coins minted

Yellow River breaks its dykes Iron production 125,000 tons p.a.

Zhezong emperor
Su Song constru astronomic clocktc

1040   1050   1060   1070   1080   1090

Internally, Taizu's reorganization of the government and administration laid the foundations for an extraordinary upsurge of economic activity and prosperity and created a certain separation of powers between the emperor and government. A Board of Censors controlled abuses and the administration was more centralized than ever before. Central authority was firmly applied through an empire-wide information and control network, and policy was decided in a Council of State after free and genuine ministerial debates; although the emperor, as chairman, had the casting vote, he deferred to the prevailing view, remaining in the background while his prime minister enjoyed the limelight and real power. The tone of government became more humane: ousted ministers were no longer killed or exiled, merely sent to minor provincial posts.

The family good sense was confirmed by Taizu's choice of successor. Reminded by his mother that his own accession was the result of an infant on the throne, he appointed his younger full brother, Taizong, rather than his young son as Heir Apparent.

TAIZONG	
Born	(2) empress Fu
939, as Zhao	(3) empress Mingde
Guangyi	(4) empress Li
Title before accession	Yuande
Prince of Jin (973)	*Children*
Accession	At least 3 sons
976	*Died*
Father	997
Zhao Hongyin (2nd	*Tomb*
son of)	Yong Xiling,
Mother	Gongxian, Henan
Du (died 961)	*Temple name*
Wives	Taizong ('Supreme
(1) empress Yin	Ancestor')

TAIZONG

Now is the moment for binding friendship and resting the people. If indeed Heaven above regrets calamity and [causes] the rogues to appreciate our humaneness and they thus accept our wish for friendly alliance and extinguish the beacons on the frontiers, that would indeed be a great fortune to our ancestral altars.

Song minister Zhang Ji advising Taizong to use diplomacy not force when dealing with the Khitan

Taizong (976–997) was nearly 40 on accession. Like his father and elder brother he had served the Later Zhou imperial family as an officer in the elite palace guards, and was active in the movement to enthrone his brother. Taizu had entrusted him with palace security and responsibility in his absence and in 973 raised him, as the prince of Jin, above the Chief Counsellor of State.

Within four years of coming to the throne Taizong completed reunification, peacefully regaining the Wu Yue kingdom in southern China in 978 and defeating the Han kingdom in Shanxi a year later. His attempts to regain the northern provinces (lost in 936), however, failed. In 979, he narrowly escaped capture by the Khitan, fleeing at night with a handful of officers and leaving his army to defeat. After a second disastrous campaign, he abandoned hope of further progress. Although the question of

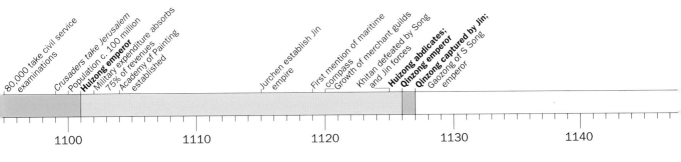

80,000 take civil service examinations

Crusaders take Jerusalem
Population c. 100 million
Huizong emperor
Military expenditure absorbs
75% of revenues
Academy of Painting
established

Jurchen establish Jin empire

First mention of maritime compass
Growth of merchant guilds
Khitan defeated by Song and Jin forces
Huizong abdicates:
Qinzong emperor
Qinzong captured by Jin:
Gaozong of S Song emperor

1100   1110   1120   1130   1140

regaining the northern lands remained an active political problem, the military remained subordinate to civil authority. Deprived of their traditional source of soldiers from the non-Han border populations, the army had to rely on mercenaries drawn from the lowest ranks of society who were no match for the warlike northerners, and the cavalry was hampered by the loss of western grazing lands. A realistic appraisal of the military balance of power thus forced the Song to follow a flexible, peaceful foreign policy and accept a loss of territory.

Taizong was a scholar. He was a good calligrapher, chess-player and was fond of writing poetry. He encouraged Confucian studies and the publication of classical texts; he commissioned encyclopedias and with his genuine love of art attracted scholars and painters to his court, building an impressive collection of paintings and calligraphy.

In domestic policy, he concentrated on improving the calibre and conditions of officials. He extended the recruitment field for candidates, increased official salaries and encouraged the promotion of able provincial officials. Civil servants with increased salaries exercised more power than at any other time in Chinese history and eunuchs and empresses' families were sidelined, minimizing the possibility of palace coups.

Taizong intended that his younger brother should succeed him, but while on the disastrous northern campaign, a plot to replace this brother with Taizu's eldest son split the family, leading to the death of both candidates; horrified by these events, Taizong's eldest son lost his reason and was demoted to commoner, and in 995 Taizong's third son, Zhao Heng (Zhenzong), was made crown prince.

An official and his servant travelling in the provinces. Tang dynasty painting from Dunhuang.

NORTHERN SONG IMPERIAL TOMBS

Over 1,000 stone statues have survived on the Northern Song imperial tombs at Gongxian, Henan. The figures, representing an imperial audience on New Year's Day, stand as if lining a courtyard, and include a wider variety of subjects than those of any other dynasty. Noteworthy are the lively depictions of foreign ambassadors (reflecting Song dependence on diplomacy) and the palace guards, over 15 ft (4.5 m) tall. The Southern Song, hoping for reunification with the north, built only temporary mausolea without the stone statuary which implied permanence.

(Right) Tomb of Zhezong, 1100. Gonxian, Henan.

Diplomacy was so important that foreign ambassadors were carved to stand in the imperial spirit roads.
(below, left to right): Southeast Asian envoy, with double turban, bearing a rhinoceros horn, tomb of Taizong, 997; Arab envoy, with gifts of precious stones, tomb of Taizong; Korean envoy, with chased mother-of pearl inlaid box of the Koryo period, tomb of Taizong; Khotan envoy, tomb of Zhezong, 1100. Gongxian, Henan.

ZHENZONG	
Born	(2) empress Guo
968, as Zhao	(3) empress Liu
Dechang	(4) empress Li
Title before accession	(5) empress Yang
Crown prince Zhao	*Children*
Heng (995)	At least 6 sons
Accession	*Died*
998	1022
Father	*Tomb*
Taizong (3rd son of)	Yong Dingling,
Mother	Gongxian, Henan
Li Yuande	*Temple name*
Wives	Zhenzong ('True
(1) empress Pan	Ancestor')

ZHENZONG

The reign of **Zhenzong** (998–1022) was overshadowed by the northern problem. A Khitan invasion in 1004 forced the court to flee to Nanjing and thence to Chengdu; leading the troops himself, Zhenzong fought back to the Yellow River where he negotiated the treaty of Shanyuan. Although no territory was ceded, he was forced to accord virtual equality – the Khitan emperor recognized him as 'elder brother' – and pay an annual tribute of 200,000 rolls of silk and 100,000 oz (2,835 kg) of silver. The treaty was regarded as a humiliation, although a flourishing trade developed with the mixed border populations – horses and hides were purchased for Chinese tea and silks – which more than compensated for the annual payments. Aware of the frailty of a title originally acquired through military force, Zhenzong sought to reinforce his legitimacy with 'revelations' and fabricated 'heavenly writings' conferring divine approval on his rule. These were derided by Confucian historians who also criticized his expenditure on lavish sacrificial ceremonies and a temple to house the heavenly documents, but these ceremonies and building works successfully secured popular agreement to his policies. Despite increasing military expenditure, the standard of living rose and the population increased rapidly thanks to the introduction of two-crop rice from southern Annam, in southeast Asia, and a doubling of the irrigation systems. The number of registered households likewise nearly doubled to 97 million in 1020.

Zhenzong died in 1022 after a two-year illness, leaving the throne to his sixth son, the 13-year-old Zhao Zhen, who became the emperor Renzong.

Contemporary paintings show the cultivation and irrigation of rice fields in the rich Yangzi valley.

PAPER MONEY

The Tang had used 'flying money' or paper certificates for government purchases in order to reduce transport costs – 1 mule load of paper equalled 40 mule loads of coins – but the world's first real paper money was printed in Chengdu, Sichuan, in 1024, during the Song emperor Renzong's reign. Economic expansion led to a rocketing demand for coins (6 million strings of 1,000 coins were cast in 1073) and paper notes were soon widely used. The quality of notes, printed in colour on special paper, was strictly controlled, with a high cash backing to prevent inflation and a time limit of three years' use. Cheques, promissory notes and bills of

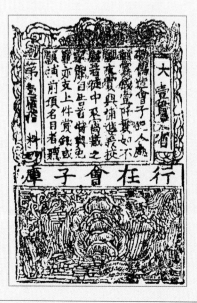

exchange were also used and by the end of the dynasty production was equivalent to 70 million strings of cash. Paper money spread to the Khitan (Liao), Jin (Jurchen) and Mongols and later to Persia, Korea and Japan.

Paper money issued in Hangzhou by the Southern Song.

RENZONG	
Born	(demoted)
1010, as Zhao	(2) empress Zhang
Zhen	(3) empress Cao
Title before accession	(4) empress Zhang
Crown prince	*Children*
(1018)	3 sons, died young
Accession	*Died*
1022	1063
Father	*Tomb*
Zhenzong (6th son	Yong Zhaoling,
of)	Gongxian, Henan
Mother	*Temple name*
consort Li	Renzong
Wives	('Benevolent
(1) empress Guo	Ancestor')

The emperor Renzong. Anon. 11th century.

The clock tower constructed by Su Song in 1090 at Kaifeng relied on water-driven gears (on the right) which rotated an armillary sphere (on the top) and a celestial globe. The intricate mechanism included a clock escapement system (invented by Yi Xing in the 8th century) which was operated by a wheel.

RENZONG

For 10 years the dowager-empress Liu (Zhenzong's able and active wife who had entered the imperial harem at 15) acted as regent for the young emperor **Renzong** (1022–1063), but on her death in 1033, Renzong took full power and immediately replaced his wife, Guo – whom Liu had chosen – with Cao, the granddaughter of a famous general. His 40-year reign (the longest of all Song reigns) is praised as a time of peace and prosperity. Although personally weak and indecisive, becoming slightly deranged in old age, Renzong appointed wise ministers, encouraged political debate and always accepted the majority view. Said to have been irresponsible when young, he developed a genuine concern for the people's welfare, meriting his temple name 'Benevolent' (*Ren*).

The northern frontier remained quiet but in 1038 China was invaded from the west by the Western Xia under their new leader, 'emperor of the Great Xia'. Under the peace treaty of 1044, the Western Xia won conditions similar to those awarded the Khitan. Their ruler accepted vassal status as 'king of Xia', but the Song agreed to pay an annual tribute of 130,000 rolls of silk, 50,000 oz (1,400 kg) of silver and 20,000 lb (9,000 kg) of tea. The Khitan raised their own demands to 300,000 rolls of silk and 200,000 oz (5,700 kg) of silver and the resulting three-way balance of power gave 80 years of peace.

These border wars brought trouble at home. Peace on such terms required the maintenance of a large army (the Western Xia had only negotiated in the face of clear Chinese numerical superiority). The Chinese army, only 378,000 in 975, more than tripled to 1,259,000 by 1045 and the consequent financial drain caused widespread hardship and popular unrest. The spiral of rising taxes became self-defeating, since peasants unable to pay were forced off the land, thus reducing the tax base. A leading statesman, Wang Anshi (1021–1086), called for an active reform of land tenure. His proposals to limit the privileges of large landowners and ease the burden on the poor were bitterly attacked by traditional conservatives. The remainder of the dynasty was racked by a struggle between the conservative and reform parties (each justifying their policies by their own interpretations of the Confucian classics), which created serious divisions and factions in the civil service.

The scholarly arguments used in political debate reflected the vigorous intellectual activity of the time. Reacting against the mysticism and foreign ideas which had attracted the Tang, the Song turned to their past for inspiration and a great classical renaissance – a conscious return to purely Chinese sources – led to the second great age of Chinese philosophy, based on rediscovering the original meaning of the classics and reformulating it in contemporary terms. This movement was helped by the spread of printing which made the ancient texts available cheaply to the educated classes. Rational and practical experimentation replaced religious meditation and revelation. Man was seen, not as the Daoist potential immortal or the Buddhist candidate for paradise, but as an integral part of the physical cosmos whose laws could and should be studied and verified.

This active curiosity led to extraordinary developments in all branches of knowledge. Wealth and energy were channelled into practical experimentation leading to advances in arts, social organization, philosophy and technology. In mathematics, Shao Yong (1011–1077) calculated the tropical year to within four seconds; the compass and abacus were discovered and the first relief maps made; one of the oldest and most perfect clockwork astronomical machines was constructed at Kaifeng in 1090; the earliest treatises on Chinese architecture (*Ying Zao Fa Shi*) and forensic medicine date from this time. Much of our knowledge of pre-Song sites and monuments derives from Song archaeological works and rubbings of ancient stelae. From the emperor downwards – Renzong's library, catalogued between 1034 and 1036, contained 80,000 volumes – a passion for information and collecting texts, ancient and modern, fuelled the production of encyclopedias.

Renzong's three sons died, and accepting that he could no longer expect a male heir, he adopted Zhao Shu (Yingzong), the 13th son of his cousin, the prince Pu (a grandson of Taizu).

YINGZONG, SHENZONG AND ZHEZONG

On accession, **Yingzong** (1064–1067) was too ill to take power and the dowager-empress Cao became regent. Honest, modest, more interested in science and arts than politics, Yingzong remained frail and his short reign was plagued by interference from the dowager-empress who favoured the conservatives. Without proper leadership, rivalry between the two parties intensified and the border situation worsened.

Shenzong (1068–1085), Yingzong's eldest son by the empress Gao, was 19 years old on accession. Conscientious, frugal and banning luxury at court, he was genuinely interested in state affairs and appointed the reformer Wang Anshi to deal with the rapidly deteriorating general situation. Renewed hostilities against the Western Xia had disastrous effects on the economy, bringing widespread unemployment, falling tax revenues and unrest. Wang's measures, aimed at helping the peasantry and small merchants, aroused bitter opposition from the landowners and wealthy merchants whose privileges were affected, but Shenzong supported Wang even when disagreeing with some of his ideas. Slowly the treasury filled and with solvency, the border situation improved.

Zhezong (1086–1101), Shenzong's heir and sixth son, was only 10 when his father died. The regent, Yingzong's widow, the dowager-

YINGZONG	

Born
  1032, as Zhao Shu
Titles before
accession
  Zhao Congshi
  (1036),
  Heir Apparent
  (1062)
Accession
  1064
Family connection
  Yingzong was the
  great-grandson of
  Taizu and was
  adopted by
  Renzong
Father
  Prince Pu, a
	grandson of Taizu
	  and a cousin of
	  Renzong
	Mother
	  Ren
	Wife
	  empress Gao
	Children
	  2 or more sons
	Died
	  1067
	Tomb
	  Yong Houling,
	  Gongxian, Henan
	Temple name
	  Yingzong ('Heroic
	  Ancestor')

SHENZONG	

Born
  1048, as Zhao Xu
Title before accession
  Heir Apparent
  (1066)
Accession
  1068
Father
  Yingzong (eldest
  son of)
Mother
  empress Gao
Wives
  (1) empress Xiang
	(2) empress Zhu
	  (3) empress Zhen
	Children
	  At least 11 sons
	Died
	  1085
	Tomb
	  Yong Yuling,
	  Gongxian, Henan
	Temple name
	  Shenzong ('Spiritual
	  Ancestor')

ZHEZONG	
Born	*Children*
1076, as Zhao Xu	None
Accession	*Died*
1086	1101
Father	*Tomb*
Shenzong (6th son of)	Yong Tailing, Gongxian, Henan
Wife	*Temple name*
(1) empress Meng (demoted 1096)	Zhezong ('Sagacious Ancestor')
(2) empress Liu	

(*Right*) Portrait of Renzong's second wife, the empress Cao.

(*Far right*) The Song replaced the Tang ostrich with a mythical bird intended to bring good fortune. Zhezong's tomb, 1100.

WANG ANSHI'S REFORMS

'One of the most original minds in Chinese history', Wang Anshi (1021–1086) was an exceedingly able, but abrasive, opinionated reformer (his opponents described him as 'repulsively dirty'). His measures have been misleadingly described as socialism, but Wang never questioned the basis of society and his aims were primarily practical, based on the belief that the financial problems caused by military expenditure could only be solved through radical government intervention to restore the productive capacity of poor peasants and traders.

Wang reduced land taxes by 50 per cent, introduced price regulation and cheap credit facilities for peasants and small merchants with state loans and pawnshops, and undertook vital water control measures. He tried to replace large-scale mercenary armies with peasant militia, making local regions responsible for their troops and giving peasants in the north horses in return for supplying one family member for the cavalry when needed. Welfare measures included the provision of reserve granaries and peasant education, and with the establishment of orphanages, hospitals and public cemeteries the state took over many of the charitable and medical functions previously performed by Buddhist monasteries.

Wang's reforms were bitterly attacked by the large landowners, merchants and moneylenders whose interests were affected. The measures were only partially enforced by officials, many of whom came from the landowning class, but they succeeded in raising revenues and allaying public distress.

Water control was vital to the economy and emperors and senior officials personally inspected waterworks during their travels.

empress Gao, dismissed Wang Anshi and reinstated the conservatives. They frittered away their power in personal disputes and when Gao died in 1093 Zhezong recalled the reformists and in 1096 replaced his wife, the empress Meng (chosen by Gao), with a favourite concubine. Selfish, irascible and nervous, Zhezong died aged 24 and with the approval of the dowager-empress Xiang (Shenzong's widow), Huizong, 11th son of Shenzong and the empress Chen, succeeded.

HUIZONG	
Born	(4) empress Liu
1082, as Zhao Ji	(5) empress Liu
Title before accession	*Children*
Prince of Duan	At least 1 son
(1096)	*Abdicated*
Accession	1125
1101	*Died*
Father	1135, in captivity in
Shenzong (11th son	Mongolia
of)	*Tomb*
Mother	Yong Yuling, near
empress Chen	Shaoxing, Zhejiang
Wives	*Temple name*
(1) empress Wang	Huizong ('Divine
(2) empress Zheng	Ancestor')
(3) empress Wei	

HUIZONG AND QINZONG

Painters are not to imitate their predecessors, but are to depict objects as they exist, true to colour and form.

The emperor Huizong's instructions to painters

Huizong (1101–1125) was fated to live at the wrong time. An aesthete, remembered chiefly as a collector and painter, he presided over the loss of northern China to the newly founded Jin kingdom and died blind and half-deaf after nine years in prison.

Once his conservative regent, the dowager-empress died in 1101, he recalled the reformists, but the economic situation was by now out of hand. Military expenditure absorbed 75 per cent of the falling revenues, political rivalry had sapped official morale, leading to corruption, and without strong leadership the central government drifted from one expedient to another. Against an increasingly sombre economic and political

THE KHITAN AND THE JIN

Both the Khitan (Liao) and the Jin (Jurchen) were semi-nomadic, semi-pastoral peoples from Manchuria who came to dominate large areas in northern China. The Khitan (whose name – with its variant, Khitai – was the origin of Cathay, the name for north China in Medieval Europe, and of Kitai, the Russian name for China) were based in the Liao Valley in the northeast (modern Liaoning province). In 926, they spread eastward to the coast, absorbing the kingdom of Po Hai; 10 years later they were given 16 prefectures around Beijing for helping the founder of the Later Jin dynasty to overthrow the Later Tang dynasty. In 946, with territory stretching from the Eastern Sea to Inner Mongolia, they established the Liao empire, and, coexisting with the Later Han and Later Zhou dynasties,

claimed the throne of China.

The Khitan had five capitals based on the four cardinal points and the centre; Beijing became their southern capital. To avoid becoming too sinicized they ran a dual administrative system with both a Chinese and a Khitan prime minister. With time, however, the combination of Chinese culture and the Khitans' own strong Buddhism weakened their martial spirit, and in 1125 they were defeated by the joint forces of the Song dynasty and a rival northern people, the Jurchen.

The Jurchen (also known as the Ruzhen Tatars) were a Tungusic people from Manchuria who had broken away from the Liao empire to form their own Jin dynasty in 1115. After defeating the Liao, the Jin turned on their former Chinese allies. In 1127 they overran the whole of northern China, and entering the

Northern Song capital, Kaifeng, took Song Huizong and most of the imperial family prisoner. The Chinese, driven south, established the capital of their Southern Song dynasty at Lin'an (modern Hangzhou). At first the Jin continued Liao administrative arrangements, but from 1140 onwards they tended to adopt Chinese Tang and Song practices. In the early 13th century, the Jin found themselves squeezed between the Southern Song and a new nomadic power in the north – the Mongols. Mongol advances in 1211 forced them to move their capital south from Beijing to Kaifeng; four years later the Mongols captured Beijing. In 1232, the Mongols and Southern Song united to attack Kaifeng; two years later the last Jin emperor committed suicide and the Jin empire was absorbed into the Mongol empire.

PRINTING

The development of printing (a purely Chinese invention) raised scholarship to a new level, making cheap copies of classical, educational and popular literature widely available. Since the 8th century, woodblocks had been used to reproduce religious texts in large numbers. One worker could produce 1,000 pages a day and each block yielded 20,000 copies. The earliest known complete woodblock-printed book with illustrations is the *Diamond Sutra* (868) from Dunhuang. In the 1040s, Bi Sheng invented a movable type using clay characters fixed with wax in an iron-framed plate. Although the system was clumsy, huge runs were printed: between 971 and 983 over 5,000 rolls of Buddhist canons were printed, copies reaching Korea in 991 and Japan in 995. In the 13th century a wooden-type process was introduced with square characters fitted in a frame and in 1298, 100 copies of a gazetteer using 60,000 different characters were printed in under a month. The reusable characters were sorted on a rhyming system and kept in revolving cases.

(Above) Extract from the earliest complete woodblock printed book with illustrations, the Diamond Sutra, *(868), found at Dunhuang.*

(Right) The fonts of movable type were sorted according to a rhyming system and stored in rotary cases like this 14th century example.

(Above) Illustration for texts referring to the 'Thousand Buddhas' were made from woodblocks like this 9th-century woodblock.

(Left) Reading was no longer confined to the scholar-class. The development of woodblocks with movable printing type provided cheap illustrated texts for the new merchant classes.

THE CIVIL SERVICE

The Song perfected the use of examinations for official recruitment. Under Taizong, provincial candidates were encouraged; after 1065 triennial examinations were held at provincial, state and imperial levels with papers numbered and copied to avoid favouritism by examiners recognizing the calligraphy. Wang Anshi broadened the examinations' scope to include mathematics, law, economics and geography and obliged the sons of princes and regional commanders to take examinations before attending the national university. Under the Song, the number of candidates rose from around 30,000 to nearly 400,000 and between 1148 and 1256, over half the successful candidates had no office holder on their father's side in the past three generations. Close business contacts were forbidden between officials related by blood or marriage and the empresses' and consorts' families were banned from high positions. The examination system, creating close links between state and scholarship, associated the ruling class with education and the civil servants' high calibre gave them an important role in government.

Examinations for the civil service dominated official life for most of the imperial period. Here Tang Xuanzong is seen assessing the results of examinations for county magistrates.

QINZONG	
Born	*Wife*
1100, as Zhao	empress Zhu
Huan	*Died*
Accession	1156
1126	*Temple name*
Father	Qinzong ('Admirable
Huizong	Ancestor')
Mother	
empress Wei	

(*Below*) Flower and bird painting by Huizong in the meticulous 'court' style.

background, the emperor, who was uninterested in public affairs, withdrew to his court to cultivate artistic and intellectual pursuits.

One of the leading poets of the day, Huizong loved music and developed a 'thin-gold' style of calligraphy, later known as the 'imperial style'. He was a competent painter and several of his paintings – with 'nervous vibrant brush stroke, evoking brilliant-eyed hawks, delicate flowers and swaying pine branches' – have survived. Huizong amassed the finest collection of paintings ever made in the Far East, over 6,000 paintings perished in the Song defeat in 1127, but the catalogue survived. In 1104, the emperor founded the first Academy of Painting, organized on the model

Example of Huizong's 'thin-gold' calligraphy.

FOOTBINDING

Footbinding, whereby the toes of young girls (aged 5 to 6) were bound with wet cloths which shrank when dried, became widespread under the Song. When the foot stopped hurting, the bandages were tightened, finally producing the deformed 'lily foot' considered erotic until rejected by republicans in this century. Possibly inspired by Tang dancing girls, its adoption marked the decline in women's status brought by urbanization. In the cities, where women's labour was no longer needed, the ability to support women who could not walk unaided was a status symbol and an obvious sign of wealth.

Peasants, minorities and non-Chinese northerners never adopted footbinding.

(Below) Pair of shoes 5.5 in long for feet which had been bound and drawing showing the forced curvature of a bound foot.

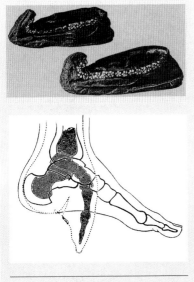

of a Confucian college, and personally instructed a group of painters at court, imposing a 'palace style' of painstaking orthodoxy and setting subjects, such as a line of poetry, which demanded intellectual agility and a literary background.

Huizong presided over a brilliant and luxurious court. When dissatisfied with the famous Dingyao porcelain, he gave official recognition to a kiln near Xi'an producing the rare Ruyao wares with their distinctive blue-grey crackled glaze; an ardent Daoist, he mounted extravagant Daoist pageants and the cost of these and the upkeep of his palaces and gardens with rare plants increased the government's financial problems. They were forced to raise taxes and issue more paper money; the resulting inflation led to a serious rebellion in 1120. When disaster struck from the north, the empire was unable to save itself. Huizong, hoping to regain the northern territories, had unwisely made an alliance with the Jin kingdom against China's ancient enemy, the Khitan (Liao), only to find himself at the mercy of his ally. In 1125, the Jin attacked and Huizong fled south. Assuming the title 'Master of Learning and the Way (Dao)', he abdicated in favour of his son, **Qinzong** (1126). Factional rivalry and imperial weakness prevented any effective regrouping of Chinese troops and when the Jin attacked again in 1126, they easily captured the capital, Kaifeng, and devastated other major cities. Huizong, Qinzong and 3,000 imperial relatives were captured and taken north as prisoners. Huizong died in 1135 and the Chinese emissary sent to bring his coffin home was himself imprisoned and died in captivity. Qinzong, white-haired at 36, spent his last 29 years in prison.

(Right) Ruyao wares, like this vase with copper rim, favoured at Huizong's court, are very rare and were made at a kiln near Xi'an.

SOUTHERN SONG
1127–1279

高 宗 **Gaozong**
1127–1162

孝 宗 **Xiaozong**
1163–1190

光 宗 **Guangzong**
1190–1194

宁 宗 **Ningzong**
1195–1224

理 宗 **Lizong**
1225–1264

度 宗 **Duzong**
1265–1274

恭 宗 **Gongzong**
1275

端 宗 **Duanzong**
1276–1278

昺 帝 **Bing Di**
1279

GAOZONG	
Born 1107, as Zhao Gou	*Wife* (1) empress Wu
Title before accession Prince of Kang (1121)	*Children* 1 son, died young
Accession 1127	*Abdicated* 1162
Father Huizong (9th son of)	*Died* 1187
Mother empress Wei	*Temple name* Gaozong ('High Ancestor')

GAOZONG

The Song dynasty was saved by yet another remarkable member of the Zhao family. As a young prince, **Gaozong** (1127–1162), ninth son of Huizong and the empress Wei, had been sent to the Jin capital as a hostage for the peace of 1125. After the fall of Kaifeng in 1126, Gaozong's elder brother, Qinzong, managed to warn him of the mass capture of the imperial family and he escaped, gathering remnants of the court *en route* and declaring himself emperor in May 1127. The army had completely disintegrated and for the next eight years he was pursued by Jin troops, only escaping capture in 1129 by fleeing to sea. The Jin took Hangzhou but the southern terrain of rivers and canals was ill-suited to their cavalry and when the Jin emperor died in 1135, they withdrew north, leaving puppet regimes in central China. Gaozong established his capital in Hangzhou and in 1141 signed a treaty admitting vassal status and paying tribute to the Jin of 500,000 units (payable in silk and silver).

Gaozong's attempts to rebuild an army were hampered by lack of money and the need to prevent a resurgence of provincial warlords. All his early skills of survival and diplomacy were needed to balance one general against another, to avoid friction between the large southern

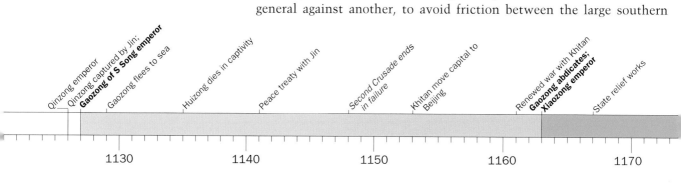

Woodcut of Gaozong from *Sancai tuhui* 1607.

landowners and newly arrived northerners and to persuade the former of the need for swingeing tax increases. Recognizing the importance of personnel, Gaozong personally supervised appointments down to provincial level, thus gaining support from all sides, and scrupulously avoided any action which might inflame north-south dislike. As long as his second wife, the empress Wu from Kaifeng, was alive, for example, he refused to take any southern girl as a concubine.

Nevertheless the army remained weak and even the newly discovered military uses of gunpowder, providing mines and grenades, could not compensate for the lack of cavalry. The government was crippled by factionalism and a new rift opened between the peace party, prepared to accept the status quo, and the revanchists, anxious to regain the lost territories. Renewed aggression by the Khitan, who had moved their capital south to Beijing in 1153, strengthened the latter and in 1161 war broke out, general Yue Fei becoming a popular hero in his attempts to free the motherland from foreign domination. Faced with increasingly violent debates on financial and foreign policy, Gaozong abdicated in 1162 in favour of his adopted son, Xiaozong and spent his last 25 years happily surrounded by southern beauties in his private quarters at the rear of the palace.

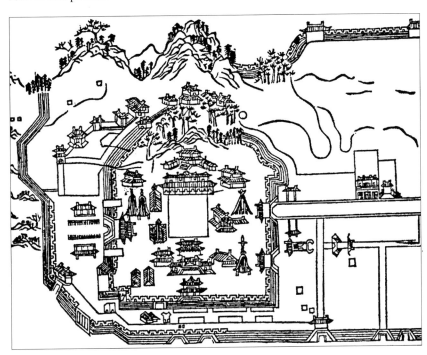

(*Right*) Artist's impression of the Southern Song capital at Hangzhou. The shape of the city, less regular than traditional Chinese capitals, lacked the earlier grid street plan.

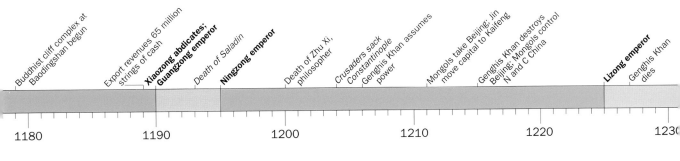

Buddhist cliff complex at Baodingshan begun

Export revenues 65 million strings of cash

Xiaozong abdicates; Guangzong emperor

Death of Saladin

Ningzong emperor

Death of Zhu Xi, philosopher

Crusaders sack Constantinople

Genghis Khan assumes power

Mongols take Beijing: Jin move capital to Kaifeng

Genghis Khan destroys Beijing; Mongols control N and C China

Lizong emperor

Genghis Khan dies

1180   1190   1200   1210   1220   1230

(*Right*) An imperial order to general Yue Fei from the emperor Gaozong.

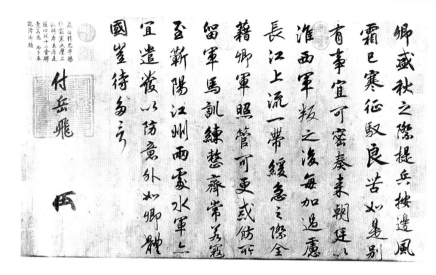

(*Below*) The reduced empire of the Southern Song in 1127 AD.

Against this unpromising background, Gaozong succeeded in reviving the cultural and intellectual glories of Kaifeng. Hangzhou soon surpassed the former capital in splendour and the Southern Song became wealthier than the Tang at their peak. The economy flourished; between the 11th and 12th centuries the population nearly doubled and under imperial patronage, Chinese civilization reached a new peak. Gaozong revived his father's Academy of Painting and this became the great age of landscape painting. The artistic and intellectual climate reflected the great renaissance in classical studies which had begun under the Northern Song. Cut off from Western influence, and in particular from Indian Buddhism, the Song turned inwards, seeking strength in their own past. Archaeology became fashionable and imperial collections of ancient ritual bronzes, jades and rubbings of stone inscriptions provided an aura of legitimacy and pride in Chinese civilization as opposed to that of the upstart conquerors. Gaozong, for example, commissioned the court painter, Ma Hezhi, to illustrate the Confucian classic, 'Book of Songs' (*Shijing*) as part of a series of paintings with themes proving the legitimacy of his rule in the face of the Jin occupation of north China.

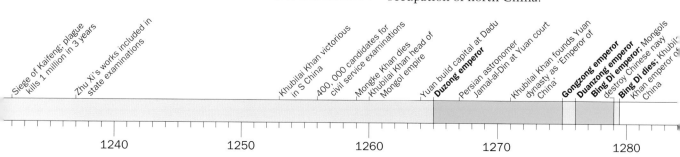

Siege of Kaifeng: plague kills 1 million in 3 years

Zhu Xi's works included in state examinations

Mongke Khan victorious in S China

400,000 candidates for civil service examinations

Mongke Khan dies Khubilai Khan head of Mongol empire

Yuan build capital at Dadu **Duzong emperor**

Persian astronomer Jamal-al-Din at Yuan court

Khubilai Khan founds Yuan dynasty as 'Emperor of China'

Gongzong emperor
Duanzong emperor
Bing Di emperor: Mongols destroy Chinese navy
Bing Di dies: Khubilai Khan emperor of China

1240   1250   1260   1270   1280

XIAOZONG	
Born 1127, as Zhao Bozong	son, Difang *Mother* Zhang
Accession 1163	*Abdicated* 1190
Father Zhao Zicheng, prince of Xiu, a 5th generation descendant of Taizu's youngest	*Died* 1194 *Temple name* Xiaozong ('Filial Ancestor')

XIAOZONG

Gaozong's only son had died early and in 1160 he adopted a descendant of Taizu's youngest son, Difang, as heir. It cannot have been easy to reign with both 'parents' living but **Xiaozong** (1163–1190) cared for them well and kept harmony at court, earning his temple name 'Filial' (*Xiao*) – he was the first to receive this name. His was the most peaceful and stable of all Southern Song reigns. Yue Fei, who was unwilling to accept the new peace policy, was recalled and executed; the peace of 1165 gave slightly improved terms and the revanchist party was kept in check.

Cut off from the transcontinental trade routes, China turned to the sea, inaugurating the first great era of oceanic commerce in world history. Improvements in navigation and ships,

(*Right*) The production of Northern Celadon wares at kilns at Yaozhou, Shaanxi, and Linru, Henan, reached its peak under the Northern Song and the Yuan.

CHINESE SHIPS

The ships which sail the Southern Sea and south of it are like houses. When their sails are spread they are like great clouds in the sky. Their rudders are several tens of feet long. A single ship carries several hundred men. It has stored on board a year's supply of grain.

Zhou Qufei 1178

Chinese ships became the most advanced in the world. Having learned from the Arabs, the Chinese, who had invented the compass (first recorded in 1119), soon surpassed them in cartography and seamanship. The junk was a natural bulk carrier, suitable for transporting rice, timber, minerals and porcelain. The vertical rudder fitted its straight stern and the great four-storey ships with 6 masts, 12 large sails and about 1,000 men were powered by sail and oar. The oars pivoted with fore-and-aft movements, and, to Arab envy, the use of capstans, canvas and rigid matting sails enabled them to sail close to the wind. The ships were built using iron nails and water-proofed with special oil; they had water-tight holds and buoyancy chambers, floating anchors and scoops for taking samples from the seabed. Carrying capacity ranged from 200–600 tons (200,000 to 600,000 kg). One excavated Southern Song junk is nearly 130 ft (40 m) long, 33 ft (10 m) wide and weighs 250 tons (250,000 kg); a 14th-century junk sunk off Korea was carrying over 10,000 ceramic wares.

Travelling on the River in Clearing Snow *by Guo Zhongshu (c. 910-977) gives a clear picture of life on luxury river craft.*

Song Painting

The Song school of landscape painting has never been surpassed. Emphasis shifted from religious to lay subjects, from figures and human events to impressionistic landscapes used to convey the artist's feelings. Brush strokes were more important than colour and there was a fashion for monochrome landscapes in which human figures were only a small detail. The use of handscrolls, unwound a section at a time, increased the viewer's impression of entering the landscape.

Another school concentrated on 'bird-and-flower painting' – exquisite vignettes of a small bird or insect on a spray of blossom or bamboo painted with extreme realism and delicacy.

Painting became a distinguished occupation which brought fame. Almost without exception, the Song emperors were genuine, enthusiastic patrons of painting; Huizong was an active painter, and his Academy of Painting was on a par with the prestigious Hanlin Academy for Confucian scholars, which had been founded by Tang Xuanzong in 754.

Since earliest times, mountains were regarded as sacred places, homes of the immortals. (Left) The towering mountain scenes of Fan Guan (active c. 1023-1031) and Guo Xi (c. 1001-1090, above) are typical of Northern Song landscape paintings, they are designed to convey the full might of the cosmos. (National Palace Museum, Taiwan and Freer Gallery, Washington).

(Below) Wild Geese, *artist anonymous* (British Museum).

(Above) Mother Hen and her Brood, *artist anonymous*. In Huizong's great catalogue of paintings, pictures were listed by subjects, such as Birds and Flowers or Feathers and Fur rather than by painters. Song masters excelled in such subjects, depicting them with a delicate accuracy which has never been surpassed (National Palace Museum, Taiwan).

(Below) Ladies Ironing Silk *by Huizong (Museum of Fine Arts, Boston).*

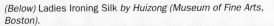

China's prosperity and an outburst of activity in western Asia following the rise of Islam, produced a flourishing maritime trade and the development of coastal trading communities along the southeast Asian coast. Earlier, such trade had been in Arab hands but Chinese ships now surpassed all others, sailing east to Korea and Japan and west to the Malabar coast of India and even to the Persian Gulf and Red Sea. Export revenues rose from 500,000 strings of cash in 960 to 65 million strings in 1189. China's clear technological superiority is reflected in trade patterns; on the whole the Chinese imported raw materials and tropical luxuries – rare woods, precious metals and gems, spices and ivory – while, apart from tea, her major exports were manufactured goods and handicrafts – silks, cotton cloth, porcelain, lacquer wares, copper cash, dyes, and, to

SONG CITIES

Coming in a palanquin to visit the medicine fair, our bearers' knees are caught in the press of the crowd...there is such a profusion it cannot be detailed....Orpiment, aconite, ginseng and glutinous millet waiting on tray after tray. Mica and frankincense the colour of sparkling crystal, aloe and sandalwood wafting their fragrant scents...Some things are costly, such as cinnabar...others bitter, like sulphate of copper...some are stale like pemmican and mince-meat pickled in brine, some fresh l ike dates and chestnuts. Many are products of barbarian tribes...Merchants have buffeted the sea-winds and the waves and foreign merchants crossed over towering crags drawn onwards by the profit to be made...Here are the rich and powerful with numerous bond-servants...carriages and horses in grand array, scattering clouds of dust. When evening comes they get completely drunk, and then go home, their bags and boxes bulging.

Du Zheng, a 13th-century poet describing the autumn medicine fair in Chengdu

The growth of trade and commerce revolutionized the nature of cities, sweeping away the Tang system of state-controlled markets and self-contained walled blocks within the city walls. From being primarily administrative units, reflecting imperial power, cities became large commercial centres with streams of itinerant traders using an empire-wide network of inns. Private trade broke the government straitjacket and commerce, no longer confined to official markets, spread throughout the city and its suburbs. Streets were crowded with vendors and lined with small shops and stalls selling every conceivable merchandise.

It was an age of luxury. Song revenues were triple those of the Tang and elegant living, previously an aristocratic privilege, was now enjoyed by a much wider class, the new scholar-gentry – landowners, merchants and traders who exerted power by becoming officials through the examination system. Rich landowners moved to the cities, centres of culture, and vied with merchants in their demands for high-quality workmanship and luxury wares. The wealthy now made gardens, used sedan chairs and played cards and dominoes; amusement quarters catered for all tastes, from tea and wine shops to brothels, and every form of spectator entertainment – theatres, puppet shows, jugglers and storytellers. The Tang curfew was a thing of the past.

The mathematician, Shao Yong, expressed the general satisfaction: 'I am happy because I am a human and not an animal, a male and not a female, a Chinese and not a barbarian, and because I live in Luoyang, the most wonderful city in the world.'

Not all approved of this extravagance which flouted imperial edicts imposing restraint. Gold and silver costume jewellery was banned but widely worn even by commoners; gold and silver vessels have been found in village teashops. A contemporary noted: 'These days the families of artisans and merchants trail white silks and brocades and adorn themselves with jades and pearls. In nine cases out of ten, if one looks a person over from head to foot, one will find that he is breaking the law.'

Another complained: 'The customs of the empire have now become extravagant. One drinking bout among

an increasing degree, books and stationery. Copper coins have been found in north Ceylon and porcelain in East Africa, Egypt, the Persian Gulf, Istanbul, Mesopotamia and across India and southeast Asia. The economic and cultural centre of China finally shifted to the south and the coastal regions acquired a growing dominance over the rest of the country.

Internally, improved communications and the growth of an urban merchant class meant that revenues from trade now exceeded those from land; central finances were so healthy that paper money was preferred to metal coins.

Two years after his father Zhao Zicheng's death in 1188, Xiaozong abdicated in favour of his son Guangzong.

the gentry may squander property worth ten gold pieces....Trifles, like women's ornaments and clasps, may cost up to 100,000 cash and adornments which make their appearance in the Rear Palace [the empress' quarters] in the morning will have become the fashion among commoners by evening.'

(Anticlockwise from below) The most famous picture of life in Kaifeng is the scroll Spring Festival on the River, *by Zhang Zeduan. The scroll, over 5m long, gives a vivid image of commercial activity and daily life in 11th-century China and depicts the city in all its bustle. Pedestrians and animal-drawn vehicles crowd the shop-lined streets while cargo boats ply the river and spectators watch a theatrical performance.*

GUANGZONG	
Born	*Abdicated*
1146, as Zhao Dun	1195 on grounds of
Accession	ill health
1190	*Died*
Father	1200
Xiaozong	*Temple name*
Wife	Guangzong
empress Li	('Glorious
	Ancestor')

GUANGZONG

The reign of **Guangzong** (1190–1194) was beset by succession problems. His wife Li's wish for their second son, Zhao Kuo, to be Heir, was opposed by Xiaozong, the head of the family, causing an open breach between him and Guangzong. When Xiaozong lay dying in 1194, Zhao Kuo visited him to say farewell and on the former emperor's death, the leading minister, Zhao Ruyu, supported Zhao Kuo 'who had always shown goodness and piety'. The old dowager-empress Wu (Gaozong's 80-year-old widow) ruled that since Guangzong was too ill to perform the mourning rites, Zhao Kuo should take the throne as Ningzong.

NINGZONG	
Born	(2) concubine (later
1168, as Zhao Kuo	empress) Yang
Accession	*Children*
1195	9 sons, all died in
Father	infancy
Guangzong (2nd	*Died*
son of)	1224
Mother	*Temple name*
empress Li	Ningzong ('Serene
Wives	Ancestor')
(1) empress Han	

NINGZONG

Ningzong (1195–1224) was a weak, indecisive character, dominated by women. Owing his throne to his mother and grandmother, Ningzong now fell under the influence of his wives' families. His first wife, the empress Han, obtained full power for her brother, Han Tuo Zhuo, leader of the war party; Ningzong was even persuaded to disgrace Zhao Ruyu who had helped him to the throne. Mongol attacks had weakened the Jin but Han Tuo Zhuo's attempts to regain the lost territories failed and peace was only regained after his execution in 1207.

Ningzong's second wife, the empress Yang, installed her brother, Yang Zishan, in power and with the chancellor Shi Miyuan, he controlled the entire central administration. Ningzong's nine sons had all died in infancy and since there was no surviving issue of Guangzong or Xiaozong, Ningzong summoned all Taizu's male descendants of the 10th generation who were over 15 to be brought up at court so that he could choose an heir. Ningzong chose Zhao Hong, his brother's adopted son, but the boy's fiery temper led to disputes with Shi Miyuan. When Ningzong lay unconscious and dying, Shi issued an edict replacing Zhao Hong with Zhao Yuju (Lizong) who ascended the throne a few days later.

LIZONG	
Born	Taizu's son, Zhao
1205, as Zhao Yuju	Dehao
Title before accession	*Mother*
Prince Gui Cheng	Chuan
(1224)	*Wife*
Accession	empress Xie
1225	*Died*
Father	1264
Zhao Xilu, a direct	*Temple name*
descendant in the	Lizong ('Logical
9th generation of	Ancestor')

LIZONG

Lizong (1225–1264), descended from Taizu's son Dehao, reigned for nearly 40 years. Internally the empire continued to prosper although the gap between landlords' riches and tenants' poverty increased greatly and the growth of bureaucratic red tape hampered the administration. The court became bound by ritual – 1,500 regulations were involved in the reception of a Korean envoy. Abroad, the rise of the Mongol empire under Genghis Khan posed the most serious threat China had ever faced. Lizong and his ministers seem to have been unaware of the extent of their danger and allied themselves with the Mongols to defeat the Jin in 1234. The Mongols then embarked on the long task of conquering the Song. They advanced in the south (taking Dali and Vietnam), west and north but their khan's sudden death in 1259 gave a respite.

Portrait of Zhu Xi.

Lizong's great contribution was to hallow the doctrines of the greatest of all Song philosophers, Zhu Xi (1130–1200). A statesman, historian, textual critic and great thinker, Zhu Xi was an ideal Confucian. His synthesis of the philosophical theories which had developed in the 11th century, known as neo-Confucianism, became the accepted political philosophy of the Ming and Qing dynasties and the 'Confucianism' we know today. The basic Confucian belief in the identity between the natural and human, moral and cosmic order, in which man was by nature good and society could be improved by education, was expanded to include moral aspects of Buddhist and Daoist teachings. Neo-Confucianism came to provide an ethical, social and political system divorced from supernatural sanctions in which moral law was the supreme controlling force – in Zhu Xi's words: 'Heaven is Law'. Centred on the family and a pattern of social relationships and obligations, it justified benevolent paternalism aided by a civil service trained in classical principles of good conduct. Good government depended on the moral character of the ruler and the cardinal virtues were benevolence, righteousness, reverence, wisdom and sincerity and a striving for balance – 'the golden mean'. During his lifetime, Zhu Xi's theories were associated with the reformers and had therefore been banned by the conservatives and he died in disgrace. In 1227, however, after the death of the conservative Shi Miyuan, Lizong formally rehabilitated Zhu Xi's doctrines, posthumously creating him a duke. He appointed men of the Zhu Xi school to introduce reforms, and in 1237 included his works in the official examinations, following this with an imperial edict commending Zhu Xi's texts to all scholars. Later, the Mongols also kept his works in the examinations.

In his later years, Lizong withdrew from practical affairs, leaving his ministers to formulate policy, and was increasingly addicted to luxury.

DUZONG	
Born	*Mother*
1240, as Zhao Mengqi	Huang
Title before accession	*Wife*
crown prince Chang Yuan (1260)	empress Chuan
Accession	*Major concubines*
1265	(1) consort Yang
Family connection	(2) consort Yu
adopted by	*Children*
Lizong in 1253,	3 sons, 4
and given the name	daughters
Qi	*Died*
Father	1274
prince Yong, the	*Temple name*
brother of Lizong	Duzong
	('Magnanimous
	Ancestor')

DUZONG

Duzong (1265–1274) was the last reigning Southern Song emperor. A nephew of Lizong, who had no male heir, he had been adopted by his uncle in 1253 and received a strict Confucian education at court. He was, however, entirely devoid of practical political experience when he ascended the throne and lacked interest in state affairs. Physically and mentally weak, he avoided all exertion and strain, leaving state affairs to his ministers. During his reign the Mongols steadily increased their power and although valiant attempts were made to bolster the northern defences, the Mongols succeeded, after a long siege, in capturing the strategic city of Xianyang, fatally weakening Song defences and leaving the route open to southern China. Increased military expenditure led to higher taxation with the inevitable result of increasing popular discontent which the government was too weak to deal with. Duzong's sudden and unexplained death in 1274 was followed by the succession of his three infant sons whose reigns lasted just four years in total.

GONGZONG

Born	Title given by
1270, as Zhao Xian	Mongols after
Title before accession	dethronement
prince Jia Guo	duke of Yingguo
(1273)	(1276)
Accession	*Died*
1275	1323, forced
Father	suicide
Duzong (2nd son of)	*Temple name*
Mother	Gongzong
empress Chuan	('Respectful
Dethroned	Ancestor')
1275	

DUANZONG

Born	Mother
1269, as Zhao	consort Yang
Shi	*Died*
Accession	1278, after a
1276	shipwreck
Father	*Temple name*
Duzong (eldest son	Duanzong ('Upright
of)	Ancestor')

BING DI

Born	son of)
1272, as Zhao Bing	*Mother*
Titles before	consort Yu
accession	*Died*
duke of Yongguo,	1279, drowned
prince of Xiu (1274)	*Temple name*
Accession	Bing Di
1279	('Promising
Father	Emperor')
Duzong (youngest	

Work on these Buddhist figures at Baodingshan, Dazu, Sichuan, was abruptly stopped when the Mongols invaded the area in 1249. Carving at the horseshoe-shaped cliff shrine had begun in 1179 at the instigation of a Buddhist monk Zhao Zhifeng, who collected money from pilgrims and local officials. The carving reflects strong local influences, both in style and choice of subject matter, and Confucian and Daoist themes are interspersed among the Buddhist figures.

GONGZONG, DUANZONG AND BING DI

Gongzong (1275), son of Duzong and the empress Chuan, was only four and Lizong's consort, the dowager-empress Xie, became regent. The Song proved unable to stem a renewed Mongol advance; after a disastrous Chinese defeat on the Yangzi the Mongol general Bayan entered the capital Hangzhou in 1276. Having sent the emperor's two brothers with their uncles to Fujian province for safety, the regent announced Song capitulation and dethroned Gongzong who was taken prisoner and sent with the entire court to Shangdu (Beijing). Khubilai Khan gave him

(*Above*) Ming watercolour of Song Gongzong from an 18th-century album of imperial portraits (British Library).

an honorary title and had him educated as a Buddhist monk in Tibet. Gongzong's unexplained suicide in 1323 led to curious rumours, including the suggestion that he was the real father of the future Mongol emperor Shundi (1333–1367), born to a Turkish woman in 1320.

Gongzong's eight-year-old brother **Duanzong** (1276–1278), son of Duzong and the concubine Yang, was declared emperor by the fugitives in Fuzhou, Fujian, but he had rapidly to flee south to Guangdong where the chief minister, Chen Yizhong, embarked the entire court to sea and anchored off the coast, slowly moving south as the Mongols advanced. When the Mongols captured Guangzhou, they launched a naval attack, driving the Chinese further out to sea. The emperor's boat was sunk in a hurricane and although he was rescued and dragged ashore, he never recovered from the shock. The survivors fought off another Mongol attack and sailed for Vietnam, eventually landing, possibly at Lantao off Hong Kong, where Duanzong died and officials named his six-year-old brother as the emperor **Bing Di** (1279).

In 1279, a new Mongol advance drove the court to sea again. When the Mongols blockaded the harbour the Chinese tried a counter-attack, chaining 1,000 vessels in a horizontal line. The battle lasted three weeks – over 800 Chinese ships were captured and 100,000 men perished. The young emperor was drowned; some say a minister tried to save him by jumping overboard with Bing Di in his arms but the Mongols later found his body on the shore. Sixteen ships, one carrying the dowager-empress Yang, escaped but the distraught mother drowned herself from grief and was later worshipped along the coast as a goddess of the sea. The Song dynasty had finally come to an end.

GUNPOWDER

The Chinese had explosives before gunpowder, using bamboo crackers to frighten evil spirits. In the 10th century incendiary projectiles or 'flying fires' were attached to arrows, and by the 11th century smoke-producing grenades, firework rockets and mines were in use followed by mortars with iron or bronze tubes. The earliest written formula for gunpowder (coal, saltpetre and sulphur) appeared in 1044, a century after Daoists searching for elixirs had warned that this mixture was dangerous and might cause singed beards.

Ming woodcuts illustrating the military uses of gunpowder.

YUAN DYNASTY
1279–1368

世祖 Khubilai (Shizu)
1279–1294

泰定 Yesun Temur (Taiding)
1323–1328

成宗 Temur Oljeitu (Chengzong)
1294–1307

文宗 Tugh Temur (Wenzong)
1328–1329; 1329–1332

武宗 Khaishan (Wuzong)
1308–1311

明宗 Khoshila (Mingzong)
1329

仁宗 Ayurbarwada (Renzong)
1311–1320

順帝 Toghon Temur (Shundi)
1333–1368

英宗 Shidebala (Yingzong)
1321–1323

KHUBILAI	
Born 1215, as Khubilai *Accession* 1279 *Father* Tolui (2nd son of) *Mother* Sorghagtani Beki *Wives* (1) Tegulun (died before 1260) (2) Chabi (3) Tarakhan (4) Bayaghucha *Children* 12 sons *Died* 1294 *Temple name* Shizu ('Genesis Progenitor')	*Note on Mongol rulers* Mongol rulers usually had four wives, each with a separate household. In some cases, the principal wife, exerting influence on the emperor, is mentioned but many of the wives' names are unknown, as are the number of their children. The Yuan emperors were buried in Mongolia and there is much uncertainty about their burial sites.

KHUBILAI KHAN

[Khubilai] always goes on four elephants, on which he has a very beautiful wooden room, which is all covered inside with cloth of beaten gold and outside it is wrapped round and covered with lion skins, in which room the great Kaan always stays when he goes hawking because he is troubled by gout.... And he sees [the hunt] always sitting in his room lying on his couch, and it is a very great amusement and great delight to him.

Marco Polo, *The Travels*

Khubilai Khan (1279–1294) was born in 1215, the year his grandfather, the great Genghis Khan, captured Beijing. His father, Tolui, was one of Genghis' younger sons; in charge of northern and western China, he was frequently away on military campaigns and Khubilai and his brothers

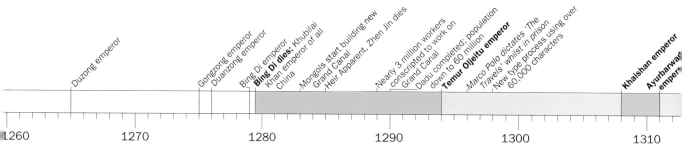

Portrait of Khubilai Khan.

were brought up by their mother, the remarkable Sorghagtani Beki. The Persian historian, Rashid-al-Din, noted that she was 'extremely intelligent and able and towered above all the women in the world', while a Hebrew physician, Bar Hebraeus, described her as 'a queen [who] trained her sons so well that all the princes marvelled at her power of administration'. She made sure that Khubilai was taught to read and write as well as being given the usual military training. More important, she showed Khubilai that the traditional Mongol occupation policies of plunder and devastation were self-defeating in China. The only way to govern the Chinese was to enlist their support; their rich farmlands would produce far higher revenue if cultivated than if reduced to pastures. A Nestorian Christian, she allowed religious freedom in her domains, conciliating her subjects by patronizing Buddhists and Daoists as well as Muslims and Christians.

Khubilai's first task was to complete the conquest of China. Since 1234 the Mongols had controlled the north, but in the south, where the terrain with its numerous waterways, mountains and forests was unsuitable for cavalry, the Southern Song had forced a stalemate. In a brilliant campaign in 1253 Khubilai outflanked the Song forces by capturing Dali (Yunnan). On his brother Mongke Khan's death in 1259, Khubilai returned north to claim the khanate. Khubilai defeated his younger brother, Arigh Boke, the leader of those opposing peaceful

Mongol horsemen, used to the dry plains of the north, were hindered in their conquest of southern China by the numerous rivers and canals. On one occasion, Khubilai surprised the Chinese forces by transporting his horsemen across a river on rafts of inflated sheepskin bags. Here Khubilai and his forces cross on pontoon boats (Asiatic Society of Bengal).

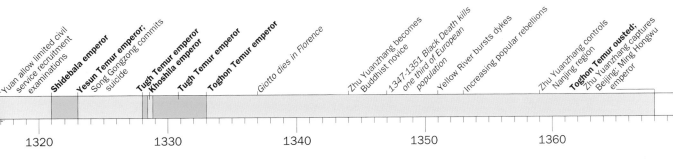

Yuan allow limited civil service recruitment examinations

Shidebala emperor

Yesun Temur emperor; Song Gongzong commits suicide

Tugh Temur emperor Khoshila emperor

Tugh Temur emperor

Toghon Temur emperor

Giotto dies in Florence

Zhu Yuanzhang becomes Buddhist novice

1347-1351 Black Death kills one third of European population

Yellow River bursts dykes

Increasing popular rebellions

Zhu Yuanzhang controls Nanjing region

Toghon Temur ousted; Zhu Yuanzhang captures Beijing; Ming Hongwu emperor

1320   1330   1340   1350   1360

(*Above*) The Mongols in China longed for the open spaces of their homeland. Hunting expeditions, lasting many days, were only possible in the open uncultivated northern lands (National Palace Museum, Taiwan).

(*Below*) Frontispiece of an edition of Marco Polo's *The Travels* published in Seville, 1503.

(*Right*) The Luguoqiao, or 'Marco Polo Bridge' was a vital link in the route joining the northeast to the Yellow River provinces.

coexistence and demanding a return to pure nomadic habits, and declared himself 'Great Khan' in 1260.

From the outset Khubilai set out to win Chinese acquiescence to his rule. He moved his capital south to Beijing and in 1271 took the title 'Emperor of China' (although the Southern Song were not finally defeated until 1279), and a dynastic name – Yuan ('Great Originator') – from the Chinese classic *Book of Changes*, to establish his position as Son of Heaven. Unlike other Mongol territories, the Chinese had a highly developed civilization and sense of identity. Although the Mongols could maintain military control, they were too few and ill-equipped (their Uighur script could not be used to write Chinese) to govern a state of that size and complexity without local assistance. Khubilai's policy was therefore to allow the Chinese to rule themselves under Mongol supervision. Within a military framework, the basic social, administrative and cultural systems were left unchanged.

The capital Dadu (Beijing) was laid out like a Chinese city, with temples of Soil and Grain for the ancient rites governing the agricultural year. Confucian temples were protected, Confucian scholars exempted from tax and traditional Confucian rites and ceremonies were performed, but Khubilai never succeeded in winning over the scholar-gentry who were excluded from high office, and the Chinese remained an underclass. They were, for example, enrolled in the army – welcomed for their technical skills in weapon-making – but had to serve under Mongol officers in an army famed for its ferocious discipline.

(*Above*) The Chinese astronomer and mathematician, Guo Shoujing (1231-1314), built 27 observatories, of which the observatory at Gaocheng zhen is the oldest surviving example. Gaocheng zhen, Dengfeng, Song Mountains, Henan, 1279.

The cultural gap between Mongols and Chinese made coexistence difficult. The Chinese were kept in their place by a legal system under which the population was divided into four classes – Mongols, non-Chinese, northern Chinese (already accustomed to Mongol rule) and, at the bottom, southern Chinese. The Mongols always maintained a homeland beyond the frontiers: they had two regions, the inner and outer, and these contacts outside China enabled them to preserve their own culture. Khubilai deliberately recruited foreign advisers and experts (entirely dependent on his favour) to avoid becoming ensnared by Chinese bureaucracy. Venetian, Flemish, French and other papal and court envoys came to the Mongol court and some, like Marco Polo, were given employ. The architects in charge of building Dadu were Muslims; a Persian astronomer Jamal-al Din was summoned to court in 1267, bringing a new more accurate calendar and globes; an Institute of Muslim Astronomy was established and Muslim and Persian doctors were employed in the newly founded hospitals and Imperial Academy of Medicine. Traders, despised in traditional China, were welcomed, and a vigorous commerce, mainly conducted by Central Asian Muslims, developed between the West and China using weights and money with multi-lingual texts. Paper notes showing Chinese and Mongolian writing spread to Japan and Korea and weights have been found which carry Chinese, Mongolian and Persian texts.

Within China, Khubilai concentrated on improving communications. The urgent problem of supplying Dadu with southern grain was solved by extending the Grand Canal northwards, joining the Yellow River and the Mongol capital. This 'connecting canal' took two and a half million workers to build it and the paved highway on its stone embankments stretched 1,090 miles (1,760 km) from Hangzhou to Beijing, a journey of 40 days. The famed Mongol postal service across Central Asia was extended to China. Manned by corvée labour, it had over 1,400 postal stations within China, with 50,000 horses, many thousand oxen and mules, 4,000 carts and 6,000 boats. A courier on horseback could cover 250 miles (400 km) a day. Postal runners wore bells to warn of their approach so that replacements could leave at once.

Like his mother, Khubilai allowed religious freedom. Mongol shamanism was exclusively concerned with material needs, leaving its followers free to accept other beliefs concerning the afterlife and spirit world. Khubilai expressed an interest in Christianity to Marco Polo; a Nestorian archbishopric was set up in Dadu under an 'Office for Christian Clergy' and Nestorians served at court. Muslim communities and mosques flourished and Khubilai at first patronized both Buddhists and Daoists. Later, under the influence of a young Tibetan monk, 'Phagsa-pa – nephew of the founder of the Lama sect in Tibet – he favoured the Buddhists at Daoist expense. Tibetan Lamaism with its necromancy and sorcery appealed to Mongol shamans; Khubilai's support for 'Phagsa-pa established Lamaistic Buddhism in both Tibet and Mongolia. In return for recognizing 'Phagsa-pa as temporal leader in

THE MONGOLS

In 1206 the Mongol leader Temujin (1162–1227) took the title Genghis Khan, 'Universal Ruler'. At its height the Mongol domination extended from the Sea of Japan to the borders of Poland and Hungary, a range beyond the wildest dreams of a Chinese 'Son of Heaven'. This internationalism enabled the Mongols, for whom China was merely part of a larger empire, to resist the sinicization and absorption which had befallen all other alien regimes in China.

This segregation was helped by an almost unbridgeable gulf in attitudes and personal habits. Chinese sedentary society was primarily civil, venerating the written word; Mongol nomadic society was a military organization. The basic military skills were similar to those used in herding; all males under 60 were liable to military service and the entire nation thus constituted a highly skilled force of cavalry.

The loose-knit Mongol clans were governed by Genghis' imperial code under which all male heirs were candidates for the throne and succession decided by the strength of a claimant's personal following and his military prestige. Family links were weak; there were no family names; marriage within the clan was forbidden and women enjoyed a much stronger position than in Chinese society.

Communication with the Chinese was hindered by language and the use of different scripts. The Mongols wore different clothes, seldom washed and ate steppe foods like cheese, mare's milk and kumiss (a fermented brew of mare's milk); the Chinese despised the Mongols' 'barbarian' use of steel knives at table and their banquets of uncontrolled gluttony and drinking which, without the activity of steppe life, led to serious obesity and alcoholism. While publicly observing many Chinese ceremonies, the Mongols continued their shamanistic rites and within the palace, Khubilai's sleeping quarters were hung with curtains and ermine in Mongol style. Even in the capital, the princes preferred to sleep in tents in the parks, planted with steppe grass, where their wives were brought to give birth. At the summer capital, Shangdu in the north (Coleridge's Xanadu), life was almost entirely Mongol, with magnificent hunts involving hundreds of men using trained leopards, lions, lynxes and over 500 gyrfalcons.

(Left) Portrait of Genghis Khan.

(Below) Chinese drawing of a typical Mongol warrior. Heavily armoured with a sword as well as his bow and arrows, the soldier wears a Chinese style belt with a lion's head.

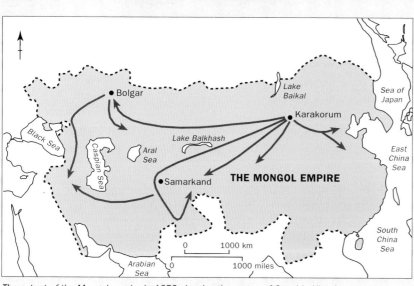

The extent of the Mongol empire in 1259 showing the routes of Genghis Khan's campaigns.

Bolgar
Lake Baikal
Karakorum
Sea of Japan
Black Sea
Caspian Sea
Aral Sea
Lake Balkhash
East China Sea
Samarkand
THE MONGOL EMPIRE
South China Sea
0   1000 km
0   1000 miles
Arabian Sea

(*Right*) Inside the Mongol archway, built in 1345 at Juyongguan, near Beijing, there are inscriptions of Buddhist incantations in Chinese, Sanskrit, Tibetan, Uighur, Mongolian and Tangut. The relief decoration on the outside shows the influence of Tibetan craftsmen brought to work at Khubilai's court in Dadu.

(*Below*) The largest surviving Yuan construction in Beijing is the *Baita si* (White Dagoba Temple), built by a Nepalese architect, Arniger, in 1271.

Tibet, 'Phagsa-pa recognized the emperor as his spiritual equal, designating him Bodhisattva of Wisdom (Manjusri) and Universal King. Numerous Lama temples were built and on Mount Wu Tai alone, the number of Buddhist establishments rose to 42,000 with nearly a quarter of a million monks and nuns.

This pro-Buddhist stance was encouraged by Khubilai's favourite wife, Chabi, an ardent Lamaistic-Buddhist. In traditional Mongol fashion, Khubilai had four wives, each with their own establishment of minor wives and concubines, but only Chabi seems to have had any influence and of his 12 sons, only hers attained eminence. Highly intelligent and well-read, Chabi strongly supported Khubilai's policy of conciliation, personally taking care of the defeated Song empresses when they arrived in Beijing. She was practical and efficient, designing a new Mongol hat with a brim to protect against the sun and sleeveless garments for Mongol soldiers in warm climates. She retained the economical habits of nomads and made the court ladies collect and spin used bowstrings into thread for cloth. After her death in 1281, her distant cousin Nambi took her place, but she never gained the same influence.

In later life, Khubilai's health deteriorated. The endless Mongol feasts of rich meats and unlimited drinking took their toll and as official portraits show, the robust, well-trimmed and determined figure of 1260 became grotesquely fat and unhealthy. He was plagued by rheumatism and gout, needing special shoes sewn from Korean fish skins for his swollen feet. Chabi's death, followed by that of her son Zhen Jin, the Heir Apparent, in 1285, plunged him into gloom and he sought distraction in unsuccessful military campaigns against Annam, Vietnam and Japan. During the suppression of a rival Mongolian's revolt in 1287 Khubilai had to be carried in a palanquin on four elephants since he could no longer walk. By 1294 he was described as ill and sunk in depression. After his death a year later his body was returned to Mongolia and lies in an unknown grave.

(*Right*) Portrait of Khubilai's favourite wife, Chabi (National Palace Museum, Taiwan).

(*Opposite*) In the lower left corner of this Tibetan-style imperial tapestry-mandala, are portraits of the Yuan emperor Tugh Temur and his brother, Khoshila; on the right are their wives (Metropolitan Museum of Art, New York).

TEMUR OLJEITU TO TOGHON TEMUR

Khubilai's successor and grandson, **Temur Oljeitu** (1294–1307), younger son of Zhen Jin, made peace with Japan and maintained reasonable prosperity. After his death in 1307, however, Mongol rule weakened rapidly with seven rulers in 26 years. The clash between pro-Chinese and pure-steppe Mongols bedevilled almost every succession and the pendulum swung with bewildering speed between Chinese-educated khans and nomadic rulers from the north. The duplication inherent in the system, the need to give employment to the élite Mongols and foreigners (one-third of all officials were non-Chinese), the use of four scripts (literary and colloquial Chinese, Uighur and Persian for Muslim traders) and the annual migration between the two capitals (the entire court with many

YUAN	
TEMUR OLJEITU	**YESUN TEMUR**
Born	*Born*
1265, as Temur Oljeitu	1293, as Yesun Temur
Accession	*Accession*
1294	1323
Father	*Father*
Third son of Zhen Jin, Khubilai and Chabi's eldest son (died 1285)	Kammala, the eldest son of Zhen Jin
Mother	*Died*
Kokojin (died 1300)	1328
Wives	*Temple name*
(1) Shirindari (died 1299)	Taiding Huangdi ('Exalted and Decisive Emperor')
(2) Bulukhan	
Died	**TUGH TEMUR**
1307	*Born*
Temple name	1304, as Tugh Temur
Chengzong ('Accomplished Ancestor')	*Accession*
	1328 (first reign); 1329 (second reign)
KHAISHAN	*Father*
Born	Khaishan (youngest son of)
1281, as Khaishan	*Principal wife*
Accession	Budashiri
1308	*Died*
Father	1332
Darmabala, Zhen Jin and Targi's 2nd son	*Temple name*
	Wenzong ('Literary Ancestor')
Died	
1311	**KHOSHILA**
Temple name	*Born*
Wuzong ('Martial Ancestor')	1300, as Khoshila
	Accession
	1329
AYURBARWADA	*Father*
Born	Khaishan (eldest son of)
1285, as Ayurbarwada	*Principal wife*
Accession	Babusha
1311	*Died*
Father	1329
Darmabala (youngest son of)	*Temple name*
Mother	Mingzong ('Brilliant Ancestor')
empress Targi	
Died	**TOGHON TEMUR**
1320	*Born*
Temple name	1320, as Toghon Temur
Renzong ('Benevolent Ancestor')	*Accession*
	1333
	Father
SHIDEBALA	Khoshila
Born	*Mother*
1303, as Shidebala	a Turkish consort
Accession	*Ousted*
1321	1368
Father	*Died*
Ayurbarwada (eldest son of)	1370, in Mongolia
Died	*Temple name*
1323	Shundi ('Submissive Emperor')
Temple name	
Yingzong ('Heroic Ancestor')	

thousands of officials spent one and a half months travelling) led to a vastly inflated bureaucracy, a gradual breakdown in control and endemic corruption. The overprinting of notes caused such inflation that eventually paper money ceased to be accepted.

Temur Oljeitu tried to continue Khubilai's policies. On his death a contest between his nephews, mirroring that of Khubilai and Arigh nearly 50 years earlier, brought **Khaishan** (1308–1311), a military hero from the steppes, to the throne. Khaishan ruled for three years. Utterly untrained in state affairs, he behaved like a nomadic chieftain. Bestowing honours and titles indiscriminately, he appointed actors, butchers, Buddhist and Daoist clergy as ministers of state, and artisans as 'dukes' or 'councillors'. Wildly extravagant, he lavished money on his palaces and Buddhist temples, supplementing revenue by selling licences in the state monopolies and tripling the amount of paper money.

His brother and successor, **Ayurbarwada** (1311–1320), the product of a Chinese education and a lover of painting and calligraphy, purged Khaishan's ministers and followed pro-Confucian policies, even restoring the examination system for civil service recruitment. (Entry was restricted to the lower ranks and never accounted for more than 4 per cent of all officials.) Such pro-Chinese sympathies led to bitter opposition at court, centred on Ayurbarwada's mother, the dowager-empress Targi, and her minister, Temudur.

The reign of Ayurbarwada's son, **Shidebala** (1321–1323), the only example of peaceful primogeniture under the Yuan, encompassed both factions. His early years were dominated by his grandmother Targi and the corrupt and despotic Temudur who launched a reign of terror against Ayurbarwada's pro-Chinese supporters. Uncowed, the Chinese-educated Shidebala became the focus for pro-Confucian sympathizers, leading his grandmother to exclaim: 'We should never have reared this boy!' On Temudur's death, the emperor and his new minister, Baiju, so successfully introduced economies and anti-corruption policies that Shidebala was assassinated by Mongol princes whose annual grants had been cut.

His successor, **Yesun Temur** (1323–1328), was the most un-Chinese of all Mongol emperors. A respected steppe ruler, he brought his ministers from Mongolia and quickly distanced himself from the regicides by purging his former supporters. Yesun reverted to the Mongol tradition of treating all religions impartially. Muslims (whom Shidebala, under Lama influence, had persecuted) were restored to favour, Muslim and Christian clergy exempted from corvée labour and Confucian and Buddhist temples, especially Lama-Buddhist establishments, were supported.

In 1328, Yesun Temur's son, Aragibag, was displaced after one month by **Tugh Temur** (1328–1329; 1329–1332) and is not included in the official list of emperors. Tugh Temur abdicated in favour of his elder brother **Khoshila** (1329) only to regain the throne, possibly through murder, when Khoshila died within a year. Tugh's own reign was disturbed by

Portrait of Khaishan Khan (Imperial Palace Museum, Beijing).

(*Below*) Tomb of Tuglug Temur, a descendant of Genghis Khan who was buried in Huocheng, Xinjiang in 1363.

eight plots against him, several led by princes. His chief ministers, El Temur and Bayan, ran a joint dictatorship, using patronage to create power bases in the bureaucracy and military; Yuan administration began to crumble in the provinces. Tugh Temur was probably the most erudite and versatile of all Yuan emperors. Well versed in Chinese, he was a good calligrapher and painter, supported educational establishments including an academy which produced a *Grand Canon for Governing the World*, and lived modestly, ruthlessly pruning the imperial establishment of over 10,000 staff, including guards, falconers and cooks.

Tugh's successor, Khoshila's younger son, the six-year-old Irinjibal, only lived 53 days and is not included in the official list of emperors. Irinjibal was followed by his elder brother, **Toghon Temur** (1333–1368), longest reigning of all Yuan emperors. Although Toghon claimed Khoshila as his father, he was widely believed to be the son of the captured Song emperor Gongzong by a Muslim mother whom Khoshila had adopted. Young and weak, he left state affairs to his ministers. His first chancellor, Bayan, blamed the decline of Mongol authority on creeping sinicization and reimposed strict segregation. He forbade Chinese people to learn Mongolian; confiscated their weapons, horses and iron tools and banned Chinese opera and storytelling, finally suggesting the extermination of all Chinese with the five most popular names, some 90 per cent of the population!

Later ministers tried in vain to restore authority, but the situation was by now beyond central control. Floods and devastating epidemics (possibly the Black Death which had broken out among Mongol soldiers in the Crimea) completed the general breakdown of administration and the Mongols were faced with revolts across the whole of China. Real power passed to the military commanders and for the last decades of the dynasty, Mongol energy was dissipated on internal fighting between warlords.

Toghon's final years were spent in semi-retirement, devoted to Lamaistic sexual orgies in the palace grounds and personal interests such as designing an elaborate water-clock and a huge pleasure boat for his lake. When the Chinese rebel leader, Zhu Yuanzhang, founder of the Ming dynasty, took Dadu in 1368, Toghon and his family fled northwards to Mongolia where he died two years later.

MING

Hongwu
1368–1398
Jianwen
1399–1402
Yongle
1403–1424
Hongxi
1425
Xuande
1426–1435
Zhengtong/
Tianshun
1436–1449;
1457–1464
Jingtai
1450–1457
Chenghua
1465–1487
Hongzhi
1488–1505
Zhengde
1506–1521
Jiajing
1522–1567
Longqing
1567–1572
Wanli
1573–1620

Taichang
1620
Tianqi
1621–1627
Chongzhen
1628–1644

QING

Shunzhi
1644–1661
Kangxi
1661–1722
Yongzheng
1723–1735
Qianlong
1736–1795
Jiaqing
1796–1820
Daoguang
1821–1850
Xianfeng
1851–1861
Tongzhi
1862–1874
Guangxu
1875–1908
Puyi
1909–1911

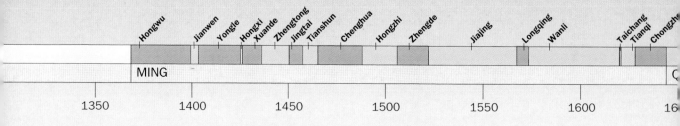

Hongwu (1368–1398)

Yongle (1403–1424)

Kangxi (1661–1722)

Qianlong (1736–1795)

REVIVAL AND COLLAPSE
The Ming Dynasty AD 1368–1644
The Qing Dynasty AD 1644–1911

THE MING RESTORED the Chinese imperial tradition. After nearly a century of alien rule by the Mongols, the Ming consciously revived ancient Chinese customs and traditions, and for nearly 300 years the empire enjoyed comparative peace. From the mid-15th century onwards, after a period of expansion, they were forced on to the defensive by the revived Mongol and newly-risen Manchu empires and became increasingly inward-looking and ethnocentric. Their highly autocratic, centralized system of government, in which all aspects of life were subordinate to the emperor, functioned well under able rulers, but with ineffectual rulers on the throne paralysis ensued. The dynasty was relatively free from succession disputes, adhering rigidly to primogeniture.

The Qing, non-Chinese Manchus, deliberately adopted Chinese ways, anxious to be accepted as legitimate heirs to the Mantle of Heaven and not foreign usurpers. Continuity in internal affairs at first brought prosperity, but later a stubborn maintenance of traditional Chinese attitudes towards foreign 'barbarians', rebuffing Western efforts to establish contact, and a refusal or inability to adopt Western technical inventions left the Qing at the mercy of 'gunboat diplomacy' which shattered the imperial fabric, leaving China's territory open to foreign annexation. With the revolution in 1911, 2,132 years of imperial rule finally came to an end.

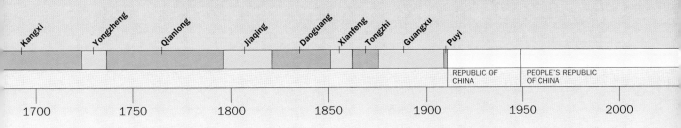

Kangxi · Yongzheng · Qianlong · Jiaqing · Daoguang · Xianfeng · Tongzhi · Guangxu · Puyi

REPUBLIC OF CHINA · PEOPLE'S REPUBLIC OF CHINA

1700   1750   1800   1850   1900   1950   2000

MING DYNASTY
1368–1434

洪 武 **Hongwu**
1368–1398

建 文 **Jianwen**
1399–1402

永 乐 **Yongle**
1403–1424

洪 熙 **Hongxi**
1425

宣 德 **Xuande**
1426–1435

Official portrait of Hongwu, painted *c.*
1377, portraying him as the ideal
emperor with regular features and
learned expression.

HONGWU	
Born 1328, as Zhu Yuanzhang	*Tomb* Xiaoling, Nanjing, Jiangsu
Accession 1368, as Hongwu ('Vast Military Power')	*Temple name* Taizu ('Supreme Progenitor')
Father Zhu Shichen	*Note on Ming burials* All but three Ming emperors are
Wife empress Ma (died 1382) Consort Wu	buried at Shisanling (the Thirteen Tombs, commonly known as the Ming
Children 36 sons, 16 daughters	Tombs) near Beijing. Ming empresses and
Died 1398; 38 concubines were immolated with him in Mongol fashion	concubines whose sons became emperors were buried with the emperor.

HONGWU

Zhu Yuanzhang was the youngest of six children; his father, an itinerant labourer, had fled from Nanjing to Anhui after defaulting on taxes and refusing corvée duties; his paternal grandfather was a goldwasher and his mother's father a popular sorcerer. During a famine in 1344 in which most of his family perished, Zhu Yuanzhang sought refuge as a novice in a Buddhist monastery where he learned to read and write. At 25 he became a rebel, eventually joining the Red Turbans, one of the major groups contesting Mongol rule, and his extraordinary organizational skills quickly brought promotion. He married the leader's daughter (née Ma) and by 1359 was in charge of the Nanjing region. Combining military skill with good administration, thus winning popular support, he soon controlled most of central and southern China and in 1368 declared himself founder of the Ming dynasty at Nanjing, taking the reign title **Hongwu** (1368–1398) ('Vast Military Power'). Like Liu Bang, founder of the Han dynasty, a poor peasant had again become the Son of Heaven.

Ming means 'brilliant' (like the Mongols, Hongwu chose a dynastic name for its significance rather than a place name) and the new ruler set out to restore the grandeur of the past. Determined to wipe out the

Toghon Temur ousted; Zhu Yuanzhang captures Beijing; **Ming Hongwu emperor**

Hongwu regains Sichuan
Major building of Great Wall in Gansu
Improvements in agriculture

Hongwu tightens personal control of government
Wat Tyler leads the Peasants' Revolt in England

China reunited
Over 50 million trees planted in Nanjing region

1350   1360   1370   1380   1390

disgrace of foreign Mongol occupation, he consciously revived tradition-al customs, following the maxim 'learn from the Tang and the Song'; even court clothing was based on Tang sumptuary regulations.

Hongwu's first task was consolidation. In 1368 his troops captured Beijing and a year later they defeated the Mongols in their summer capital Shangdu; in 1370 he drove the Mongols further north; in 1371 he regained Sichuan, and by 1387 all China, including Yunnan and Gansu, was reunited. Military expeditions in Central and Southeast Asia were accompanied by a major diplomatic offensive, with envoys requesting acceptance of tributary status sent to Korea, Japan, Annam, Champa (north Vietnam), Tibet and later, Borneo, Java, Sumatra and Coromandel on the Indian coast. While foreign envoys were welcomed at court in Nanjing, foreign students studied in Chinese universities and traders settled in her ports.

At home, decades of warfare, natural disasters and Mongol exploitation had devastated agriculture. Hongwu, reversing the Song and Yuan trend towards basing revenue on commerce and foreign trade, restored agriculture to its key position in the economy. A huge number of peasants were resettled on waste land with state help and tax exemptions, and from 1371 to 1379 the area of land under cultiva-tion and revenues paid in grain tripled.

(Below) The memorial stele on Xiaoling, Hongwu's tomb at Nanjing, is the largest in China. Its base is carved into the form of an enormous tortoise – a design almost exactly replicated by a memorial stele at the later Ming tombs. Hongwu's son, Yongle, originally ordered a much larger tablet which proved impossible to move and can still be seen outside Nanjing in the Yangshan quarry at Death's Head Valley, so-called after the horrific death toll among those who worked there.

(Below, right) Many foreign rulers paid their respects at the Nanjing court. This military official stands on the tomb of a young king of Borneo who died in 1408 while visiting Hongwu and was buried in a traditional Chinese tomb with an avenue of stone officials and animals.

Hongwu dies

Jianwen emperor; Civil war rages between Jianwen and Yongle

Jianwen disappears

Yongle emperor

Zheng He's first naval expedition

Building work starts in Beijing

King of Borneo dies in Nanjing

Extensive work on Yuan Grand Canal begins

First giraffe brought to China

Temple of Heaven built in Beijing

Hongxi emperor

Xuande emperor; palace school for eunuchs founded

Admiral Zheng He begins 7th and final naval expedition

Xuande dies; Zhengtong emperor

1400   1410   1420   1430   1440

(*Above*) Qing dynasty portrait of Hongwu making the most of his ugliness. The Ming family name, Zhu, was a homophone for the word pig, reinforcing popular references to his porcine appearance.

Neglected dykes and canals were repaired and in 1395 alone, 41,000 reservoirs were rebuilt or restored. To provide wood for shipbuilding, Hongwu launched a major reforestation campaign: each family on colonized land had to plant 200 each of mulberry, jujube and persimmon trees. In 1391 over 50 million trees were planted in the Nanjing area and probably around a billion trees were planted during Hongwu's reign.

Hongwu's intelligence, farsightedness and ability to choose and heed good officials while using superstition to manipulate the ignorant made him an excellent administrator. He was decisive, paid attention to detail, exhorting Confucian filial behaviour, and kept order, forbidding his troops to plunder and kill. His peasant upbringing and lack of education, however, left him self-conscious, with an inferiority complex. He was ugly, with a protruding lower jaw and slightly pig-like face. He feared rivals, banning all secret societies and conducting massive purges and trials of former supporters (possible rivals) who were tortured, killed or disgraced. In 1380, he abolished the post of prime minister, bringing the three branches of government – the administration, military and censorate – under his personal control, and two years later he established the imperial 'Embroidered Brocade Guards' – a secret service directed against senior officials. The Song system of checks, balances and free discussion was thus replaced by an autocratic, highly centralized system in which all power was in the emperor's hands and government was increasingly conducted in isolation or in secret councils supported by secret police. This led to friction between the Inner and Outer Courts (between the emperor's advisory Grand Secretaries and later, the eunuchs, and the administration). The contrast between Hongwu's

(*Opposite, below*) Horse and groom on the tomb of a Ming prince at Guilin, where a complete set of royal tombs (dating from 1408–1612) has survived. The founding prince, Hongwu's son Zhu Zanyi, was sent to Guilin by his father before the Ming capital was moved to Beijing and the tomb plan and statuary at Guilin are similar to those of the Northern Song dynasty, with eunuchs and grooms not found in later Ming tombs. Officials often have the non-Han features of the local minority people and columns are carved with almost three-dimensional dragons.

JIANWEN	
Born	*Wife*
1377, as Zhu Yunwen	empress Ma (died 1395)
Other title	*Children*
Prince of Qin	2 sons
Accession	*Died*
1399, as Jianwen	?1402
Father	*Tomb*
Zhu Biao, Hongwu's eldest son (2nd son of)	unknown
	Temple name
	Huidi ('Beneficial Emperor')

YONGLE	
Born	*Children*
1360, as Zhu Di	at least 3 sons
Title before accession	*Died*
Prince of Yan	1424; 16 concubines immolated with him
Accession	
1403, as Yongle ('Perpetual Happiness')	*Tomb*
Father	Changling, Shisanling, Hebei
Hongwu (4th son of)	*Temple name*
Mother	Chengzu ('Accomplished Progenitor')
Officially, empress Ma; probably a lesser consort	
Wife	
empress Xu (died 1407)	

public support for Confucian principles and his arbitrary and very un-Confucian acts of cruelty created an atmosphere of insecurity and factionalism. He restored the examination system for civil service recruitment, for example, but treated his officials in Mongol fashion with unpredictable public beatings which occasionally led to death.

His wife, the kindhearted empress Ma, died in 1382 and the loneliness and uncertainties of Hongwu's later years are reflected in his final will: 'For 31 years I have laboured to discharge Heaven's will, tormented by worries and fears without relaxing for a day.'

Hongwu had 36 sons and 16 daughters. To minimize friction at court, he appointed his sons hereditary governors of provincial regions; on the whole highly capable, these princes enjoyed real authority, responsible in border areas for imperial defence, but were forbidden to return to the capital, even on their father's death. Hongwu ordered a simple funeral and when he died in 1398, aged 70, 38 concubines were immolated with him in the Mongol fashion.

JIANWEN AND YONGLE

[Yongle was] of middle height; his beard neither very large nor very small; nevertheless about two or three hundred hairs of his middle beard were long enough to form three or four curls on the chair on which he was seated.

An Arab envoy's description of Yongle in 1420

Hongwu's death was followed by four years of bitter civil war in which his grandson and successor, the 16-year-old **Jianwen** (1399–1402), disappeared. Jianwen had tried to reduce the power of the hereditary princes but gentle, indecisive and scholarly, he was no match for his uncle, Yongle, Hongwu's fourth son, prince of Yan and commander of the important northern region. Against numerical odds, Yongle's crack troops captured and burned Nanjing, seizing power for emperor Yongle ('Perpetual Happiness'). Jianwen's body was never found and he was popularly believed to have fled the country or survived disguised as a monk.

Yongle (1403–1424) was a born ruler. Vigorous and highly intelligent, he had received an excellent military and scholarly education and had successfully campaigned against the Mongols during his father's reign. On accession, he ruthlessly exterminated his opponents, their families and associates including neighbours, teachers, students, servants and friends. In 1421, he moved the capital north to his old power base, Beijing. The Mongols were still China's greatest enemy and Beijing was strategically placed, guarding the northern approaches through the mountains and Great Wall. Yongle's city, with its beautiful monuments such as the Forbidden City and Temple of Heaven, remained virtually unchanged until the mid-20th century.

Yongle reaped the fruits of his father's policies, his reign proving to be one of the most brilliant in China's history. The people were content

THE FORBIDDEN CITY IN BEIJING

Yongle's Beijing, built slightly south of Khubilai Khan's Dadu and retaining the Yuan parks, lakes and hills, consists of three sections – the imperial palaces of the Forbidden City, the Imperial City where the officials and nobility dwelled, and to the south, the Outer City for the ordinary people. The central north–south axis runs through the heart of the Forbidden City whose three main halls are the only buildings crossing it. The two main temples of Heaven and Agriculture lie in the south, east and west of the main axis.

Building started in 1406, employing 200,000 workers, and the emperor and court moved in before the outer walls and gates were completed in 1421. Although the Qing made certain additions, the main city, with its large north–south and east–west thoroughfares and small twisting lanes (*hutungs*) with grey, walled courtyard houses remained basically unchanged until the last quarter of this century.

Towering above its surroundings, the Forbidden City is a triumph of Ming architecture. It is a real city, with streets, walled enclosures and over 9,000 rooms, covering 250 acres. In the central southern section, the way leads through imposing gateways and long courtyards to the three official halls where the emperor conducted state affairs. The clear lines and perfect proportions, emphasizing the grandeur of the buildings and the dramatic use of colour and material – red-brick walls, white-marble terraces and staircases and brilliant yellow-tiled roofs – create an architectural complex unmatched in history.

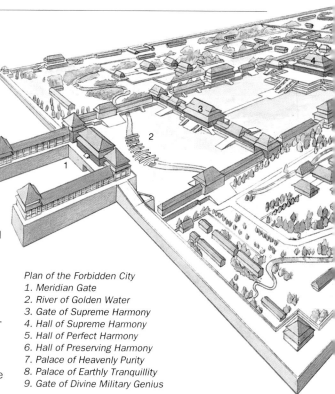

Plan of the Forbidden City
1. Meridian Gate
2. River of Golden Water
3. Gate of Supreme Harmony
4. Hall of Supreme Harmony
5. Hall of Perfect Harmony
6. Hall of Preserving Harmony
7. Palace of Heavenly Purity
8. Palace of Earthly Tranquillity
9. Gate of Divine Military Genius

(Below) In summer, emperors and their attendants drank in the garden Pavilion of the Ceremony of Purification in which the floor was carved with a maze-like stream. Their empty wine cups were refilled as they floated round the maze to return to their owner.

This ceramic Nine Dragon Screen, protecting the entrance to the northeast section of the Forbidden City where Qianlong retired after his abdication, expresses the full glory of imperial power.

(Below) The first courtyard within the Meridian gate is crossed by a bow-shaped stream with five elegant marble bridges. The stream served a double purpose, fulfilling the geomantic requirement for running water south of a building and, through an underground pipe, connecting the palace to a stream bringing water for the Forbidden City from the Jade Spring in the Western Hills.

Behind and on either side of the state apartments, lie the private quarters for the imperial family and their attendants (including 70,000 eunuchs), with libraries, temples, a three-storey theatre and garden in Chinese style with strange shaped rocks, small pavilions and winding paths. To the west are Khubilai's lakes and parks and to the north, Coal Hill where the last Ming emperor hanged himself.

The Forbidden City was in continuous use for 500 years: the last emperor, Puyi, lived here until 1924, and on 1 October 1949, Chairman Mao stood on its main gateway, the Gate of Heavenly Peace (Tiananmen) to make his historic declaration: 'The Chinese people have stood up.'

(Right) The great wooden palace doors were studded with nine rows of nine bronze knobs (nine was the imperial number) and their bronze handles were shaped like mythical horned beasts.

MARITIME EXPEDITIONS

In 1405, 63 ships carrying 27,870 men set sail for the West, the first of seven great naval expeditions under the eunuch admiral, Zheng He. Since the 11th century, Chinese ships and charts had surpassed all others but hitherto they had remained in eastern waters. Now, at the height of Ming expansion, they led the world in maritime exploration. Over the next three decades they sailed round Southeast Asia, crossing the Indian Ocean to East Africa, the Red Sea and Persian Gulf.

Zheng He, a Muslim from Yunnan and therefore well equipped to deal with the predominantly Muslim rulers he would encounter, was a brilliant organizer and diplomat but, unlike later Westerners, uninterested in trade. His aims were political and geographical, not commercial. Wherever they went, the Chinese established diplomatic contacts, extending the tributary network (Chinese ambassadors even reached Egypt). Zheng He carried messages from the emperor and returned with pledges of loyalty or even the rulers themselves, or their sons or emissaries. His fleet collected rare spices, plants and animals – in 1414 they returned with the first giraffe ever seen in China – and Zheng He's reputation was such that memorial temples sprang up throughout Southeast Asia, called after his official title, *Sanbao Taijian*.

The emperor Zhengtong stopped the maritime expeditions. The age of expansion was over; faced with the mounting expense of defending the northern frontiers against the Mongols, officials decided that such ventures, bringing little visible reward and under eunuch command, could no longer be justified. This decision had disastrous long-term consequences, leaving China's long coastline unprotected against Japanese pirates and the more aggressive European traders from the West.

(Below) Ming woodcut showing one of Zheng He's vessels. Each expedition consisted of several dozen very large junks carrying over 20,000 men. In the early 14th century Ibn Batuta, an Arab traveller, noted that Chinese ships had four decks and 'there are cabins and public rooms for the merchants. Some … [sailors] carry with them their wives or concubines.'

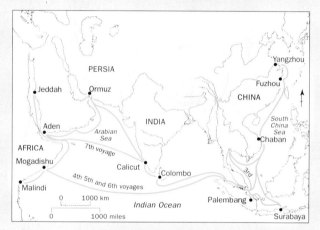

(Above) Chinese maritime compass. Although the use of a 'south-pointer' is mentioned in Chinese texts from the 4th century BC, they were not adapted for maritime use until the 10th/11th centuries.

(Below, centre) Ming woodcut of an Arab leading a zebra from East Africa.

(Below) Silk painting of a tributary leading a giraffe with an inscription referring to a qilin, a mythical beast which appeared only when a sage was on the throne. When courtiers reported the arrival of a 'qilin' to Yongle, he said that since he was no sage, the animal could not be a qilin, but later, curiosity overcame his scruples and Yongle and his entire court greeted the giraffe at the palace entrance.

(Above) Between 1405 and 1411, three expeditions sailed to Vietnam, Java, Sumatra, Ceylon and the southwest coast of India; the next three, from 1413 to 1422, reached Ormuz and the entrance of the Persian Gulf, one sailing 3,700 miles (6,000 km) without stopping from Sumatra to Mogadishu in Somalia, and landing in Aden. On the last trip (1431–1433), Chinese ships reached Jeddah and some Chinese even went to Mecca.

Anonymous 15th-century portrait of the emperor Yonglé (National Palace Museum, Taiwan).

and prosperous. With high revenues from agriculture Yonglé extended his country's influence by military campaigns, naval expeditions and diplomatic offensives. As emperor, he personally led five remarkable campaigns against the Mongols. Military commanderies were set up in Manchuria, the Amur region and maritime Siberia, and Korea accepted vassal status. In the south, China occupied Annam (north and central Vietnam). Diplomatic envoys travelled east, west and south, from Korea and Japan (where they concluded a commercial agreement) to Java, throughout Indo-China and across Central Asia to the Middle East, reaching Tamerlaine's court in Transoxania. Under the great eunuch admiral, Zheng He, Chinese ships sailed through the Indian Ocean, reaching the Persian Gulf, Red Sea and coast of East Africa. Zheng He established contacts and a tributary network throughout this vast region, bringing kings and chieftains back to Beijing as vassals.

At home, Yonglé encouraged scholarship, commissioning compilations of the classics and literature, and the publication of the complete Buddhist *Tripitaka* with 6,771 sections. In a move of far-reaching consequence, he reversed Hongwu's policy of excluding eunuchs from politics and deliberately employed them as envoys, military officers and spies to counterbalance the officials, thus exacerbating friction between the Inner and Outer Courts.

Yonglé died in 1424 during a campaign against the Mongols and was buried with his wife and 16 concubines in the great imperial cemetery he had built northwest of Beijing.

HONGXI	
Born 1378, as Zhu Gaozhi	(died 1442)
Titles before accession Prince of Yan (1395); Heir Apparent (1404)	*Children* 10 sons, 7 daughters
	Died 1425; 10 concubines buried with him
Accession 1425, as Hongxi	
Father Yonglé (eldest son of)	*Tomb* Xianling, Shisanling, Hebei
Mother empress Xu	*Temple name* Renzong ('Benevolent Ancestor')
Wife empress Zhang	

HONGXI

Forthwith issue it [grain] in relief! What would loans accomplish? Relieving people's poverty ought to be handled as though one were rescuing them from fire or saving them from drowning. One cannot hesitate.

Hongxi's order to officials to give the people grain during famine

Yonglé's eldest son, Hongxi (1425), was fat and sickly. Suffering from gout, he was distinctly unmilitary, abandoning manoeuvres when he was too cold. A very good administrator, however, who had frequently acted as regent when his father was campaigning, he was genuinely humane.

Hongxi died within a year, leaving 10 sons and 7 daughters. His wife, the empress Zhang, lived until 1442, becoming a powerful and

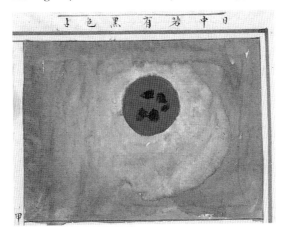

Hongxi had an avid interest in astronomy. This painting from 1425 is one of several surviving paintings by the emperor of sunspots and atmospheric effects around the sun (Cambridge University Library).

THE TEMPLE OF HEAVEN

This beautiful temple is the visible expression of the belief which lies at the heart of Chinese philosophy, that all power, and hence all good, flows from a non-personal Heaven transmitted through the emperor with his Mantle of Heaven. Here, at the Winter Solstice, the emperor performed his most important task: to pay homage and report to Heaven on the state of the realm. (The service was last performed in 1915, by Yuan Shikai, President of the Republic, who had imperial pretensions.)

The complex consists of three sections on a north–south axis: the Temple of Annual Prayers where the emperor prayed for good harvest; the Temple of the Universe housing the tablets of Heaven and the Ancestors; and the Altar of Heaven, a beautiful, round marble altar in a square enclosure, reflecting the ancient Chinese maxim 'Heaven round, earth square'. The altar has three tiers and all its measurements, number of steps and columns are multiples of nine, the imperial number. During the two-day service, all traffic in Beijing ceased (in later centuries the railway was stopped); all windows and doors were closed while the emperor proceeded from the Forbidden City to the temple. After fasting and donning special robes, he ascended the open altar to stand alone before Heaven. Prostrating himself nine times, he offered his report and asked for help and blessings for the empire.

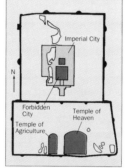

(Above) Temple of Annual Prayers, built in 1420. The blue roof tiles symbolized heaven while its round shape reflected the Chinese belief that heaven was round. The 4 central columns represent the seasons; the 24 outer columns stand for the 12 months and 12 hours into which the Chinese divided the day.

(Left) Plan showing the Temple of Heaven in relation to the Forbidden City.

The annual ceremony on the Altar of Heaven (above) epitomized the unique relationship between the emperor and heaven. As the sole link with this world and heaven, it was here that he reported on the state of the empire. After a night spent in fasting and purification, he ascended the altar alone, and, facing north, reported and paid homage to heaven. Sacrificial animals and bundles of silk were then offered to heaven.

(Right) The painted ceiling of the Temple of Annual Prayers.

(*Below*) The use of reign marks became well established under Xuande. The characters on this bowl mean 'made in the reign of Xuande of the great Ming dynasty'.

respected regent and stabilizing influence in the next two reigns. Ten concubines were buried with Hongxi.

XUANDE

Xuande (1426–1435), the eldest of Hongxi's 10 sons, had something of the Renaissance 'perfect man' about him. His military skills had endeared him to his grandfather, Yongle; he had administrative ability and a genuine sense of responsibility for his people and was a patron of the arts. After an early uprising in which an uncle contested the throne, his reign was an era of stability, prosperity and cultural achievement. He followed a peaceful foreign policy, withdrawing from Annam and keeping relative peace in the north where the Mongols were now split into rival factions. He reduced friction between the court and administration, maintaining excellent relations with the able ministers he had inherited from his father and grandfather and developing the Grand Secretariat (previously only advisory) into a distinctive institution for screening and drafting memorials. A reformer, Xuande genuinely tried to check injustices, opposing death sentences and the imprisonment of the poor for debt. Perhaps his greatest fault was to extend eunuch power, establishing a palace school for eunuchs and appointing them as military supervisors, 'Grand Defenders'.

Xuande was the first Ming emperor who seriously patronized the arts, being himself a talented poet and competent artist (who often signed his works 'playfully painted by the imperial brush'). Xuande gathered painters at court, embellished the Ming Tombs with beautiful columns and the largest marble archway in China, and sponsored the manufacture of ceramics which became world famous. An avid collector, he sent eunuchs throughout the realm to find valuable rarities – luxury goods, precious stones and unusual animals including fighting crickets – and used eunuch messengers to procure Korean virgins for his harem.

Xuande was succeeded by the son of his second wife, Sun, his first, the empress Hu, having no heir. Ten concubines were buried with him.

XUANDE	
Born 1399, as Zhu Zhanji	(2) empress Sun (died 1462)
Title before accession Heir Apparent (1424)	*Principal concubine* consort Wu
Accession 1426, as Xuande	*Children* 2 sons, 2 daughters
Father Hongxi (eldest son of)	*Died* 1435; 10 concubines immolated on his death
Mother empress Zhang	*Tomb* Jingling, Shisanling, Hebei
Wives (1) empress Hu, childless, retired 1425 (died 1443)	*Temple name* Xuanzong ('Proclaimed Ancestor')

(*Right*) Anonymous painting showing Xuande on horseback. As a child, Xuande was taken hunting by his grandfather, Yongle, and he never lost his enjoyment of riding and military sports, frequently inspecting northern border posts in person.

MING
1436–1644

正统 天顺	Zhengtong/ Tianshun 1436–1449; 1457–1464	嘉靖	Jiajing 1522–1567
景泰	Jingtai 1450–1457	隆庆	Longqing 1567–1572
成化	Chenghua 1465–1487	万历	Wanli 1573–1620
弘治	Hongzhi 1488–1505	泰昌	Taichang 1620
正德	Zhengde 1506–1521	天启	Tianqi 1621–1627
		崇祯	Chongzhen 1628–1644

ZHENGTONG/TIANSHUN	
Born 1427, as Zhu Qizhen *Title before accession* Heir Apparent (1428) *Accession* 1436, as Zhengtong; 1457, as Tianshun *Father* Xuande (eldest son of) *Mother* empress Sun	*Wives* (1) empress Qian, childless (died 1468) (2) empress Zhou (died 1504) *Children* At least 1 son (Chenghua) *Died* 1464 *Tomb* Yuling, Shisanling, Hebei *Temple name* Yingzong ('Heroic Ancestor')

ZHENGTONG/TIANSHUN AND JINGTAI

The empress Qian shall lie with me in the same grave for more than a thousand autumns and ten thousand years.

Zhengtong expressing his gratitude to his wife, the empress Qian, who stood by him during the long years of house-arrest after his return from Mongol captivity

Emperor at 8, prisoner of the Mongols at 22, emperor again at 30 and dead before he was 40, **Zhengtong's** (1436–1449; 1457–1464) life spans an important turning point in the Ming dynasty. His father's peaceful reign presaged the waning of Ming military power and henceforth the Ming, menaced in the north by the reunited Mongols under Esen Khan, were on the defensive. Turning their backs on the outside world, they withdrew physically and mentally within their borders.

Under the de facto regency of his able grandmother Zhang (Hongxi's widow) and three excellent ministers, Zhengtong's early reign was a model of good government. His father's favourite, the boy was precocious and well-taught, and is said to have had such a large forehead that

Xuande dies; **Zhengtong emperor** · Zhengtong captured by Esen Khan · **Jingtai emperor;** Zhengtong freed by Mongols, held in palace arrest in Beijing · Constantinople falls to Turks · Jingtai deposed: **Zhengtong returns to throne as Emperor Tianshun** · c.1460 Zhengtong bans burying of live concubines · **Chenghua emperor** · Caxton sets up first printing press in England

1430 · 1440 · 1450 · 1460 · 1470

JINGTAI

Born
  1428, as Zhu Qiyu
Accession
  1450, as Jingtai
Father
  Xuande
  (2nd son of)
Wives
  (1) empress Wang
  (died 1507)
  (2) consort (later
  empress) Hang
  (died 1456)

Children
  one son (died
  1454), 1 daughter
Died
  1457
Tomb
  Western Hills,
  near Beijing,
  Hebei
Temple name
  Jingdi ('Admired
  Emperor')

A Ming silk painting of a Mongol horseman. Mongol military strength was based on their unrivalled horsemanship. Both men and women rode from the earliest age and their hunting skills, needed for survival, laid the base for their military prowess. The population of northern China were familiar with Mongol horsemen whose frequent incursions brought them to the gates of the Great Wall (Victoria and Albert Museum, London).

he needed special hats. In 1449, however, encouraged by his tutor, the eunuch Wang Zhen, he was inspired by Chinese victories in the south to lead an expedition against Esen Khan. It was an unmitigated disaster. The emperor had no military experience; his army of half a million was ill-equipped and ill-prepared, many dying from hunger on the march north. When Zhengtong tried to retreat, his rearguard and a large relief force had already been annihilated and the army was massacred almost to a man. The Mongols, unprepared for such a victory, seized the emperor and returned north, losing the chance to capture Beijing.

In Beijing, after an ineffectual attempt to place Zhengtong's infant son on the throne, his younger brother, Zhu Qiyu, was installed as the emperor **Jingtai** (1450–1457). Jingtai was weak and irresolute but his ministers successfully fortified the capital and when Esen returned two months later they kept him at bay.

Meanwhile the imperial captive was well treated and became personal friends with Esen. By installing a new emperor, the Chinese had reduced Zhengtong's hostage value; they refused to pay ransom and when he was released after a year they sent only a sedan chair and two horses to meet him. The new emperor placed Zhengtong and his wife in confinement in the palace and for six-and-a-half years they lived as prisoners, incommunicado. Jingtai's son was appointed Heir but died, and when the emperor fell ill in 1457, he was deposed in a sudden palace coup which replaced Zhengtong on the throne as **Tianshun**. Jingtai died soon afterwards, possibly strangled, and was buried outside the imperial cemetery in the Western Hills.

Zhengtong's long confinement left him suspicious and vindictive, and he used the eunuchs and their secret police to launch a purge in which even the coup leaders lost their lives. The war and Jingtai's interregnum had left the country unsettled and over 1,500,000 were killed or expelled in uprisings during the

Hongzhi emperor;

Columbus reaches the New World

Vasco da Gama discovers sea route to India

Zhengde emperor; attempt to curb eunuchs fails

Rebellion in Ningxia

Portuguese reach China by sea

1517–1519 Zhengde tours northwest frontier

Zhengde sails to Nanjing

Jiajing emperor; start of 'Single Whip' tax reforms

Ottomans retreat from siege of Vienna

1490   1500   1510   1520   1530

EUNUCH POWER

Aware of the dangers of court plots, Hongwu excluded eunuchs from politics on pain of death, hanging a tablet one metre high in the palace saying 'Eunuchs must have nothing to do with politics'. His intensely personal, autocratic and secretive system of government, however, made the growth of eunuch power inevitable. Yongle, suspicious of his nephew Jianwen's former advisers, deliberately used eunuchs (dependent on imperial favour) to counterbalance the officials. He appointed them to high posts – Admiral Zheng He was a eunuch – entrusting them to oversee and report on others and encouraging them to form their own secret service with files on officials.

These moves were irreversible and by the mid-15th century eunuchs, now numbering tens of thousands, virtually controlled the administration, deciding appointments and promotions for central and provincial posts. In 1426 a palace school was established for eunuchs, strengthening their already unique position *vis-à-vis* the emperors, many of whom had been brought up by eunuchs and regarded them as trusted friends. As commanders of the palace guards, with responsibility for imperial workshops and foreign tribute and trade, they controlled the sources of military power and commercial wealth. Their greed was legendary. When Zhengde had a particularly

corrupt eunuch from a poor family, Liu Jin, removed after four years in office, his property included 15,723,975 lb (7,132,395 kg) of gold and silver, 20 lb (9 kg) of precious stones, two suits of gold armour, 500 gold plates, 3,000 gold rings and brooches and 4,000 belts studded with gems as well as a palatial house.

Political friction was compounded by personal factors: eunuchs tended to come from poor northern families, scholars from the southern scholar-gentry. The eunuch secret service provided limitless opportunities for blackmail and corruption, leaving officials helpless in the face of false accusations. In the long run, the in-fighting between eunuchs and officials paralysed government, leading to the fall of the Ming dynasty.

(Left) A eunuch on Zuling, the tomb of Hongwu's grandparents. The figures, flooded by irrigation works in the mid-17th century, remained under water for 300 years and were only rediscovered in the late 1960s.

(Above) Silk panel on back of eunuch's robe, Zuling. The muddy lake floor acted as a perfect preservative, and the Zuling carvings are among the finest Ming statuary we have.

1450s. Zhengtong tried to eliminate Mongol influence in Chinese life, stopping the burying of live concubines and prohibiting Mongol dress and speech in Beijing. (Statues of Confucius in Mongol clothing were changed to Chinese style.) To protect the imperial monopoly on fine porcelain, the emperor banned the manufacture for sale of the most valuable wares such as the famous 'blue-and-white'.

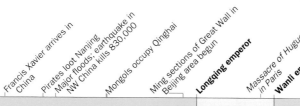

Jiajing escapes assassination attempt

Martin Luther dies

Francis Xavier arrives in China

Pirates loot Nanjing

Major floods; earthquake in NW China kills 830,000

Mongols occupy Qinghai

Ming sections of Great Wall in Beijing area begun

Longqing emperor

Massacre of Huguenots in Paris

Wanli emperor

Matteo Ricci arrives in China; Adoption of Gregorian calendar in Europe

Wanli withdraws from public duties

1540　　1550　　1560　　1570　　1580　　1590

CHENGHUA	

Born
   1447, as Zhu
   Jianshen (also
   known as Zhu Jianji
   and Zhu Jianru)
 Accession
   1465, as Chenghua
 Father
   Zhengtong (eldest
   son of)
 Mother
   empress Zhou (died
   1504)
 Wives
   (1) empress Wu,
   dethroned after one
   month for beating
   emperor's favourite
   concubine
   (2) empress Wang,
	no sons (died
	   1518)
	   (3) empress Ji (died
	   1475)
	   (4) empress Shao
	   (died 1522)
	 Principal concubine
	   consort Wan Guifei
	 Children
	   11 sons, 6
	   daughters
	 Died
	   1487
	 Tomb
	   Maoling,
	   Shisanling, Hebei
	 Temple name
	   Xianzong
	   ('Constitutional
	   Ancestor')

CHENGHUA

Zhengtong's eldest son, **Chenghua** (1465–1487), had a troubled upbringing. Only 20 months old when his father was captured by the Mongols, he was thrust from being Heir Apparent to being under palace arrest and back to Heir Apparent before he was 10. An indecisive personality, weak, kind and permissive and speaking with a stutter, he was plagued by problems with women. On accession, his mother and Zhengtong's official widow, empress Qian, disputed the title of dowager-empress and in later years he was dominated by a concubine, Wan Guifei.

During the early part of his reign a council of 12 regents followed an enlightened policy, redressing the wrongs of the previous reign, rehabilitating the unjustly punished and giving generous famine relief. They reorganized the military, reviving the imperial palace guards with highly trained divisions of 10,000 men, each under a eunuch commander responsible for their weapons. The new force distinguished itself against the Mongols and Jurchens (Manchus) between 1471 and 1479 and the military position improved in both south and north, where nearly 3,100 miles (5,000 km) of Great Wall had been rebuilt.

In the palace, however, Chenghua's former nurse, the concubine Wan Guifei, ruled supreme. His first wife, the empress Wu, had been dethroned for having Wan beaten; his second empress, Wang, gave Wan free rein. Wan, whose own son had died, was extremely jealous, and after it became clear that she was having possible heirs by other concubines murdered, Chenghua kept his distance but left her authority intact. When a palace maid became pregnant, the first empress hid her and kept the birth of the maid's son secret. Five years later, when Chenghua lamented his lack of an heir, the boy was produced to his father's delight but Wan immediately had his mother killed.

With Chenghua's tacit consent, the concubine Wan and her favourite eunuch, Liang Fang, aided by the notorious eunuch chief of police, Wang Zhi, set about milking the country. Blatantly abusing their power, they sold titles at an imperial shop and sent agents to mine and collect copper, silver, gold and precious stones throughout the empire. Imperial greed and lack of control brought a collapse of public morality: Buddhist, Daoist and Tibetan monks specializing in pornography and aphrodisiacs were ennobled. Eunuchs and officials were rewarded with large grants of land, and the imperial farmland, only a smallholding in Hongwu's time, grew from 200,000 acres (80,000 hectares) to over 3 million acres (1,200,000 hectares) by the early 16th century.

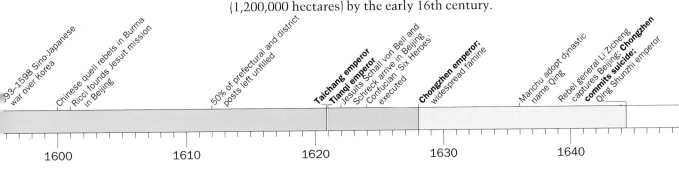

HONGZHI	
Born	(died 1541)
1470, as Zhu	*Children*
Yutang	2 sons, 3
Accession	daughters
1488, as Hongzhi	*Died*
Father	1505
Chenghua (3rd and	*Tomb*
eldest surviving son	Tailing, Shisanling,
of)	Hebei
Mother	*Temple name*
Concubine (later	Xiaozong ('Filial
Empress) Ji	Ancestor')
Wife	
Empress Zhang	

Chenghua loved music and theatre; he was a good calligrapher, could paint and was a great connoisseur of porcelain, reviving the use of reign marks (Chenghua porcelain is among the finest ever made) and encouraging the development of polychrome wares, the best of which were considered as valuable as the finest jade.

HONGZHI

Despite his dramatic childhood, during which he was hidden from the murderous consort Wan, **Hongzhi** (1488–1505) seems to have been a well-balanced and unexceptionable ruler. He received a strict Confucian education and was a good family man, the only monogamous Ming emperor, having two sons and three daughters by the empress Zhang. He tried in vain to trace his mother's family (she was from a minority tribe, bought by a eunuch in Guangxi), posthumously ennobled her and built her a temple in Guangxi. He banished the most corrupt eunuchs including Liang Fang and demoted over 3,000 who had bought official posts. Certain sales of titles, particularly to Buddhist and Daoist priests, however, were continued to raise revenue.

As a good Confucian, Hongzhi listened to advice from his Grand Secretaries, was punctilious in state affairs, seldom lost his temper, inflicted no public humiliations or beatings on officials and showed no martial spirit. Despite two instances when officials attacked the eunuchs, the administration worked well and the reign was on the whole harmonious and uneventful. The increasing development of fine manufactured goods which had begun under Chenghua – such as the silk wares of Suzhou – created a new rich class who vied with the nobility in their acquisition of *objets d'art*. The centre of culture shifted south to the lower Yangzi region and the influence of southerners at the expense of northerners increased. On the land, the increasing growth of very large estates dispossessed poor farmers and tenants who drifted to the towns, creating a floating urban proletariat.

(*Above*) The emperor Hongzhi on a silk scroll (National Palace Museum, Taiwan).

(*Opposite*) Late 15th-century hanging scroll by Du Jin showing two wealthy gentlemen admiring their newly acquired antiques (National Palace Museum, Taiwan) .

(*Right*) Statue of a Grand Secretary, at the Ming Tombs, near Beijing. Grand Secretaries were accomplished scholars and the emperor's closest mentors, particularly during Hongzhi's reign. In the early years of the Ming dynasty they worked as an advisory team and polished the imperial edicts, but later, when the administrative system began to fail, they often assumed direct responsibility for administrative actions, acting as individuals in the emperor's name.

ZHENGDE	
Born	1535)
1491, as Zhu	*Children*
Houzhao	none survived
Accession	*Died*
1506, as Zhengde	1521
Father	*Tomb*
Hongzhi	Kangling,
(eldest son of)	Shisanling,
Mother	Hebei
empress Zhang	*Temple name*
Wife	Wuzong ('Martial
empress Xia (died	Ancestor')

The emperor Zhengde was fascinated by Tibetan culture, and had a Lama temple built in the Forbidden City in Beijing. Tibetans frequently used tankas – portable icons painted on cloth which could be rolled up for travelling – like this example from the Lama Temple, Beijing.

ZHENGDE

Zhengde (1506–1521), aged 14 on accession, was adored by his father, Hongzhi, but the latter was aware of the boy's faults and on his death bed (he was only 35), bade the Grand Secretaries look after him, for he 'was intelligent but loved ease and pleasure'. The warning was justified. Zhengde, reacting against his father's Confucianism, was uninterested in state affairs, impatient with ritual and disliked his orthodox officials, preferring the flattery of eunuchs. He embarked on a life of leisure – riding, archery, hunting and music; he filled the court with entertainers such as wrestlers, acrobats and magicians and acted as merchant in specially established eunuch-run shops in the Forbidden City. Alarmed by his behaviour, the officials tried but failed in 1506 to remove the leading eunuch advisers, and government passed under eunuch control.

Zhengde was drawn to all things Tibetan, building a new temple in the Forbidden City for Lama services; sometimes he donned Tibetan garb and at his grandmother's funeral service personally led the Lama monks. He was fascinated by fire, commenting when a palace caught fire in a lantern pageant: 'What a magnificent display of fireworks'. He loved women and wine and was often drunk for days at a time. His guards were ordered to commandeer beautiful girls, including his own commanders' concubines; one girl was snatched from a senior official's boat, and prostitutes were brought to the palace and paraded for inspection. One of Zhengde's greatest delights was to disguise himself and slip out of the palace into the streets of Beijing. The already tarnished reputation of the court was brought to a new low by the frequent visits of an ill-disguised Son of Heaven to the city brothels. Although this behaviour shocked the Confucians, it earned Zhengde the reputation of a great lover among the populace.

A serious rebellion by a prince in Ningxia in 1510 was followed by two years of banditry and popular risings in Sichuan. The anti-bandit campaigns infected the emperor with a passion for the military. He adopted 127 young officers as his sons, giving them the imperial family name, and played at soldiers, drilling a group of eunuchs in the palace and practising with explosives. Military dress became the fashion at court and civilians wore yellow mesh-like armour over their silk

Detail of a silk scroll, *The Emperor's Approach*, showing the luxury in which the emperor Xuande travelled. Elephants were kept in the imperial elephant stables until around 1900 and were often used for ceremonial occasions, such as the emperor's visits to the Temple of Heaven. Here, however, the large number of horsemen accompanying the emperor's carriage suggests that the emperor was on a much longer journey in the countryside (National Palace Museum, Taiwan).

clothing and large sunshade hats with goose plumes. After a camping trip with 162 specially luxurious yurts (tents), he gave the officers silk for new costumes and headgear in which to welcome him as he rode home by torchlight, wearing uniform and carrying a sword, claiming that he had decapitated a barbarian. After touring the northwest frontier for two years (1517–1519) and building a new headquarters there, Zhengde turned his attention south. Overriding officials protesting at the expense (140 officials were flogged, many to death), he sailed down the Grand Canal as Supreme Military Commander. He arrived in

JIAJING	
Born 1507, as Zhu Houcong *Accession* 1522, as Jiajing *Father* Zhu Yuyuan – 3rd son of Chenghua and empress Shao – (died 1519) *Mother* Jiang *Wives* (1) empress Chen, 1522 (died 1528) (2) empress Zhang, 1528, deposed 1534 (died 1536)	(3) empress Fang, 1534 (died 1547) *Major concubines* consort (posthumously empress) Du (died 1554) *Children* 8 sons, 5 daughters *Died* 1567 *Tomb* Yongling, Shisanling, Hebei *Temple name* Shizong ('Genesis Ancestor')

Nanjing in 1520, where he forbade the populace to raise hogs since their Chinese name sounded like his family name, Zhu. On the return journey, the imperial boat capsized and Zhengde fell ill, spitting blood at a ceremony and fainting. Three months later, he died.

Zhengde's neglect of state affairs led first to eunuch control and then to government by favourites, often military men with no political aptitude. In desperation, the Grand Secretaries and ministers finally intervened and the chief Grand Secretary became virtual ruler of the empire. This relaxation of imperial control led to a rise in status of scholar-officials in the provinces who became steadily more powerful, securing tax exemptions and large estates, thus increasing the tax burden on the poor.

JIAJING

Zhengde had no sons and the throne passed to his adopted son, **Jiajing** (1522–1567), descendant of a younger son of Chenghua and a concubine from Hangzhou whom a eunuch had bought and educated, teaching her to recite hundreds of Tang poems. Although Jiajing had been accepted as Heir since the age of 12, he refused to accept his adopted status, and insisted that he had inherited through his real parents, giving his father a posthumous imperial title and making his mother dowager-empress. Their tomb was rebuilt as an imperial mausoleum. As founder of a new branch of the ruling family, he made his own tomb as large as and even more luxurious than that of Yongle.

Jiajing was the only Ming emperor to follow Daoism. As well as producing spells and elixirs for immortality, Daoists specialized in soothsaying, reading fortunes from omens and interpreting diagrams, like the Daoist is shown doing in the woodcut below.

Unique among Ming emperors, Jiajing was an ardent Daoist, actively seeking immortality. Vast sums of money were poured into Daoist temples along with special materials for elixirs such as pearls, ambergris and gold. Thousands of ounces of gold were used in single services lasting over 12 hours – the texts were written with gold dust which the scholars collected happily from their brushes. Jiajing consulted the planchette board to gather messages from the spirit-world, heeded omens and tried to suppress Buddhism. When the Buddhist temple in the Forbidden City was dismantled in 1536 over 3,000 catties of so-called Buddhist bones were destroyed and scattered. (One catty weighs approximately 1.3 lb (0.6 kg.) He also forbade the use of images in Confucian temples.

In 1542, Jiajing narrowly escaped assassination by his concubines. Eighteen palace girls tried to strangle him while he slept but they used the wrong knot and after one girl warned the empress, all but she were executed. Jiajing's first wife, Chen, died after a miscarriage brought on by his rage in 1528; his second, Zhang, was deposed without official reason in 1534 and died shortly

The spirit road leading to Jiajing's parents' tomb, Xianling, Zhongxian, Hubei, built in 1539. On accession, Jiajing raised his parents to imperial rank and when his mother died in 1538 he personally supervised the transformation of his parents' tomb into an imperial mausoleum. The tomb plan is unusual, reflecting Daoist influences. His parents were buried in separate tombs, each with a tumulus, one behind the other and connected by an underground passage. In front of the stele tower a circular pond reflects the tomb buildings.

afterwards; the third, Fang, was the girl who gave the warning in 1542. His consort, Du, was raised posthumously to the rank of empress when her son, Wanli, became emperor.

On accession, Jiajing, with the support of the dowager-empress and the Grand Secretary, had rid the court of the worst eunuchs (confiscating 70 chests of gold and 2,200 chests of silver from one alone), and although his absorption in Daoism led him to neglect state affairs he appointed able ministers. The length of Jiajing's reign gave stability. Major tax reforms – the 'Single Whip' reforms transformed the traditional levies on land and labour into money payments, and amalgamated small items into a single payment – helped to restore the economy despite a disastrous earthquake in central China in 1556, when 830,000 perished in the resulting Yellow and Wei rivers floods. He was, however, unable to stem growing threats from abroad. In the north, Altan Khan (1507–1582) had reunited the Mongols and invaded at will; in one month in 1542 his troops massacred or captured 200,000 Chinese and a million cattle and horses, burning thousands of dwellings. In the southeast, Japanese and other pirates dominated the coast. Attempts to limit trade with Japan

Jiajing on his state barge. Scroll *c.* 1538, artists unknown. Imperial journeys were used to impress the population with the emperor's power and wealth, and he travelled in luxury with a vast entourage. Journeys by water provided a useful opportunity for inspecting the upkeep of the all-important water-transport system and the maintenance of irrigation works and dykes (National Palace Museum, Taiwan).

led to large-scale smuggling and piracy which the Chinese were unable to control. In 1555 a group of only 70 pirates looted their way to Nanjing and back for 2 and a half months unhindered; in 1660, 6,000 Japanese were to land and ravage Fujian province.

LONGQING	
Born	1596)
1537, as Zhu Zaihou	(3) empress Ci (concubine Lishi)
Accession	(died 1614)
1567, as Longqing	*Children*
Father	4 sons
Jiajing (3rd son of)	*Died*
Mother	1572
concubine Kang, later empress Du	*Tomb*
	Zhaoling,
Wives	Shisanling, Hebei
(1) empress Li (died 1558)	*Temple name*
	Muzong ('Reverent
(2) empress Chen, childless (died	Ancestor')

LONGQING

Jiajing disliked his Heir, preferring the son of another concubine who was one month younger, but the tradition of primogeniture was too strong to break and in 1567, aged 29, **Longqing** (1567–1572) ascended the throne without any experience of state affairs. Weak and unambitious, he remained indifferent to politics, silent at court audiences, keeping his ministers at a distance, preferring the eunuchs and enjoying luxury. He redressed some of Jiajing's wrongs, rehabilitating unjustly accused officials and expelling Daoists from court. Under his able minister Zhang Zhuzheng, peace was made with Altan Khan who accepted vassal status, and coastal piracy was largely brought under control.

WANLI

Wanli (1573–1620) ruled for 47 years, the longest reign since Han Wudi in the 2nd century BC. Third (but eldest surviving) son of Longqing, he was 10 years old on accession.

During Wanli's reign the social and economic transformation of China into a modern state which had begun in the early 16th century

Woodcut illustration from the Ming novel, *Journey to the West* – written by Wu Chengen (c. 1505–1580) during the florescence of popular literature – in which Monkey, a hero with magical powers, and his companions, Pigsy and Sandy, help the famous Tang Buddhist pilgrim, Xuanzang, overcome gods, demons and men on his perilous journey to seek Buddhist scriptures in the west.

continued. New crops from America such as maize, sweet potatoes and peanuts increased food production and the population reached over 100 million, double that of the early Ming. The 'Single Whip' tax reforms and the spread of silver currency produced an economic boom. Wealth shifted from land to commercial and manufacturing enterprises: the growing of industrial crops like cotton, sugar-cane and tobacco with mills and factories centred in special regions – silk wares in Suzhou, paper factories and the Jingdezhen porcelain kilns in Jiangxi. Technical advances improved the standard of manufactured goods, and with the general expansion of maritime trade in east Asia the demand for Chinese exports of luxury products rocketed, leading to the rise of a new class of extremely wealthy merchants, bankers and businessmen. The new rich class vied with the nobility in conspicuous consumption, building elaborate mansions and gardens and acquiring *objets d'art*, thus further stimulating production. It was a vigorous, creative and productive age and the great cities like Beijing, Nanjing, Suzhou and Hangzhou became centres of intellectual activity. Private academies promoted education and there was a blossoming of popular literature, novels and encyclopedias. This activity took place in spite of government policies, for politically it was a period of decline. After the first decade, Wanli's inaction led to a creeping paralysis of the administration and an inner decay which was to prove fatal.

The reign had started well. Under the leadership of the most able of all Ming ministers, Zhang Zhuzheng, supported by Wanli's mother, Lishi, discipline and efficiency in the administration were restored,

As the administration deteriorated, floods caused by the neglect of dykes increased; in this contemporary woodcut peasants seek refuge from the flood waters in trees.

WANLI	
Born 1563, as Zhu Yizhun	Wang (died 1611) *Principal concubines* (1) consort Liu (died 1642)
Title before accession Heir Apparent (1568)	(2) consort Zheng (died 1630)
Accession 1573, as Wanli	*Children* 8 sons (3 died in infancy); 10
Father Longqing (3rd but eldest surviving son of)	daughters (8 died young)
Mother concubine Lishi, later empress Ci	*Died* 1620 *Tomb* Dingling, Shisanling, Hebei
Wives (1) empress Wang (died 1620) (2) empress	*Temple name* Shenzong ('Spiritual Ancestor')

One of the many headdresses found in Wanli's tomb. This black and gold hat, adorned with strings of precious stones, was worn when the emperor made official journeys.

border attacks repelled and the financial situation stabilized. Wanli became restless under Zhang's strict control, however, and on his death, increasingly withdrew from state affairs. From the age of 25 onwards he blatantly neglected state duties and for the next quarter century, from 1589 to 1615, never appeared at imperial audiences, leaving ministers and foreign envoys to kowtow and pay respects to an empty throne. After 1591, Wanli ceased to perform public ceremonies, refusing even to attend his mother's funeral in 1614. The entire Ming administrative system revolved round the emperor and when he refused to act responsibility fell on the Grand Secretaries or was usurped by the eunuchs. The Grand Secretaries, however, were held at a distance. In 30 years (from 1590 to 1620) Wanli only saw them five times, and it was left to the eunuchs to transmit memorials to the emperor who steadily ignored displeasing subjects, finally refusing to consider all but the most urgent matters of finance and defence.

Slowly, the system ground to a halt. Posts were left unfilled and there were no promotions. By 1603 two-thirds of the censorate posts were unfilled; in 1612 there was only one Grand Secretary and he was ill; 50 per cent of all prefectural and district posts were vacant. Prisoners languished and died in prison for lack of judges to try them. The emperor, totally egoistic and irresponsible, brooked no opposition. When unduly harsh sentences were appealed against, he increased the punishments, and officials who remonstrated were flogged or exiled. The eunuchs with their secret service created a miasma of distrust and bitter factionalism. Senior officials, falsely accused and without redress, simply left their posts without authorization. By the end of the reign, there was an atmosphere of frustration and despair.

Military problems abounded. There were Mongol raids in the north (in 1560 the Mongols occupied Qinghai) and serious troubles with minority tribes in the southwest where Chinese troops had to enter Burma to quell the rebels in 1599–1600. The Japanese invasion of Korea led to five years of ruinous war (1593–1598) to expel them. Finally a new and far more serious threat appeared: the newly-risen Manchus (Jurchen) invaded and by 1620 occupied the far northeast under their emperor, Nurhachi.

These campaigns were extremely expensive. Although the army had doubled since the 14th century, it was ill-organized and inefficient, mainly composed of mercenaries drawn from the homeless and dregs of society. To raise money, Wanli reopened the silver mines in 1594 and appointed eunuch tax commissioners to supervise mining and to collect heavy new taxes imposed on trade, shops, market stalls and boats. Their extortionate behaviour, which often included physical attacks and murder, led to bitter resentment in the provinces; even when the emperor ordered tax relief for areas hit by serious earthquakes, floods and famine, the voracious eunuchs continued their exactions; much of the revenue

Ivory figure of a Ming magistrate. The portly figure reflects the common belief in the wealth of magistrates while the long beard, combed into strands, indicates age and wisdom. During Wanli's reign the administrative system began to break down because the emperor neglected to fill official posts. Criminals remained in prison without trial due to the lack of judges and magistrates.

TAICHANG	
Born 1582, as Zhu Changle	(2) empress Wang (died 1619)
Title before accession Heir Apparent (1601)	*Principal concubine* (1) consort Li (2) consort (posthumously created empress) Liu (died 1615)
Accession 1620, as Taichang	*Children* 15
Father Wanli (eldest son of)	*Died* 1620
Mother concubine, later empress, Wang	*Tomb* Qingling, Shisanling, Hebei
Wives (1) empress Guo, no sons (died 1613)	*Temple name* Guangzong ('Lustrous Ancestor')

never reached the imperial coffers and the desperate population turned increasingly to banditry and rebellion.

Financial problems were compounded by the emperor's extravagance. Greedy – he suffered from dizzy spells, his feet and legs hurt and he grew so fat that he could no longer stand unaided – and sensually self-indulgent, he spent vast sums on his tomb and palaces, ordering expensive materials from the outermost parts of the empire. The Jesuit, Matteo Ricci (the first European ever to set foot in the Forbidden City), records seeing a convoy of wood 2 miles (3 km) long on the Grand Canal, pulled by tens of thousands of workers, which he was told was being brought from the southwest to Beijing to rebuild two palaces which had burned down; the journey was going to take four years. Inordinately vain, Wanli spent a fortune on his family, clothing, jewellery and other luxuries: his wedding clothes cost 90,000 oz of silver, those for two daughters' weddings over 1 million, and the investiture of five sons in 1601, 21 million oz. These expenses were all taken from state money, leaving his private purse intact. (The contents of his tomb confirm his interest in clothes.) In addition, there was the cost of supporting the imperial family. Hongwu's decision to send his sons to the provinces proved an expensive one, for these princes enjoyed huge estates and salaries, keeping personal guards of many thousands; under Jiajing the court was supporting over 33,000 not including wives, concubines, female staff and sons-in-law; under Wanli, there were 45 princes of the first rank and over 23,000 lesser nobility. In some provinces half the revenue went on their support.

During Wanli's reign, the Jesuit Matteo Ricci reintroduced Christianity into China. (The Nestorian Christians and William of Rubruck's tiny Roman Catholic mission under the Mongols had perished when the Mongols were driven out.)

TAICHANG

Taichang (1620), son of the concubine (later empress) Wang, only ruled for a month. Another unwanted heir, he grew up, however, neglected in a world of court intrigues led by the concubine Zheng whose son his father preferred. Soon after succession, he fell ill and when the Chief Minister gave him a 'wonder-working' pill and banished his favourite concubine 'Western Li' he weakened and died, popularly believed to have been poisoned by the lady Zheng and her associates.

TIANQI

Taichang's son, **Tianqi** (1621–1627), was a sorry figure. Succeeding at 15, he had grown up in the depraved court of his grandfather Wanli and was good with his hands but illiterate. Chinese sources put it more politely: 'he did not have sufficient leisure to learn to write', but once at his workbench 'he forgot cold and heat, hunger and thirst' in pursuit of his carpentry.

THE MING TOMBS

The Ming Tombs undoubtedly formed one of the largest and most gorgeous royal cemeteries ever laid out by the hand of man. They yield the palm to the Egyptian pyramids in point of bulk, but certainly not in that of style and grandeur.

Jan Jakob Maria de Groot, 1894

The Ming revived the importance of ancestor worship at the tomb and one of Yongle's first acts on moving to Beijing was to choose a site for the imperial cemetery. No other dynasty has left such a complete set of tombs in a single burial ground; this is also the earliest dynasty for which the surface architecture has survived.

The site, a valley some 45 km (30 miles) northwest of Beijing, illustrates the best principles of Chinese geomancy or *fengshui* – the conscious harmonization of man and nature in which buildings fit into rather than dominate the landscape. A magnificent single approach and Spirit Road leads from the southern entrance to the first tomb in the valley, Yongle's Changling, under the highest peak in the north. All later Ming emperors, except for Jingtai who was denied an imperial tomb, are buried in the foothills east and west of Changling. Changling and Longqing's Zhaoling have been restored; Wanli's Dingling was excavated in the late 1950s and the remainder are in varying states of decay, enabling one to see the basic construction methods.

Acting on the principle 'Treat the dead as if alive', the tomb buildings are based on ordinary palace architecture: the sacrificial hall at Changling, for example, is an exact replica of the largest hall in the Forbidden City (until the 20th century these were the two largest buildings in China). The tomb plan, based on 'heaven round, earth square', consists of highly coloured halls and courtyards where the sacrifices and ceremonies were held, and a round, fortified, unadorned artificial hill planted with trees which covers the underground chamber containing the coffin.

Excavations of Wanli's tomb, Dingling, from 1956 to 1958 under Dr Xia Nai revealed a wealth of treasure. The tomb had not been robbed and included a jewel-studded headdress made with kingfisher feathers, a gold and pearl military helmet, exquisite jade objects such as a jug carved in one piece with its handle and lid held by a delicate chain, gold chopsticks and goblets, money and vast quantities of finest woven embroidered silk, each bolt marked with the date and place of origin and name of the pattern and responsible foreman.

(Left) Civil official in the spirit road, representing a president of one of the Six Boards responsible for imperial administration. Stone camels (above), horses and elephants in the spirit road showed the extent of the Ming domain, symbolizing north, west and south respectively.

(Far left, below) The memorial archway (pai lou) erected by Jiajing in 1540 to mark the approach to the Ming tombs. The dedication plaque over the central arch was left blank since it was forbidden to write the imperial name.

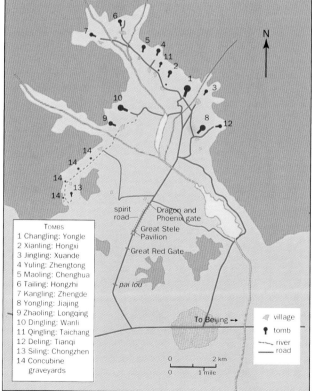

TOMBS
1 Changling: Yongle
2 Xianling: Hongxi
3 Jingling: Xuande
4 Yuling: Zhengtong
5 Maoling: Chenghua
6 Tailing: Hongzhi
7 Kangling: Zhengde
8 Yongling: Jiajing
9 Zhaoling: Longqing
10 Dingling: Wanli
11 Qingling: Taichang
12 Deling: Tianqi
13 Siling: Chongzhen
14 Concubine graveyards

spirit road — Dragon and Phoenix gate
Great Stele Pavilion
Great Red Gate
pai lou
To Beijing →

village
tomb
river
road

0   2 km
0   1 mile

(Above) The shape of the Valley of the Thirteen Tombs (Ming Tombs) and the layout of its monuments stress the unity of the empire and the continuity of the dynasty. A single spirit road serves all the emperors buried here and the memorial stele at the valley entrance is dedicated to the dynasty rather than a single emperor.

(Above) Hall of Heavenly Favours, Changling, tomb of Yongle, the first emperor buried in the valley (1424). Restored in 1950, this tomb is the oldest and most perfect surviving example of a self-contained palatial complex. Sacrifices to the Ming emperors were held in this hall until 1924 when the ex-emperor, Puyi, went into exile.

(Below) Plan of the underground tomb chambers of Dingling, the tomb of Wanli.

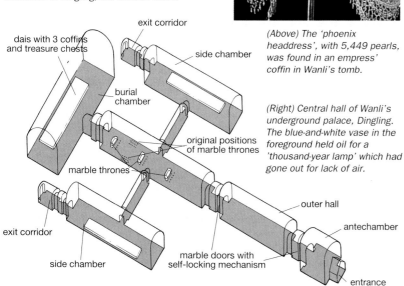

dais with 3 coffins and treasure chests

exit corridor

side chamber

burial chamber

original positions of marble thrones

marble thrones

exit corridor

outer hall

side chamber

antechamber

marble doors with self-locking mechanism

entrance

(Above) The 'phoenix headdress', with 5,449 pearls, was found in an empress' coffin in Wanli's tomb.

(Right) Central hall of Wanli's underground palace, Dingling. The blue-and-white vase in the foreground held oil for a 'thousand-year lamp' which had gone out for lack of air.

JESUITS IN CHINA

The first European to enter the Forbidden City was the great Jesuit priest, Matteo Ricci (1552–1616). Born near Rome in 1552, he reached China 30 years later and quickly realized that in a country where merit was equated with knowledge of the classics the only way to influence the Chinese was to meet them on their own ground. Learning Chinese and mastering the Classics, he was eventually accepted by Chinese scholars and nobility; his early training in mathematics, geography, astronomy and music put him ahead of his Chinese counterparts in those fields and he won admiration by his prodigious feats of memory which enabled him to read a page of 500 characters once and the repeat them either forward or backward.

After years in the provinces and an earlier unsuccessful visit to Beijing, Ricci was allowed to settle and found a small mission in the capital in 1601, becoming a familiar Beijing figure with 'his curly beard, blue eyes and voice like a bell'. Ricci never saw the emperor Wanli, now firmly in seclusion, but he was summoned to the palace when one of his gifts, a striking clock, stopped. For three days he remained, instructing the eunuchs on its workings and during this time was bombarded with questions from the emperor about conditions in Europe. Later he was summoned to teach the eunuchs to

play the clavichord and in 1608 the emperor ordered a copy of Ricci's *Mappa Mundi* as a screen and was sufficiently curious to get the court artist to paint Ricci and his companion, Pantoja.

Ricci's work was continued by the Jesuits Adam Schall von Bell and John Schreck (Terrentius), who arrived in Beijing in 1622 bringing the first telescope ever seen in China. Their astronomical skills impressed Tianqi's court and after predicting an eclipse more accurately than the Chinese astronomers they were given the task of reforming the imperial calendar.

18th-century portrait of Matteo Ricci, who was buried in the Christian cemetery outside the city walls in a coffin presented by Wanli.

Ricci believed that the Chinese could only be converted by presenting Christianity in a form compatible with Confucianism (allowing ancestor worship, for example), and on this basis converted several influential Chinese. Under Schall, Terrentius and their successors, converts rose to several thousand but the papal decision in the Rites Controversy in the early 18th century that Christianity must be taught in its pure form undermined their work and the later Jesuits were either expelled or imprisoned for trying to subvert traditional Chinese beliefs.

(Left) Ricci's map from 1600, the first in China to show the American continent, was bitterly attacked by Chinese scholars for failing to place China in the centre.

(Below) Adam Schall von Bell (1591–1666) in mandarin robes, 1665.

(Left) Both Adam Schall von Bell and Ferdinand Verbiest were directors of the observatory in Beijing. Originally built by the Yuan, it was refitted by Verbiest, many of whose instruments have survived.

TIANQI	
Born 1605, as Zhu Yujiao *Accession* 1621, as Tianqi *Father* Taichang (eldest son of) *Mother* empress Wang (died 1619) *Wife* empress Zhang	(died 1644) *Children* 5, all died in infancy *Died* 1627 *Tomb* Deling, Shisanling, Hebei *Temple name* Xizong ('Bright Ancestor')

CHONGZHEN	
Born 1611, as Zhu Yujian *Accession* 1628, as Chongzhen *Father* Taichang (5th son of) *Mother* consort Liu (died 1615, posthumous title of empress) *Wife* empress Zhou (died 1644)	*Principal concubine* consort Tian (died 1642) *Children* 7 sons (4 died early) *Died* 1644 *Tomb* Siling, Shisanling, Hebei *Temple name* Sizong ('Thoughtful Ancestor')

View of Chongzhen's modest funeral mound and stele, Siling, at the Ming Tombs. Wang Chengen's loyalty was rewarded by a burial close to his master, a unique privilege for a eunuch. Wang's grave is to the southwest, out of picture.

Tianqi entrusted power to his nurse's close friend, the eunuch Wei Zhongxian (1568–1627), who had been his mother's butler. Wei was a gangster of the first order, who tyrannized the court and administration with his secret service, appointing officials on the basis of their loyalty to him and ability to exact taxes. In 1624, an attempt by reformers campaigning for a moral revival of pure Confucianism failed and the leaders, the 'Six Heroes', were tortured and beaten to death; 700 of their supporters were purged and for the remainder of the reign Wei operated a rule of terror. Tianqi's passive acceptance of these events finally persuaded the people that the Ming had lost the Mantle of Heaven and were no longer fit to rule. Tianqi's widow, the empress Zhang, lived until the fall of the dynasty when she strangled herself and was buried with her husband.

CHONGZHEN

I, feeble and of small virtue, have offended against Heaven; the rebels have seized my capital because my ministers deceived me. Ashamed to face my ancestors, I die. Removing my imperial cap and with my hair dishevelled about my face, I leave to the rebels the dismemberment of my body. Let them not harm my people!

The emperor Chongzhen's final message written on his robe

The last Ming emperor, Tianqi's younger brother, **Chongzhen** (1628–1644), inherited a discredited administration and never had a chance. Ironically, intellectual life at court revived and two Jesuits, Adam von Schall and John Schreck (Terrentius), were given the important task of reforming the imperial calendar after predicting an eclipse more accurately than the court astronomers. The official system had, however, broken down and when a severe famine broke out in 1628, the government was helpless; bandit groups sprang up all over the country; the people rose against corrupt, inefficient and harsh rule and the situation was similar to that when the first Ming emperor had seized power from the Yuan. In April 1644, while powerful Manchu forces advanced in the northeast, a Chinese rebel leader, the 'Dashing General', Li Zicheng, who occupied western and northwestern China, swept unopposed into Beijing, sacking the Ming Tombs *en route*.

The final drama was worthy of a Greek tragedy. The emperor called a last council in which 'all were silent and many wept'; the imperial troops fled or surrendered, and the emperor, after helping his two sons to escape in disguise, got drunk and rushed through the palace ordering the women to kill themselves. The empress and Tianqi's widow committed suicide; the emperor hacked the arm off one daughter before killing her sister and the concubines. At dawn he laid his dragon robe aside and dressed in purple and yellow, with one foot bare, climbed the hill behind the now silent palace and hanged himself on a locust tree. His faithful eunuch, Wang Chengen, followed suit and was buried beside him in the Ming Tombs.

MING PORCELAIN

The Ming emperors actively patronized the production of ceramics, establishing imperial kilns at Jingdezhen, Jiangxi, in the late 14th century. Their wares were reserved for the imperial court and upper classes and with their privileged position the Jingdezhen potters were able to perfect new techniques and styles to satisfy the exigent court. Most famous are the blue-and-white underglaze wares with expressive and naturalistic designs painted in cobalt blues on white porcelain (a mixture of local kaolin clay with Chinese stone (petuntse) fired at 1400°C (2500°F) producing a delicate white ware so hard that steel cannot scratch it), and covered with translucent glaze before firing.

Although a few early reign marks have been found, they only came into regular use under Xuande (1425–1435); after a hiatus under Zhengtong and Jingtai, production revived in the Jiajing period when there were at least 58 official and 20 unofficial kilns producing tens of thousands of pieces annually.

(Below and above right) Ming woodcuts illustrating pottery techniques. By the 15th century, production at the imperial kilns of Jingdezhen was divided into 23 different processes with specialized kilns for firing different wares. The scale of production was staggering. A single order from the Board of Public Works in 1433 specified that 433,500 pieces of porcelain were to be decorated with dragons and phoenixes according to the patterns enclosed. Porcelain was now a more valuable trading commodity than silk and a large proportion of production was geared to foreign markets, particularly Japan, Southeast Asia and the Near East.

(Right) Early 15th-century blue and white flask (Percival David Foundation of Chinese Art, London).

(Below) Glazed pottery dish with a design of dragons, flowers and fruits in three colours against a yellow background. On the base is a six-character Wanli reign mark (National Palace Museum, Taiwan).

洪武 年製 Hongwu 1368–1398	永樂 年製 Yongle 1403–1424	永樂 年製 Yongle 1403–1424	大明宣 德年製 Xuande 1426–1435
化年製 大明成 Chenghua 1465–1487	治年製 大明弘 Hongzhi 1488–1505	德年製 大明正 Zhengde 1506–1521	靖年製 大明嘉 Jiajing 1522–1566
慶年製 大明隆 Longqing 1567–1572	曆年製 大明萬 Wanli 1573–1619	啟年製 大明天 Tianqi 1621–1627	年製 崇禎 Chongzhen 1628–1643

(Above) Reign marks, in sets of four or six characters, were painted with underglaze cobalt, generally on the centre of the base of the vessel and usually enclosed with a double circle. Such marks are not always reliable; many vessels from 1435–1465, for example, bear Xuande reign marks.

(Below) Monochrome vessels, rare in the 15th century, became more common in the 16th. The turquoise for this Chenghua (late 15th-century) wine jar was derived from copper and had to be fired on the porcelaineous stoneware like enamel.

(Left) Early 17th-century De-hua porcelain. Immortals in a celestial boat bound for the Daoist Island Paradise.

QING DYNASTY
1644–1735

順治 **Shunzhi**
1644–1661

康熙 **Kangxi**
1661–1722

雍正 **Yongzheng**
1723–1735

Watercolour of Shunzhi from an 18th-century album of imperial portraits (British Library).

SHUNZHI	
Born 1638, as Fulin	(died 1660, posthumously raised to empress)
Accession 1644, as Shunzhi	*Children* 8 sons (4 died young), 6 daughters (5 died young)
Father Aberhai (9th son of)	
Mother secondary consort Xiao Zhuang (later became empress Wen), the daughter of a Mongolian prince	*Died* 1661
	Tomb Xiaoling, Eastern Tombs, Hebei
Wives (1) empress Berjijit, Xiao Kang (deposed 1653) (2) empress Xiao Hui (died 1718)	*Temple name* Shizu ('Sage Progenitor')
	Note on Qing emperors All Qing emperors had the clan name Aisin Gioro.
Major concubine consort Xiao Xian	

The Manchus were Jurchens from southeast Manchuria, descendants of the Jin who had ruled northern China in the 12th century. In the early 17th century, under Nurhachi and his son, Aberhai, the Manchus occupied the Liaoning area in north China and established a strong Chinese-style state with its capital at Mukden (Shenyang), adopting a Chinese dynastic name, the 'Great Qing' – 'Qing' means 'pure' – in 1636. Enlisting Chinese support, they made Korea and Mongolia vassal states and when the Ming collapsed in 1644, profited from Chinese rebel dissension by occupying Beijing, declaring Nurhachi's six-year-old grandson, Shunzhi, emperor of China.

The Manchus were never more than two per cent of the population in China and their rule depended on creating a highly authoritarian and centralized Sino-Manchu empire in which the Ming administrative system functioned under Manchu supervision; ultimately their power rested on the efficient military banner system (see p. 194) and Chinese veneration for the throne, bolstered by the imposition of a neo-Confucian moral orthodoxy stressing the virtues of obedience. For a century and a half, they were eminently successful, but from the early 19th century onwards, the system ossified; population growth and economic crises led to widespread popular rebellions and when confronted with

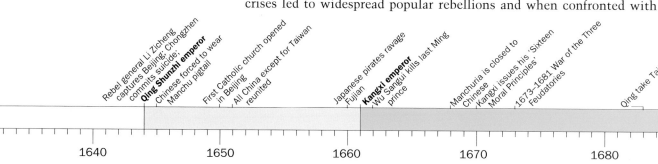

Rebel general Li Zicheng captures Beijing; Chongzhen commits suicide; **Qing Shunzhi emperor** Chinese forced to wear Manchu pigtail

First Catholic church opened in Beijing

All China except for Taiwan reunited

Japanese pirates ravage Fujian

Kangxi emperor Wu Sangui kills last Ming prince

Manchuria is closed to Chinese Kangxi issues his 'Sixteen Moral Principles'

1673–1681 War of the Three Feudatories

Qing take Taiwan

1640   1650   1660   1670   1680

(*Above*) A typical battle scene between Chinese and attacking northern horsemen. The Chinese had always depended on defensive walls, and the Manchus could never have conquered northern China so easily had it not been for support within China.

(*Above*) Civil official on the spirit road leading to Shunzhi's tomb, Xiaoling, 1661. Qing Eastern Tombs, near Beijing, Hebei.

European military aggression, the empire toppled.

The Manchus, with a loose-knit family pattern, did not observe primogeniture.

SHUNZHI

Until **Shunzhi** (1644–1661) was 14, his uncle, Dorghon, ran the state, concentrating on consolidating the Qing occupation. In 1646, the eastern provinces of Fujian and Zhejiang were brought under control and Sichuan fell in the southwest. In the following year, Canton (Guangzhou) was taken and by 1651, when Dorghon died, only Taiwan (which held out until 1683) and the last of the Ming forces in Yunnan remained unsubdued. On Dorghon's death Shunzhi assumed full power. Conscientious and studious, he learned Chinese in order to read documents and replaced Manchu household officials with Chinese eunuchs. He was sympathetic to the Jesuits, but later turned to Zen Buddhism. After deposing his first empress, he fell in love with a concubine, Xiao Xian, of noble Mongol birth, formerly the wife of a Tartar prince, who shared Shunzhi's interests in Buddhism and Chinese culture. When she died aged 22, the distraught emperor tried to follow suit and then to become a monk. His health failed, he lost weight and spat blood (possibly due to tuberculosis) and suffered uncontrollable rages – on one occasion he attacked his throne with a sword and only Adam Schall, the Jesuit, could calm him. When Shunzhi caught smallpox the end was swift and he died barely four and a half months after Xiao Xian.

KANGXI

Be kind to men from afar and keep the able ones near, nourish the people, think of the profit of all as being the real profit and the mind of the whole country as being the real mind, protect the state before danger comes and govern well before there is any disturbance, be always diligent and always careful ...

I am now close to seventy and have been sixty-one years on the throne – this is all due to the quiet protection of heaven and earth and the ancestral spirits; it was not my meagre virtue that did it.

Kangxi's Valedictory Edict, 20 December 1722, issued to the people on his death

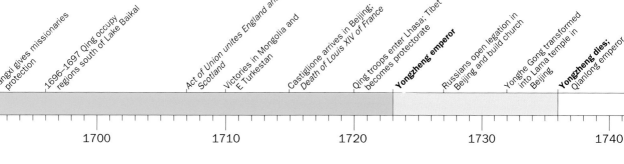

Kangxi gives missionaries protection

1696–1697 Qing occupy regions south of Lake Baikal

Act of Union unites England and Scotland

Victories in Mongolia and E Turkestan

Castiglione arrives in Beijing; Death of Louis XIV of France

Qing troops enter Lhasa; Tibet becomes protectorate

Yongzheng emperor

Russians open legation in Beijing and build church

Yonghe Gong transformed into Lama temple in Beijing

Yongzheng dies; Qianlong emperor

690   1700   1710   1720   1730   1740

IMPERIAL THOUGHTS

But it is when one is beyond the Great Wall that the air and soil refresh the spirit: one leaves the beaten road and strikes out into the untamed country; the mountains are densely packed with woods, 'green and thick as standing corn'. As one moves further north the views open up, one's eyes travel hundreds of miles; instead of feeling hemmed in, there is a sense of freedom. It may be the height of summer, but there is dew on the trees, and some of the leaves are turning yellow already, as if it were late autumn; you have to wear a fur jacket in the mornings, even though in Peking it is so hot that you hesitate about having the eunuchs lead the consorts out of the palaces to greet you on your return.

The emperor Kangxi's thoughts on motion

I have enjoyed the veneration of my country and the riches of the world; there is no object I do not have, nothing I have not experienced. But now that I have reached old age I cannot rest easy for a moment. Therefore, I regard the whole country as a worn-out sandal, and all riches as mud and sand. If I can die without there being an outbreak of trouble, my desires will be fulfilled...

I have revealed my entrails and shown my guts, there's nothing left for me to reveal.

I will say no more.

The end of Kangxi's Valedictory Edict

The young emperor Kangxi at his studies (Imperial Palace Museum, Beijing).

Is it possible that you are always concerned about a world you have not entered and count for almost nothing the one in which you are now living? Believe me, everything in its own time.

Kangxi to the Jesuits

Thus wrote **Kangxi** (1661–1722) in his Valedictory Edict, three years before his death. Chosen to succeed at the age of eight, partly because he had already had smallpox and was therefore likely to survive, Kangxi reigned longer than any other Chinese emperor and was the first of three remarkable rulers who gave China over a century of prosperity and internal peace.

Kangxi showed his ability to govern at an early age. For the first six years of his reign, Kangxi had a regency, but on reaching 14, with the help of Songgotu – his wife the empress Ren's uncle – he removed the chief regent, Oboi, and assumed full powers. When a serious revolt broke out in 1673, the 18-year-old Kangxi took personal responsibility for deal-

(*Above*) Kangxi seated in his library with his collection of scrolls on the shelves behind him.

KANGXI	
Born 1654, as Xuan Ye	*Children* 36 sons (20
Accession 1661, as Kangxi	reached adulthood), 20 daughters (8
Father Shunzhi (3rd son of)	survived) *Died* 1722
Mother empress Xiao Kang	*Tomb* Jingling, Eastern Tombs, Hebei
Wife empress Xiao Cheng (died 1674)	*Temple name* Shengzu ('Sacred Progenitor')

ing with the crisis. Three powerful generals, led by Wu Sangui (who had successfully defeated the remnants of the Ming forces in Yunnan, capturing and killing the last Ming claimant to the throne in 1662), rebelled and took control of most of southern and western China. Kangxi realized that it was necessary to act swiftly to prevent his empire from falling apart, but later he blamed himself for failing to prevent this bitter 'War of the Three Feudatories' which lasted eight years. On its successful conclusion, he inaugurated a deliberate policy of pacification. Hitherto the Manchus had treated the Chinese as a subject race. They had expelled all Chinese from Manchuria and confiscated large areas of land inside China, treating the peasants as slaves. Manchus and Chinese were segregated, intermarriage was banned and while footbinding was forbidden for Manchus, the Chinese men were forced to shave their hair in front and wear the hated Manchu queue (plait). In Beijing, Chinese were expelled from the northern city (the Forbidden City and official dwellings) and forced to live in the 'Chinese city' in the south.

Kangxi softened these policies. He prohibited further confiscation of land and lowered taxes, thus creating a prosperous agricultural basis which provided stable revenue. He reduced corruption by raising official salaries and conciliated the intelligentsia with his genuine love of Chinese literature and the commissioning of vast histories, including the *History of the Ming*, compilations, and dictionaries which gave employment to thousands of scholars. Workshops and studios were set up in the Forbidden City for artists, mechanics and architects. He studied the various sciences and music with the Jesuits at court and appointed them as astronomers, physicians and cartographers. Loving travel, he made six Grand Tours to show himself to the people, to oversee the control of vital dykes and water systems and to visit the centres of Chinese learning in the south. Above all, he imposed moral neo-Confucian orthodoxy, issuing 'Sixteen Moral Principles' stressing the virtues of obedience, which had to be read twice monthly throughout the empire.

Abroad, Kangxi re-established China's dominance in Central Asia and Tibet. Russian ambitions in the Amur region (modern Heilongjiang) to the northwest were checked in 1689 with a commercial treaty; in the 1690s Kangxi personally led two military expeditions against the powerful tribal leader, Galdan, who was trying to establish a nomadic tribal empire in Central Asia, and in 1720 sent a force to Tibet, thus securing China's frontiers in the north and west.

(*Right*) Kangxi's tours of inspection gave him a chance to show himself to people in the provinces and to meet local officials. Here the emperor is being greeted by the inhabitants of a small town who may well have brought him a petition for help (Musée Guimet, Paris).

THE BANNERS

Under the Manchu 'banner system', all tribesmen were enrolled under different coloured banners and the entire population – including captives, slaves and serfs – were registered, taxed and mobilized through these units which provided a transition from tribal to bureaucratic organization. Originally 4 in number, then 8, the banners were finally increased to 24, including 8 Chinese and 8 Mongol banners. In 1644 the conquest of China was accomplished by 278 Manchu companies, about 169,000 men, fewer than half of whom were Manchu. Banners did not fight as units but were dispersed in small numbers in banner garrisons around China and along the borders. These élite banner troops were supplemented by a larger, less mobile and untrained Chinese army of ex-Ming troops and local forces. Bannermen formed an aristocracy and imperial concubines, for example, were restricted to bannermen's daughters between the ages of 13 and 17.

Military display by Manchu bannermen, 1884.

Personal details are tantalizingly rare in Chinese imperial history, but Kangxi has left an extraordinary record of his life and thoughts in his palace memorials, personal letters and a moving Valedictory Edict in which he encapsulated the governing principles of his life. He comes across as a humane man (avoiding the death penalty where possible), driven by an overriding sense of duty. Happiest when hunting or on a military expedition – he enjoyed the chase, the landscape and living rough – Kangxi lived a frugal life, with only two meals a day, one taken in his private quarters. Throughout his reign he followed the same routine, rising at 5a.m., washing, drinking tea with milk and bird's-nest broth followed by a short period of prayer and contemplation at a small Buddhist shrine. He then read extracts from the classics, histories or other subjects before being carried to the Palace of Heavenly Purity where he conducted official audiences and business. After eating at 2p.m., he relaxed with reading, calligraphy, painting or hunting, but in the evening, returned to paperwork, often dealing with documents until late at night. When old, he noted: 'The palace memorials were read by me in person, and I wrote the rescripts on them myself, using my left hand if my right was paining me too much', and he envied the officials who could retire with old age.

Kangxi's later years were clouded by the succession question. Of his 56 children, only his second son, Yinreng, was born to an empress. (After Shunzhi's infatuation for Xiao Xian, no concubine was now allowed to spend the whole night with the emperor.) Naturally affectionate, Kangxi adored the boy, educating him with care, but Yinreng grew up dissolute, lawless and mentally unstable. His open immorality with young boys deeply shocked Kangxi and when Yinreng was involved in an apparent conspiracy, he was demoted and his associates exterminated. Kangxi refused to name a new heir until his deathbed when his fourth son, Yongzhen, claimed that he had been chosen.

YONGZHENG	
Born	Xian
1678, as Yinchen	*Children*
Accession	10 sons
1723, as Yongzhen	(4 survived),
Father	4 daughters
Kangxi (4th son of)	(1 survived)
Mother	*Died*
empress Xiao Gong,	1735
the daughter of a	*Tomb*
palace bodyguard	Tailing, Western
Wives	Tombs, Hebei
(1) empress Xiao	*Temple name*
Sheng	Shizong ('Genesis
(2) empress Xiao	Ancestor')

YONGZHENG

Many questioned whether **Yongzheng** (1723–1735), the son of a maidservant, had really been named heir in Kangxi's will and he acted swiftly to eliminate possible rivals, killing or imprisoning brothers or uncles who posed a threat, and removing the princes' power to control bannermen assigned to their service. Throughout his reign he used spies to crush opponents and ruthlessly edited the official histories for Kangxi which might have thrown light on the succession question, leaving them the shortest of all Qing imperial biographies.

Yongzheng was, however, an able, conscientious ruler. Aged 45 on accession, he further tightened imperial control by insisting that all major decisions needed imperial approval. He controlled the officials strictly, introducing rewards for honesty; he abolished hereditary servitude and replaced the patchwork of taxes inherited from the Ming with simple public levies. He promoted education and the imposition of moral orthodoxy, issuing a textbook justifying the Manchu emperors' right to the throne and thus their claim to obedience as Sons of Heaven. Like his grandfather, he was a devout Zen Buddhist and in 1732 transformed the palace, Yonghe Gong, where he had been born into a Lama Temple.

Fearing court intrigues, Yongzheng kept the name of his heir (Qianlong, his fourth son) secret in a sealed box behind the ancestral tablet, only to be opened after his death.

(*Right*) The emperor Yongzheng. The symbols embroidered on his robes — dragons, mythical beasts and birds and magic fungi — are all symbols of protection, supernatural power and longevity (Imperial Palace Museum, Beijing).

(*Below*) The tomb of Yongzheng, the first Qing emperor to be buried in the Qing Western Tombs. Qing tomb complexes were smaller and less elaborate than those of the Ming emperors. Unlike the Ming, the Qing never opened an imperial tomb once it had been closed and empresses who survived their husbands were given their own tombs east of the imperial tomb. Tailing, Western Tombs, Hebei, 1735.

QING DYNASTY
1736–1795

乾 隆 # Qianlong
1736–1795

Qianlong. Detail from *Inauguration Portraits of Emperor Qianlong, the Empress and the Eleven Imperial Consorts*, 1736, by Long Shih-ning (Giuseppe Castiglione), Chinese, 1688-1768, Qing dynasty. Handscroll.

QIANLONG	
Born	(10 survived),
1711, as Hongli	10 daughters
Accession	(5 survived)
1736, as Qianlong	*Abdicated*
Father	1795, taking the
Yongzheng (4th son of)	title Tai Shang Huang ('Super
Mother	Emperor')
Xiao Sheng	*Died*
Wives	1799
(1) empress Xiao Xian	*Tomb*
	Yuling, Eastern
(2) empress Xiao Yi, née Ula Nara	Tombs, Hebei
	Temple name
Children	Gaozong ('High
17 sons	Ancestor')

In his reception of us [Qianlong] has been very gracious and satisfactory. He is a fine old gentleman, still healthy and vigorous, not having the appearance of a man of more than sixty.

Lord Macartney after his first meeting with Qianlong in 1793, 10 days before the emperor was 80

The reign of **Qianlong** (1736–1795) was a watershed in the Qing dynasty. China expanded to its greatest extent ever, and by 1775 was easily the most wealthy and populous nation in the world. Its rapid expansion, however, brought problems and the last decades of Qianlong's rule saw a decline which eventually brought the empire down.

Qianlong's mother, Xiao Sheng, was of noble Manchu birth and the boy was Kangxi's favourite grandson. Kangxi appointed an eminent scholar to tutor him and took him on hunting trips where he displayed his courage at the age of eight, sitting unflinching on his horse when attacked by a bear. Throughout his life, Qianlong kept his grandfather as a model, retiring after 60 years on the throne so as not to reign longer than Kangxi.

Intelligent, combining Manchu military skills with the virtues of a Confucian scholar, Qianlong's first 40 years were an almost unmitigated

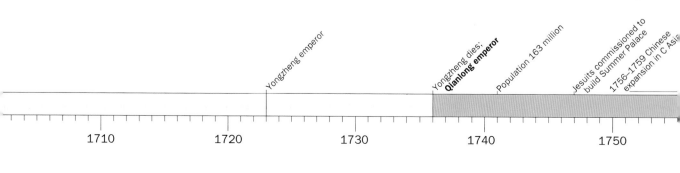

Yongzheng emperor

Yongzheng dies; **Qianlong emperor**

Population 163 million

Jesuits commissioned to build Summer Palace

1756–1759 Chinese expansion in C Asia

1710　　1720　　1730　　1740　　1750

THE JESUITS AND THE SUMMER PALACE

It [Christianity] is contrary to orthodoxy and it is only because these apostles have a thorough knowledge of the mathematical sciences that the state employs them. Take care not to forget that.

Kangxi to the Jesuits

Both Kangxi and Qianlong welcomed Jesuits at court. Kangxi, after an initial repression of the order, formed a lasting friendship with Verbiest who corrected the imperial calendar and cast cannons for him (salving his conscience by naming them after saints). In 1692, Kangxi granted the missionaries official protection and by 1700 there were nearly 300,000 Christians in China, with churches at Macao, Guangzhou and Beijing. When the Italian Jesuit Giuseppe Castiglione arrived in Beijing in 1715 he was welcomed at court and, surviving the repressions of the emperor Yongzheng, enjoyed a high position under Qianlong.

The Jesuits were valued for their artistic and technical skills; they, like Matteo Ricci before them, bore the restrictions and confinement of court life in the hope of spreading their faith. Father Denis Attiret bewailed: 'To be on a chain from one sun to the next; barely to have Sundays and feast days on which to pray to God; to paint almost nothing in keeping with one's own taste and genius; to have to put up with a thousand other harassments … all this would quickly make me return to Europe if I did not believe my brush useful for the good of religion and a means of making the Emperor favourable towards the Missionaries…'.

In 1747, Qianlong commissioned the Jesuits to design his summer resort to the northwest of Beijing with palaces in 'the manner of European barbarians' in the midst of multitudes of fountains. Castiglione, aided by the German Ignatius Sickelpart and the Florentine Bonaventura Moggi, acted as architect, while the Frenchman Michel Benoit planned the hydraulic systems. The resulting Summer Palace (Yuanmingyuan) was a fascinating blend of European and Chinese styles. Behind the façade of apparently two-storey pavilions inspired by the Trianon and Versailles were traditional single-

storey Chinese halls, for Qianlong had no wish 'to live in the air' like Europeans who must be 'very poverty-stricken and lack land' to live like that. The gardens were filled with *trompe l'oeil* European street scenes and the ingenious waterworks included a beautiful waterclock flanked by 12 fountains in the form of Chinese zodiac animals.

The Summer Palace was the target for Anglo-French revenge in 1860 when a French officer noted: 'The second night we spent at the Summer Palace was impossible, crazy, giddy. Every trooper had his bird, his musical box, his alarm clock and … bells were ringing everywhere.' The pillage ended with a fire in which delirious soldiers used tapestries threaded with silver to try to put out the blaze.

(Left) European facade and gardens of the Belvedere with monumental marble staircases — one of the palaces designed by the Jesuits for Qianlong at his Summer Palace (the Yuanmingyuan) outside Beijing.

(Below) Ruined pavilion, 'old Summer Palace'.

Qing territory peaks at 11.5 million sq kms

Annual drain of silver to West 3 million ozs

Population 200 million

American Declaration of Independence

Heshan gains power

Brutal suppression of rebellion in Shandong

French Revolution begins

Macartney's embassy to Qianlong

Qianlong abdicates; Jiajing emperor

760   1770   1780   1790   1800   1810

(*Above*) Scroll by Castiglione showing Qianlong receiving Kazakh envoys presenting tribute horses.

(*Above*) Stupa, Putuozongcheng miao (Temple of the Putuo Sect) or Potala Temple, Chengde, built 1767–1771.

success. After an early period of consolidation, he embarked on a policy of expansion abroad and magnificence at home. A series of campaigns doubled the size of the empire. Tibet was brought under Chinese control by a display of military strength in 1751 accompanied by favours for the Lama religious authorities. Since the end of the 17th century Beijing had been the centre for publishing Tibetan and Mongolian works and Qianlong encouraged the translation of Lama texts into Manchu and Mongolian. Between 1756 and 1757 Chinese armies swept through Central Asia, bringing the entire area from Dunhuang to the Pamir mountains under their control and incorporating the 'New Territories', modern Xinjiang, into the empire. By 1759 the empire covered nearly 4 and a half million sq miles (12 million sq km), including Outer Mongolia and parts of Russia, while Korea, Nepal, Burma, Thailand, Vietnam and the Philippines recognized Chinese dominance. Within this cosmopolitan empire, official texts, already in both Chinese and Manchu, were often in Turkish Arabic and Tibetan scripts and valuable multilingual dictionaries were compiled.

Qianlong's reputation as a great Chinese emperor, however, rests on his scholarship and patronage of the arts. Like Kangxi, he was a genuine lover of Chinese classics and sponsored major publications including an extraordinary compilation of rare works known as the *Four Treasuries* – classics, history, philosophy and *belles lettres* – in which over 3,450 complete works were collected and copied by 15,000 scholars in 36,000 volumes. He was a good calligrapher and is credited with over 42,000 poems. He painted and collected pictures, attracting painters to court and employing the best architects and artists to build new palaces. Eight great temples were built, including a replica of the Tibetan Potala – the imposing palace-monastery of the Dalai Lama in Lhasa – at the summer resort of Jehol (Chengde) and the Jesuits were ordered to make a Summer Palace (Yuanmingyuan) outside Beijing. With buildings designed by Giuseppe Castiglione and mechanical fountains by Michel Benoit, the Summer Palace presented a fascinating blend of West and East.

The entire complex was sacked and looted by Anglo-French forces in 1860. Like Kangxi, Qianlong appreciated the Jesuits' superior knowledge in certain fields and enjoyed their company as long as there was no interference from Rome. And again, like his grandfather, he undertook six Grand Tours in the south, commissioning paintings of his favourite scenic spots.

Qianlong was a strong man. Father Benoit, painting him in 1773, commented on his remarkable posture and vitality; 20 years later, George Staunton noted that the emperor, now 83, 'walked firm and erect'. His routine was similar to Kangxi's. He rose at 6a.m., ate at 8a.m. and 2p.m., each meal only lasting 15 minutes. In the morning he dealt with official business; in the afternoon he read, painted or wrote verse, following the same pattern whether at Beijing, Jehol or the Summer Palace. He could read and write without spectacles until his death and hunted until he was 86. Open-minded, truthful and responsible, Qianlong was a good family man, devoted to his first wife, Xiao Xian, and educating his sons well although denying them responsibility. When his second wife, Xiao Yi, suddenly tonsured her hair to become a nun while on tour in Shandong she was declared mad.

The very success of Qianlong's reign, however, brought problems. The 18th century saw an unprecedented expansion in Chinese agriculture and population. New crops from America (sweet potatoes, groundnuts and sorghum) and improved technology and irrigation brought

(*Below*) Qianlong's spectacular autumn hunting expeditions at Mulan, north of Jehol, were painted by Castiglione in collaboration with Chinese artists. The emperor and his entourage lived in Manchu style, sleeping in yurts within a round stockade. Provisions were brought by camel and 1,250 Mongol beaters were employed for the hunting. Details from Mulan scroll, II, Musée Guimet, Paris. (Cat.49).

COMMERCIAL EXPANSION AND TRADE

Production of industrial crops and fine manufactured goods soared, creating industrial centres and raising the peasants' standard of living. Cotton goods became a major export and British imports of tea increased 50-fold in 80 years. Tens of thousands of workers at the porcelain kilns in Jingdezhen produced celadons and porcelains for export; as well as manufactured silk and cotton wares, Europeans sought Chinese furniture and lacquerware and China became a major exporter of paper and books in the East. Trade was conducted in silver and since China was largely self-sufficient, the balance was in her favour. Between 1760 and 1780 the net drain of silver from the West to China rose from 3 million to 16 million oz (85,000 kg to 450,000 kg).

Chinese workers packing porcelain for export to Europe.

(*Above, right*) New strains of seed made it possible to produce three crops of rice a year in some areas. The work was very labour-intensive: to get faster growth, the soil had to be heavily manured and ploughed, when possible, by buffalo. Seedlings were transplanted by hand after a month and the small fields were then irrigated and drained according to the plants' stage of growth.

(*Box, left*) During the 18th century, tea became the English national drink and imports of tea rose to a staggering £20,000,000 p.a. Since the Chinese did not want to buy goods from England, the ships carrying tea to the west returned eastward empty and there was a steady flow of silver to China.

year-round harvests, and with increased prosperity the population rocketed. Chinese population statistics are unreliable, but official figures show a rise from 143 million in 1741 to 200 million in 1762, 360 million in 1812, reaching 432 million by 1851. Pressure for land led to colonization of minority regions, provoking tribal rebellions against Chinese and Manchu exploitation. These were all peripheral risings, posing no threat to central rule, but by the late 18th century land shortages caused hunger and poverty in China itself, leading to serious peasant unrest with an anti-Manchu bias.

Commercial expansion also brought a backlash. A dramatic increase in industrial production and export of agricultural products (tea, cotton, paper) and fine manufactured products had created a very favourable balance of trade, but in the late 18th century the British started to redress the imbalance by importing opium from India into China (see.p 207). Under Qianlong the problem was still in its infancy, but by the 1830s the flow of silver had already been reversed and was thereafter a serious drain on Chinese resources.

With age, Qianlong's judgment failed. In 1780, at 69, having lost his favourite wife and son, he fell under the spell of a good-looking palace guard, Heshan (1750–1799), aged 30. Charming and intelligent, he won the emperor's confidence, was rapidly promoted and dominated the last 15 years of Qianlong's reign. Heshan was completely unscrupulous. He installed his family in high posts, married his daughter into the imperial family, and, through a network of corrupt henchmen, levied a 'squeeze' on officialdom throughout the empire which permanently undermined the foundations of government. On his death, his private wealth was estimated at one and a half billion American dollars in modern terms.

Despite growing hardship at home, Qianlong embarked on further foreign ventures. After abortive invasions of Burma (1766–1769) and Tongking (1788), he sent expeditions to Nepal (1788–1792) and Tibet to ward off possible Russian, French and British infiltration. These distant, difficult campaigns exhausted the exchequer while Heshan's exactions undermined the army. In suppressing a peasant revolt in 1782 in Shandong Heshan's minions had ruthlessly bled the already starving peasantry; now they embezzled army allocations, undermining the vital bannermen, leaving them ill equipped and demoralized.

The serious financial situation was made worse by court extravagance. Qianlong's Grand Tours and new building projects were extremely expensive and the sheer magnificence of his daily life – the splendid palaces and gardens, his exquisite collections and the luxury of his lifestyle – set a pattern of extravagant living among the upper and official classes. The first British embassy to China thus took place when the outwardly prosperous empire was in the first stages of a terminal disease. In 1793, Lord George Macartney was sent to ask the Chinese emperor for permission to increase the opportunities for British trade and to accept a permanent ambassador in Beijing. As George III's envoy, Macartney was transported in a British warship, but the trip was paid for by the British East India Company.

Macartney was received in Jehol on Qianlong's 83rd birthday. The visit was kept under Heshan's control and doomed from the start. As ruler of the Middle Kingdom, whose moral base and culture placed it above the barbarian world outside, Qianlong expected Macartney to kowtow in the accepted fashion. Much has been made of Macartney's refusal to do so, but this was only a symptom of the fundamental, irreconcilable differences between China and the West. The envoy from a great maritime, trading empire, Macartney came to offer western technology and trade. To the continental, self-sufficient China this was of little interest. Even at the peak of her exports, income from commercial taxes never exceeded 5.4 per cent of state revenues. Macartney's requests seemed impertinent. His impressive gifts were received as tribute, but Qianlong commented: 'I set no value on strange or ingenious objects and have no use for your country's manufactures.'

From the British point of view, the mission was a failure and the stage was set for the tragedies of the next century.

MACARTNEY'S EMBASSY

If magnificence and splendour could impress the Chinese, Lord George Macartney's mission would have been a success. A nobleman with wide diplomatic experience and an entourage of nearly a hundred men, he brought 600 packages of gifts carried by 90 wagons, 40 barrows, 200 horses and 3,000 coolies. At the imperial audience: 'Over rich embroidered velvet I wore the mantle of the Order of the Bath with the collar, a diamond badge and a diamond star.'

Material display could not, however, confer equality. For the semi-divine emperor Qianlong, Macartney remained a bearer of tribute from a powerful nation best kept at bay. The gifts, carefully chosen to reflect the newest European technology, made little impression on the Chinese, who ignored those they could not understand and regarded the remainder as superfluous luxuries. The meeting exposed an unbridgeable gulf between Europe and China; Macartney's comparison of the Qing empire to 'an old, crazy, first-rate man-of-war, which a fortunate succession of able and vigilant officers has contrived to keep afloat', but which would, with lesser men at the helm, slowly drift until 'dashed to pieces on the shore' proved fair. The mission's failure hardened British attitudes towards China, increasing the likelihood of future conflict.

The gulf separating East and West: In this Chinese tapestry-picture (below) of 'the arrival of Ma-Kha-Erh-Ni bringing tribute from the King of the Red-haired People of England', the Westerners are seen in a disorderly procession; William Alexander's watercolour (below left) is filled with accurate details but the overall impression of equality between Qianlong and Lord Macartney reflects an entirely European viewpoint.

QING DYNASTY
1796–1911

嘉庆 Jiaqing
1796–1820

道光 Daoguang
1821–1850

咸丰 Xianfeng
1851–1861

同治 Tongzhi
1862–1874

光绪 Guangxu
1875–1908

溥仪 Puyi
1909–1911

Portrait of Puyi, 1909.

JIAQING	
Born 1760, as Yongyan	9 daughters (eldest son and 7 daughters died in infancy)
Accession 1796, as Jiaqing	
Father Qianlong (5th son of)	*Died* 1820
Mother empress Xiao Yi	*Tomb* Changling, Western Tombs, Hebei
Wives empress Xiao Shu	*Temple name* Renzong ('Benevolent Ancestor')
Children 5 sons,	

JIAQING

Jiaqing (1796–1820) was Qianlong's fifteenth son; his mother was Qianlong's favourite secondary consort Xiao Yi, who had been elevated to the rank of empress in 1750. On Qianlong's death in 1799, he acted swiftly against the powerful Heshan who still controlled the government, forcing him to commit suicide and sharing his fabulous fortune with his brothers. Healthy, well proportioned and fond of military sports, Jiaqing was intelligent and conscientious, rising early and working hard, but Heshan's depredations had fatally weakened the empire. The treasury was empty; sheer hunger was causing widespread rebellion and the bannermen, corrupted by luxury, could no longer maintain order.

From 1799 until 1803, Jiaqing struggled against risings in central and southern China; anti-Manchu feeling spread, however, notably in secret societies like the White Lotus Society and Triads; in 1813 he narrowly avoided assassination when rebels, aided by palace eunuchs, attacked in Beijing. Eastern China was meanwhile laid waste by major Yellow River floods and coastal piracy. Jiaqing and his son, Daoguang, were hampered in their attempts to help by their Confucian upbringing. The scholarly

Qianlong abdicates; **Jiaqing emperor**

Napoleon becomes Emperor; White Lotus rebellion finally suppressed

Population 360 million

1770   1780   1790   1800   1810

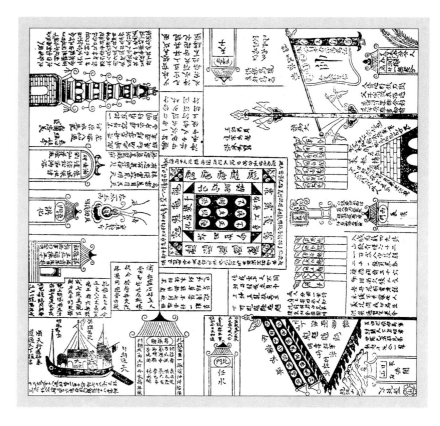

(Right) Daoism had often been associated with popular rebellions and secret societies. Part of a credential, with Daoist symbols, of a member of the Triad Society.

emphasis on precedent, virtuous behaviour and frugality was useful in settled times but left them ill-equipped to deal with problems demanding radical initiatives. Jiaqing's attempt to regain authority by moral example and ruthless economies alienated family and officials (cutting salaries merely increased the attractions of embezzlement), and he had to raise money by selling official posts.

Jiaqing died from heat stroke in Jehol in 1820, having secretly named his second son, Daoguang, as Heir in 1799.

DAOGUANG

Daoguang (1821–1850), who had helped his father in the 1813 revolt, inherited Jiaqing's lack of political clout. He was a good friend and supported his officials, but lacked imagination and courage, and his attempt to solve the financial crisis by wearing old, patched clothes, stopping visits to Jehol and further cutting salaries was a pathetic failure.

DAOGUANG	
Born	*Children*
1782, as Min Ning	9 sons (2 died
Accession	young), 10
1821, as Daoguang	daughters
Father	*Died*
Jiaqing (2nd son of)	1850
Mother	*Tomb*
empress Xiao Shu	Muling, Western
Wives	Tombs, Hebei
(1) empress	*Temple name*
Xiaomu	Xuanzong
(2) empress Xiao	('Proclaimed
Zhuan (died 1840)	Ancestor')

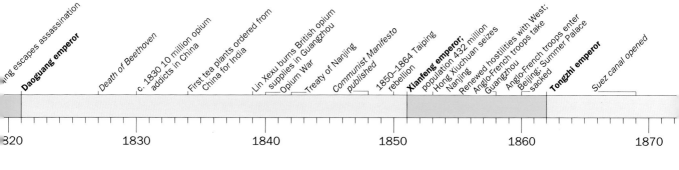

...ing escapes assassination

Daoguang emperor

Death of Beethoven

c. 1830 10 million opium addicts in China

First tea plants ordered from China for India

Lin Xexu burns British opium supplies in Guangzhou

Opium War

Treaty of Nanjing

Communist Manifesto published

1850–1864 Taiping rebellion

Xianfeng emperor; population 432 million

Hong Xiuchuan seizes Nanjing

Renewed hostilities with West; Anglo-French troops take Guangzhou

Anglo-French troops enter Beijing; Summer Palace sacked

Tongzhi emperor

Suez canal opened

320   1830   1840   1850   1860   1870

(*Above*) The emperor Daoguang with his family (Imperial Palace Museum, Beijing).

(*Below*) Foreign traders were confined to foreign 'factories', each with a narrow coastal strip and houses behind it, on the Pearl River, Guangzhou. There were 13 factories belonging to 8 nations – England, Spain, Java (Dutch), France, Austria, Sweden, Denmark and later the U.S.A.
Foreign Factories at Shameen, *c.*1800.

It was a time of internal disorder and external aggression. After a quiet start, popular unrest revived, particularly in minority and border regions. In 1807 the Tibetans had risen near Kokonor; in the late 1820s, the Muslims rose in Xinjiang and the oases of Yarkand and Kashgar were in open rebellion, undermining the Chinese domination of Central Asia.

At this point, the West struck. Dissatisfaction with trade restrictions and reacting against Chinese attempts to ban opium imports, British warships attacked and the resulting Opium War (1840–1842) revealed the extent of Western military superiority. Daoguang became the first Chinese emperor to be humiliated by a Western power; by the Treaty of Nanjing, China was forced to yield territory (Hong Kong), pay an indemnity and open five ports to Westerners who were exempted from Chinese laws. The cosmic framework of the Chinese imperial system had finally been pierced.

Daoguang was a poor, indecisive war leader lacking contact with reality, and this defeat, exposing government weakness, fanned anti-Manchu feelings. He made the already suffering coastal inhabitants pay the war indemnity, ordered officials to make good a treasury deficit of 13 million oz (368,550 kg) of silver from their salaries, and dealt with lack of maintenance on the Grand Canal by having rice shipments sent by sea, causing massive unemployment along the canal.

Aware of his own failings, Daoguang refused a funeral tablet praising him and arranged for his clothing to be distributed among the courtiers, not buried with him.

Tongzhi dies; Alute commits suicide
Guangxu emperor
First trains run on British-owned Shanghai–Woosung railway
Karl Benz builds the first motor car
Guangxu comes of age
Summer Palace partially restored
Japanese defeat China; Sun Yatsen founds Revive China secret society
Treaty of Shimonoseki
Hundred Days' Reforms; Guangxu under palace arrest
Boxer Rebellion; international force lifts siege of foreign legations
Abolition of state examination system based on the classics
Puyi emperor
Anti-Manchu rebellion; **Puyi ousted**; birth of the Republic
Sun Yatsen resigns to let Yuan Shikai take presidency

1880　　　1890　　　1900　　　1910　　　1920

THE OPIUM WAR

Suppose there were people from another country who carried opium for sale to England and seduced your people into buying and smoking it; certainly you would deeply hate it and be bitterly aroused…

Commissioner Lin to Queen Victoria, 1839

Employed delivering opium briskly. No time to read my bible.

British Captain on Sunday 2 December 1839

The Opium War (1840–1842) was a clash between irreconcilable cultures. The opium trade provided the fuse, but the underlying cause was the inability of the Chinese tributary system to accommodate the increasingly aggressive demands of Western traders. Western trade was still confined to Guangzhou (Canton), conducted through monopolistic official Chinese agents, *co-hongs*; European merchants, forced to spend half the year in Macao, were only allowed to live in the 'factory area', a small strip of land opposite Guangzhou, and were forbidden to enter the city and bring wives. Since Macartney's failed mission, Britain's triangular trade, by which imports of tea and silks were paid for by opium exports from India to China, had increased dramatically. By the late 18th century the tea trade was worth £20 million while Chinese imports of opium rose in 40 years from around 1,000 chests to 40,000 chests; by the 1830s there were some 10 million opium addicts in China, leading to a serious drain of silver westwards. In 1839, Daoguang ordered commissioner Lin Zexu (1785–1850) to suppress the entire opium trade, imposing the death penalty on any involved in it. Lin's valiant efforts were undermined by Chinese dealers and smugglers and his confiscation of British opium stocks in the factories led to hostilities in which British warships easily reduced the antiquated Chinese coastal defences. When an expeditionary force took Shanghai and advanced on Nanjing, the emperor conceded defeat. The Treaty of Nanjing (1842) abolished the Guangzhou monopoly; the Chinese agreed to set 'fair and regular' tariffs, to pay an indemnity of 20 million silver dollars, to cede Hong Kong to Britain and open five ports (Guangzhou, Xiamen (Amoy), Fuzhou, Ningpo and Shanghai) to foreign traders who were given 'extra-territorial rights', exempted from Chinese laws.

In 1858 trouble flared up again and when Xianfeng undermined an agreement to accept foreign ambassadors at Beijing, the British seized Guangzhou and in 1860 Anglo-French troops marched on Beijing, where they destroyed and looted the old Summer Palace in retaliation for the murder of a truce envoy. The peace treaties of 1858 and 1860 gave Britain Kowloon, established further 'treaty ports' and gave foreigners rights to trade on inland and coastal waters, leaving virtually the whole empire open to infiltration.

(Left) Lin Zexu seizing and burning opium.

(Below) The Nemesis, *one of the East India Company's iron-clad paddle-steamers, bombarding Chinese junks off Guangzhou in 1841 (National Maritime Museum, Greenwich).*

(Below) The opium trade had begun as an atttempt to stem the outflow of silver from England caused by huge tea imports. Opium smoking was highly addictive and Chinese imports rose from 4,500 chests p.a. between 1800-1821 to 40,000 chests by 1838. Opium den, by Thomas Allom, 1843.

XIANFENG	
Born 1831, as Yichu	(2) empress Xiao Qin, Yehonala family, dowager-empress Cixi (died 1908)
Accession 1851, as Xianfeng	
Father Daoguang (4th son of)	
Mother empress Xiao Zhuan	*Children* 2 sons, 1 daughter
Wives (1) empress Niuhuru, Xiao Chen, dowager-empress Ci An (died 1881)	*Died* 1861
	Tomb Dingling, Eastern Tombs, Hebei
	Temple name Wenzong ('Literary Ancestor')

XIANFENG

Vast columns of smoke were seen rising to the northwest.... The barbarians had entered the Summer Palace and after plundering the three main halls ... had set fire to the buildings. Their excuse for this abominable behaviour is that their troops got out of hand. After this they issued notices, placarded everywhere, in very bad Chinese.

A Chinese resident in Beijing on the day the emperor Xianfeng reached safety in Jehol, 13 October 1860

Daoguang's fourth son, **Xianfeng** (1851–1861), was only 20 on his accession. Well-meaning but inexperienced and incompetent, inheriting a crumbling empire and depleted treasury, Xianfeng was unable to cope

THE TAIPING REBELLION

All of you should be at ease and try your hardest.... This enterprise is directed by Heaven, not by men; it is too difficult to be handled by men alone. Trust completely in your Heavenly Father and Heavenly Brother; they will take charge of everything, so you need not worry or be nervous.

Hong Xiuchuan to his followers 30 March 1851

The Taiping rebellion (1850–1864), one of the strangest and most violent events in human history, cost over 20 million lives. Its leader, Hong Xiuchuan, was a failed civil servant from a peasant family, convinced by a dream that he was the son of the Christian God with a mission to save the world. His messianic preaching attracted a fanatical army of followers from the myriad landless peasants and bandits and he eventually established power over vast areas in northern China. The Taiping believed in the Ten Commandments and chastity; they banned footbinding, opium and the queue (the Manchu pigtail), and practised a primitive form of communism with land distribution and a common treasury. When banned by the Qing, the movement turned anti-Manchu and its followers

(Right) End of the Taiping rebellion. Imperial troops take Nanjing.

swept through the country seizing cities and, with Christian intolerance, destroying all Buddhist and Daoist temples.

The Qing only survived this anti-Manchu onslaught because they were supported by the Chinese scholar-gentry who preferred Manchu rule to the destruction of their established way of life and beliefs. As fellow Christians, the Taiping were pro-European, but the Western powers, fearing the rebels' strength, preferred to support the weak imperial government. British and French troops helped the Chinese at Shanghai, Suzhou, and Hangzhou and in 1864 the Qing finally ended the rebellion by retaking Nanjing.

(Above) Hong Xiuchuan, leader of the Taiping rebellion.

(*Right*) While Xianfeng remained in Jehol, unwilling to face the foreign victors, his younger brother, the prince Kong, negotiated with the allied troops and in addition to accepting humiliating territorial concessions, was forced to express 'deep regret' for the Chinese treatment of British representatives.

with the mounting problems and soon retired to the Summer Palace, leaving state affairs to his officials. For his entire reign, the empire was rent by the Taiping rebellion, the most destructive civil war China had ever known. The Taiping leader, Hong Xiuchuan (1814–1864) preached a Chinese form of Protestant Christianity and primitive socialism which spread like wildfire among the dispossessed. In 1853 Hong Xiuchuan declared himself 'Heavenly King', making Nanjing his capital. Over 600 walled cities were sacked and millions slaughtered before government forces aided by Western troops restored order 11 years later. To compound the general misery, in 1855 the Yellow River changed course from the north to the south of Shandong, inundating vast areas and reducing further millions to destitution. The administration, paralysed by corruption, did nothing to help and the surviving peasants turned to brigandry.

Meanwhile, the Westerners increased their hold along the coast and revived demands for permanent representation at court. When Xianfeng, thoroughly anti-foreign, undermined an agreement, the British and French renewed hostilities and in 1860 marched on Beijing. The emperor fled to the summer resort of Jehol; when a Westerner carrying a flag of truce was murdered, Western troops destroyed the Summer Palace, burning all they could not loot. Rare silks were used to cart the spoils away and Queen Victoria was brought a Pekinese dog which she named 'Looty'. The peace treaties which followed increased China's humiliation, ceding Kowloon, opening more ports and all waterways to Westerners and protecting foreign missionaries.

Xianfeng, ashamed to meet officials and foreign envoys demanding audience, never returned from Jehol and died in 1861, weakened by debauchery, drugs and palsy at 30. His most lasting contribution had been to lie with the daughter of a minor Manchu nobleman, the concubine Cixi, who placed her six-year-old son, Tongzhi, on the throne and went on to dominate the last half-century of imperial rule.

TONGZHI	
Born	*Children*
1856, as Zaichun	none
Accession	*Died*
1862, as Tongzhi	1874
Father	*Tomb*
Xianfeng	Huiling, Eastern
Mother	Tombs, Hebei
Cixi	*Temple name*
Wife	Muzong ('Reverent
empress Xiao Che,	Ancestor')
Alute	

TONGZHI TO PUYI

The Dowager Empress wore yellow silk, with blue and gold embroidery. Lady Macdonald...wore an astrakhan cape with a large collar, black hat with feathers, light dress and white gloves...The ladies of the Court were dressed in pink, light green, and light blue, with dark embroidery. They wore flowers and hairpins.

A caption for a photograph in the *Illustrated London News* c. 1902 showing the emperor Guangxu (not mentioned) and the dowager-empress receiving foreign ladies at the Forbidden City

On Xianfeng's deathbed, Cixi secured **Tongzhi's** (1862–1874) accession by skilfully allying herself with the empress, Xiao Chen, who only had a daughter. Xianfeng's brother, the prince Kong, supported the two, overthrowing a chauvinistic regency and making them both dowager-empress. (They were buried in twin tombs attached to Xianfeng's mausoleum.)

Cixi was the second great woman ruler in Chinese imperial history. Unlike Wu Zetian, however, she never became emperor, but for 50 years she effectively ruled China from 'behind the curtain'.

Kong belonged to a small group of reformers who believed that cooperation with the West was preferable to conflict. In an uneasy partnership with Cixi, this strong man with powerful backing gave the new reign firm Manchu leadership. He supported Chinese generals, such as Zeng Guofan, in modernizing the army, and enlisted Western help against the Taiping who were finally crushed in 1864. In 1868, the last northern bandits were suppressed and when Muslim and tribal risings in Yunnan and Guizhou were crushed in 1873, internal order was restored throughout the empire.

(*Above*) A Westerner's photograph of Prince Kong.

(*Right*) Unable to appear in public at official ceremonies, Cixi exerted her power from behind this screen which stood behind the imperial throne. Hall of Supreme Harmony, Forbidden City, Beijing.

(*Above*) Li Lienying, the chief eunuch. The volumes on the desk behind him include some of the many Buddhist sutras which he used to recite to Cixi.

(*Right*) Tower of the Fragrance of Buddha, Longevity Hill, Summer Palace.

(*Below*) Cixi was attracted by some western ideas. In 1893, the empress appropriated money designated for rebuilding the Chinese navy to build a marble boat resembling a Mississippi paddle-steamer.

China moved into the international field, establishing a Ministry of Foreign Affairs and an Institute for Foreign Languages. When Tongzhi came of age in 1873, he received the ambassadors of Japan, Russia, Britain, France, Holland and United States of America at court without the traditional kowtow. Foreigners, who had virtually monopolized coastal trade since 1860, were now enlisted to collect revenue and excise duties in the Imperial Maritime Customs Service, a foreign-staffed arm of the Chinese government run by an Englishman, Robert Hart.

Tongzhi was a cipher. Although he had assumed full imperial powers, Cixi continued to control state affairs. Reacting against her domination, Tongzhi turned to the eunuchs who pampered his natural instincts for dissipation. At 15, he was visiting brothels incognito and his bisexual debauchery gave him venereal disease while his drinking seriously undermined his health. At 16, Cixi married him to Alute, the daughter of a powerful Manchu clan, and tried to persuade him to rebuild a residence in part of Qianlong's Summer Palace where certain stone and metal buildings had survived the 1860 sacking. When Kong vetoed the

IMPERIAL COLLAPSE

By the 19th century, the imperial system was close to collapse. An excessive reliance on neo-Confucian orthodoxy with its emphasis on the classics and veneration for the emperor led to imperial isolation and official rigidity. The examination system ossified, rigorously confined to textual and stylistic exercises with no relevance to the modern world. The bureaucracy was grossly understaffed – a district manager often governed 300 sq miles (780 sq km) and a quarter of a million people – and revenues were increasingly gathered by local gentry 'tax farmers', who exempted themselves from taxation in return for raising levies on the peasants. The system was bedevilled by excessive centralization (all major decisions needed imperial approval) and the need to duplicate all documents into Manchu and Chinese. The entire administration was riddled with corruption. Eunuch extortions and the custom of 'squeeze', whereby each official kept part of the moneys passing through his hands, brought public services to a standstill.

China's weakness whetted foreign appetites and each new military defeat brought crushing indemnities leading to further foreign control of finances and loss of territory. Two years after the Japanese victory in 1895, Germany seized the Qingdao peninsula in Shandong; a year later the British took Weihaiwei, the Russians Dalien and the Liaodong peninsula; while the French, having occupied Vietnam, settled in Guangdong. The process of foreign occupation was speeded by a Most Favoured Nation agreement, by which the Chinese were obliged to treat all foreign powers equally, so that concessions won by one nation, were automatically gained by all the others.

Rebellions were largely caused by famine and corruption. Here peasants seize a cargo of grain from the local authorities.

(*Above*) The Forbidden City on the occasion of Guangxu's wedding. Contemporary coloured woodcut.

QING	
GUANGXU	**PUYI**
Born	*Born*
1871, as Zai Tian	1905, as Aisin
Accession	Gioro Puyi (known
1875, as Guangxu	to Europeans as
Father	Henry Puyi)
Yi Huan, prince Jun	*Accession*
(2nd son of)	1909
Mother	*Father*
Cixi's younger	prince Chun II, the
sister	brother of Guangxu,
Wife	and grand-nephew
empress Long Yu,	of Cixi
Xiao Ding (died	*Ousted*
1913)	1911
Children	*Died*
none	1967
Died	*Burial*
1908	cremated in Beijing
Tomb	*Temple name*
Chongling, Western	Xuandi ('Proclaimed
Tombs, Hebei	Emperor'); also
Temple name	Xuanzong
Dezong ('Virtuous	
Ancestor')	

project on grounds of expense, Tongzhi wept and raged in vain. In 1874 he caught smallpox and, after an apparent recovery, died suddenly, leading to suspicions that Cixi, fearing Alute's influence over him, was responsible. Blatantly flouting the principles of succession, Cixi installed her own nephew, the four-year-old son of her sister who had married Xianfeng's brother, promising that his first son would be regarded as Tongzhi's proper heir. Two months later, Alute committed suicide. Once again the two dowager-empresses governed from behind the curtain and after Xiao Chen's death in 1881, Cixi ruled supreme. In 1887, **Guangxu** (1875–1908) came of age but Cixi hung on for another two years to 'instruct him in state affairs'.

Cixi was an astute manipulator, playing her ministers against each other in order to retain power. The natural isolation of her position was reinforced by her violent rages which deterred criticism and unwelcome information, and she never seems to have appreciated the dire condition of the empire. She was personally vivacious, only 5 ft (152 cm) tall but wore 6 inch (15 cm) heels, heavy makeup with rouged cheeks and whitened face and, like other Manchu ladies, cultivated long fingernails, scratching the cheeks of servant girls when displeased. Her morals were dubious; certain young officers and eunuchs freely enjoyed her company and she rewarded them with profitable posts. (On her favourite eunuch An Dehai's death, observers were shocked to see that 'his teapot had a spout'.) Rapacious and extravagant, Cixi poured money into the Forbidden City and the Summer Palace (finally restored in 1888) where she had a special theatre built and diverted money earmarked for modernizing the naval fleet to build a marble boat on the lake.

Guangxu, slightly built, with large melancholy eyes and a sensitive mouth, had chronic lung trouble. His voice was 'light and thin like a mosquito'. As a child he was terrified of Cixi, running to his tutor on her

I have often thought that I am the most clever woman that ever lived, and others cannot compare with me.... Although I have heard much about Queen Victoria ... and read a part of her life which someone has translated into Chinese, still I don't think her life was half so interesting and eventful as mine.... She had the able men of parliament at the back of her at all times ... and had really nothing to say about the policy of the country. Now look at me, I have 400,000,000 people dependent on my judgment ...

Cixi, quoted by the princess Der Ling in
Two Years in the Forbidden City

Portrait of Cixi, painted from a photograph taken in 1903.

approach 'as if facing lions and tigers'. He never grew out of this fear. Well-educated, interested in Western technology and even learning English, Guangxu was a conscientious ruler with strong moral convictions, bitterly aware of his country's helplessness and need for modernization. As the foreign stranglehold on China tightened, the foreigners' control of emerging industries and the new railways, their financial hold on the economy and imperious behaviour – particularly that of the missionaries – infuriated the population and prompted serious demands for reform. In 1894, the Chinese army and fleet were destroyed in a devastating defeat by the Japanese over Korea; under the Treaty of Shimonoseki (1895), China had to pay a crippling indemnity and cede territory to Japan. The Europeans quickly profited from her defenceless situation, seizing 'concessions' along the coast.

In these desperate straits, Guangxu supported a group of reformers led by Kang Yuwei (1858–1927). In 1898 a series of reforms derived from Russian and Japanese models to modernize education and check corruption were imposed against the opposition of the conservatives. From her retirement in the Summer Palace, where she still supervised state affairs, Cixi opposed the movement and when Guangxu's plans to curb her were betrayed, she struck swiftly, imprisoning the emperor in the Summer Palace and crushing the 'Hundred Days' reforms' with edicts issued in his name.

Guangxu never recovered, remaining a virtual prisoner for the rest of his life. Cixi even walled up the windows of his quarters in the Summer Palace. He enjoyed Western support, however, and Cixi dared not dethrone him. Instead she tried to rid herself of Westerners by supporting the violently xenophobic Boxer Movement which was sweeping China. Fortified by magic spells promising protection against modern weapons, the Boxers attacked all foreigners and, encouraged by Cixi, advanced on Beijing where they besieged the foreign legations. When a Western relief force arrived, Cixi forced the emperor to flee to Xi'an disguised as a peasant in a cart. His favourite consort, the beautiful Pearl Concubine, urged him to remain and face the enemy, but Cixi had her drowned in a palace well, and Beijing and the Forbidden City were left to the mercy of Western troops.

After sacking the new Summer Palace, the Westerners imposed numerous demands including a staggering indemnity of some 450 million oz (12.7 million kg) of silver (*c.* $333 million), to be deducted from customs and salt revenues over 40 years, and the right to fortify and garrison the Legation Quarter

THE BOXER REBELLION

The Boxers (based on the secret society of 'Righteous and Harmonious Fists') began in 1898 as a typical anti-dynastic peasant rebellion supported by the hungry and dispossessed. They rapidly acquired an anti-foreign, particularly anti-Christian, complexion, attributing China's misery to the foreigners and were soon supported by anti-foreign, anti-reform elements at court. They adopted the slogan 'Support the Qing, destroy the foreigner'. Invoking supernatural support, they believed their magical amulets and spells gave them immunity to foreign bullets.

After initial hesitation, Cixi wholeheartedly supported the movement, appointing the pro-Boxer Manchu prince Duan as head of the Foreign Office. When the rebels, chanting 'Burn, burn, burn. Kill, kill, kill', entered Beijing and besieged the Legation Quarter where all foreigners had gathered, Cixi declared war on Britain, the USA, France, Germany, Austria, Belgium, Holland and Japan. The siege lasted 55 days, with some of the worst fighting around the Catholic cathedral

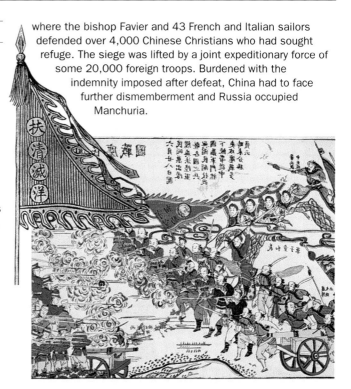

where the bishop Favier and 43 French and Italian sailors defended over 4,000 Chinese Christians who had sought refuge. The siege was lifted by a joint expeditionary force of some 20,000 foreign troops. Burdened with the indemnity imposed after defeat, China had to face further dismemberment and Russia occupied Manchuria.

(Above right) This Boxer banner bears the inscription 'Support the Qing, destroy the foreigner'.

(Right) Contemporary print of Boxer forces attacking British and French troops.

(Below) Contemporary print of foreign prisoners brought before General Tung.

in Beijing. In January 1902, the court returned to Beijing and Cixi cordially received foreign envoys and later, their ladies in the Forbidden City.

Cixi and her ministers now began reluctantly to introduce reforms along the lines of the 1898 measures, modernizing education and establishing a modern police force. In 1905, the traditional examination system based on the classics was abolished, a bitter blow to the conservative scholar-gentry. In 1908, she announced a nine-year plan for constitutional reform, but it was too late. After a slight stroke, the 'old Buddha', as she was popularly known, died aged 73 on 15 November 1908, and it was announced that Guangxu, aged 37, who had retained his reforming enthusiasm, had died the previous day. Cixi had named her three-year-old great-nephew, **Puyi** (1909–1911), as Heir, and power passed to a group of ignorant, vainglorious Manchu princes with Puyi's father, the prince Chun II, as regent.

While the Manchus stumbled towards reform, a more serious movement was afoot. After the 1898 fiasco, many Chinese intellectuals had fled to Japan – by 1906, 15,000 Chinese were there studying 'dangerous thoughts'. Under Dr Sun Yatsen – the father of the republic who had in 1894 founded the 'Revive China' secret society – a nationalist republican movement developed with undercover branches inside China. On 9 October 1911, the accidental detonation of a bomb in Wuhan ignited an anti-Manchu rebellion which spread throughout the empire. Sun Yatsen returned to China and was elected provisional president of the Chinese republic in Nanjing. General Yuan Shikai, commander of the northern troops, negotiated a settlement with the Manchus whereby Puyi, the emperor Xuanzong, bowed 'to the Mandate of Heaven ... manifested through the wish of the people' and in February 1912, Sun Yatsen resigned to allow Yuan Shikai to become the first president.

After 2,000 years the imperial system had collapsed almost without a struggle. It had been one of the most successful political systems ever devised. Its extraordinary

(*Below*) Puyi (seated) with his tutor, Reginald Johnson, in the gardens of the Forbidden City.

(*Right*) A contemporary impression of the anti-Manchu rebellion in 1911 which led to the fall of the imperial system.

success had lain in its flexibility and cosmic nature, providing a philosophical and moral basis for the relationship between human society and heaven. It provided a centralized form of government with a safety valve based on morality. If the emperor erred, he forfeited the divine mantle and could be replaced, but, until the late 19th century, the system as such was never questioned.

It fell because it had ceased to adapt and no longer presented an acceptable view of reality. The rise of the West shattered the notion of a Middle Kingdom with a special relationship to heaven; the modern age with industrialization created a society too large and complex for a system in which, theoretically at least, all power rested ultimately with one man, and under the Manchus, the underlying philosophy ossified. Their rigid insistence on obedience and veneration for the emperor stifled indigenous intellectual developments which might have modernized it. The imperial system became associated with the non-Chinese Manchus and much of the impetus for the 1911 revolution was the conscious desire to return to Chinese roots. On 15 February 1912, Sun Yatsen solemnly gave the land back to the imperial ancestors in a ceremony at the tomb of the first Ming emperor, Hongwu, in Nanjing.

Epilogue

Puyi was allowed to remain in the Forbidden City with a stipend of $4 million per year and all the imperial treasures until 1924 when he was expelled by a warlord. Seeking protection in the Japanese concession in Tientsin (Tianjin), he was made puppet emperor of Manchuria under the Japanese in 1934. A prisoner of the Soviets in 1945, after years of re-education under the Communist government, Puyi ended his life as a gardener in the People's Republic of China, dying in 1967.

SELECT BIBLIOGRAPHY

The following list gives some of the main sources for further information; more detailed bibliographies will be found in these works, particularly in the *Cambridge History of China*.

General

Arlington, L. and Lewisohn, W. *In Search of Old Peking*. Peking 1935, reprint New York 1967.

Birch, C. ed. *Anthology of Chinese Literature*. Harmondsworth 1967.

Cameron, N. *Peking, A Tale of Three Cities*. New York and Tokyo 1965.

– *Barbarians and Mandarins*. New York and Tokyo 1970.

Carrington-Goodrich, L. *A Short History of the Chinese People*. London 1948.

Ch'en,K. *The Chinese Transformation of Buddhism*. Princeton University Press 1973.

Clunas, C. *Art in China*. Oxford 1997.

Dun, J. Li. *The Essence of Chinese Civilization*. Toronto and London 1967.

Ebrey, P. *Cambridge Illustrated History of China*. Cambridge 1996.

Fisher, R. *Buddhist Art and Architecture*. Singapore 1993.

Fitzgerald, C.P. *China, A Short Cultural History*. London 1965.

Gernet, J. *A History of Chinese Civilization*. Transl. J.R. Foster. Cambridge 1982.

Giles, H. *A Chinese Biographical Dictionary*. London 1898.

Lu Hsun [Xun]. *A Brief History of Chinese Fiction*. Peking 1959.

Medley, M. *The Chinese Potter*. Oxford 1976.

Meishu Yishu [Great Treasury of Chinese Arts], Sculpture, vol.2, Qin, Han (Beijing 1985); vol. 3, Wei, Jin, Northern and Southern Dynasties (Beijing 1988); vol. 4, Sui, Tang (Beijing 1988); vol.5, Five Dynasties, Song (Beijing 1988); vol. 6, Yuan, Ming, Qing (Beijing 1988). These volumes contain excellent illustrations of the major sculptural works of each period; the text is in Chinese.

Paludan, A. *The Chinese Spirit Road – the Classical Tradition of Stone Tomb Sculpture*. New Haven 1991.

– *Chinese Tomb Figurines*. Hong Kong 1994.

Rawson, J. ed. *Chinese Art*. British Museum, London 1992.

Reischauer, E.O. and Fairbanks, J.K. *East Asia, The Great Tradition*, vol.1. Boston 1958.

Sickman, L. and Soper, A. *The Art and Architecture of China*, Harmondsworth 1971.

Sullivan, M. *A Short History of Chinese Art*. London 1967, Hong Kong 1982.

Twitchett, D and Fairbank, J.F., eds. *Cambridge History of China*,
– vol.1, *The Qin and Han Empires*. eds. Twitchett, D. and Loewe, M. 1986;
– vol.3, part 1, *Sui and T'ang China*. eds. Twitchett and Fairbank 1979;
– vol.6, *Alien Regimes and Border States*. eds. Franke, H. and Twitchett, D.1994;
– vol. 7, part 1, *The Ming Dynasty*. eds. Mote, F. and Twitchett, D. 1988;
– vol.10, part 1, *Late Ch'ing*. eds. Twitchett and Fairbank, 1978.

Waley, A. *Chinese Poems*. London 1946.

– *Anthology of Chinese Literature*. Harmondsworth 1967.

Watson, W. *Art of Dynastic China*. New York 1981.

Welch, H. and Seidel, A. *Facets of Taoism*. New Haven 1979.

Wood, F. *China*. Blue Guide. London 1992.

Wright, A. *Buddhism in Chinese History*. California and London 1959.

Zhewen, Luo. *China's Imperial Tombs and Mausoleums*. Beijing 1993.

Zurcher, E. *The Buddhist Conquest of China*, 2 vols. Leiden 1972.

Qin, Han

Cotterell, A. *The First Emperor of China*. New York 1981.

Fontein, J. and Wu Tung. *Han and T'ang Murals*. Boston 1976.

Ledderose, L. and Schlombs, A. *Jenseits des Grossen Mauer, Der Erste Kaiser von China und seine Terrakotta-Armee*. Munich 1990.

Loewe, M. *Chinese Ideas of Life and Death*. London 1982.

Pirazzoli-t'Serstevens, M. *The Han Dynasty*. New York 1982.

Rawson, J., ed. *Mysteries of Ancient China*. London 1996.

Szuma Chien [Sima Qian]. *Records of the Historian*, selections transl. Yang Hsienyi and Gladys Yang. Beijing 1979.

Wang Zhongshu. *Han Civilization*. New Haven 1982.

Wen Fong ed. *The Great Bronze Age of China*. New York 1980.

Three Kingdoms, Northern and Southern Dynasties

Grantham, A. *Hills of Blue*. London 1927.

Till, B. and Swart, P. *In Search of Old Nanking*. Hong Kong 1982.

Zhong, Luo Guan. *Romance of the Three Kingdoms*. Transl. C.H. Brewitt-Taylor. Shanghai 1925, republished Singapore 1985.

Sui, Tang and Song

Barrett, T.H. *Taoism under the T'ang*. London 1996.

Capon, E. *Tang China*. London 1989.

Ebrey, P. *Religion and Society in T'ang and Sung China*. Honolulu 1993.

Fitzgerald, C.P. *Son of Heaven, A Biography of Li Shih-Min, founder of the T'ang Dynasty*. Cambridge University Press 1933.

– *The Empress Wu*. London 1956.

Franke, H. ed. *Sung Biographies*. 4 vols. Wiesbaden 1976.

Rossabi, M. ed. *China among Equals*. California 1983.

Schafer, E. *The Golden Peaches of Samarkand*. University of California Press: Berkeley and Los Angeles 1963.

Yuan

Morgan, D. *The Mongols*. Oxford 1986.

Rossabi, M., ed. *Khubilai Khan*. California 1988.

Wood, F. *Did Marco Polo go to China?*. London 1995.

Ming, Qing

Beurdely, C. and M. *Giuseppe Castiglione*. Fribourg 1971; English ed. London 1972.

Bickers, R. *Ritual and Diplomacy, The Macartney Mission to China, 1792-1294*. London 1993.

Carrington-Goodrich, L. and Fang Chaoying, ed. *Dictionary of Ming Biography*, 2 vols. New York and London 1976.

Holdsworth M. and Courtauld, C. *The Forbidden City – the Great Within*. London 1995.

Huang, R. *1587 – A Year of No Significance*. New Haven 1981.

Hucker, C. *The Traditional Chinese State in Ming Times*. Arizona 1961.

Hummell, A. ed. *Eminent Chinese of the Ch'ing Period*. Washington 1943, reprint Taipei 1967.

Paludan, A. *The Imperial Ming Tombs*. New Haven and Hong Kong 1981.

– *The Ming Tombs*. Hong Kong 1991.

Ricci, M. *China in the Sixteenth Century: the Journals of Matteo Ricci, 1583-1610*. tranls. Gallagher, L. New York 1953.

Spence, J. *Emperor of China, Self-Portrait of K'ang-hsi*. Penguin Books USA 1974.

– *God's Chinese Son*. New York 1996.

Warner, M. *The Dragon Empress*. London 1972.

ILLUSTRATION AND TEXT CREDITS

a=above, c=centre, b=bottom, l=left, r=right

The following abbreviations are used to identify sources and locate illustrations. AP – Ann Paludan; BL – By Kind Permission of the British Library; BM – Copyright The British Museum; CL/CI – Catherine Lawrence and Claire Ivison (cartographers); IPM – Imperial Palace Museum, Beijing; MFA – Courtesy, Museum of Fine Arts, Boston; NPM – The National Palace Museum, Taipei, Taiwan, Republic of China; PW – Philip Winton (illustrator); RHPL – Robert Harding Picture Library; TW – Tracy Wellman (illustrator); WFA – Werner Forman Archive.
All maps drawn using Mountain High Maps® Copyright 1993 Digital Wisdom, Inc.

The author would like to thank Mr. Bai Jingcheng for the characters used on p. 10 and Mrs. Luo Bing who drew the characters used throughout for the reign titles.

1 V&A Picture Library. 2 NPM. 5a-b NPM; NPM; IPM; IPM. 6l RHPL; b NPM. 7a BL. 8a&b BL. 9a NPM; b BM. 10-11 CL/CI. 12a BL; b BL. 15l&cl BL; cr&r MFA, Denman Waldo Ross Collection. 16 BL. 17 Shaanxi Historical Museum, Xian. 18al Morning Glory Publishers, Beijing; bl © 1997 Daniel Schwartz/Lookat Photos. 18-19 c.C.Bowman/RHPL. 19al CL/CI; bl Morning Glory Publishers, Beijing. 20 Chinese Classical Architecture, 1979. 20-21 PW. 21c Morning Glory Publishers, Beijing; b Historical Relics Unearthed in New China, 1972. 22-23 © 1997 Daniel Schwartz/Lookat Photos. 24cl TW; r RHPL; r Shaanxi Provincial Museum, Xian; b Museum of Qin Shihuangdi's tomb, Mount Li, Shaanxi. 25a,c&br Shaanxi Provincial Museum, Xian; bl TW. 26a BL. 28 BL. 29 Chinese Classical Architecture, 1979. 30l PW; c Chinese Classical Architecture, 1979; b Science Museum/Science and Society Photo Library. 31 Morning Glory Publishers, Beijing. 32r China Pictorial, Beijing; bl Private Collection; br Luoyang City Museum, Henan Province. 34l Morning Glory Publishers, Beijing; r Institute of Archaeology, Beijing; b Hebei Provincial Museum. 35c Historical Relics Unearthed in New China, 1972; br BM. 36 O.Louis Mazzatenta/National Geographic Image Collection. 38 CL/CI. 39a&b Morning Glory Publishers, Beijing. 41 BL. 43a BL; b NPM. 44 BL. 45a Sichuan Provincial Museum, Chengdu; c Tokyo National Museum; b SichuanProvincial Museum, Chengdu. 46a-b AP. 47a-b AP. 48a Morning Glory Publishers, Beijing; b Royal Ontario Museum, Canada. 49 NPM. 52 NPM. 53l BL; c BL; br Historical Relics Unearthed in New China, 1972. 54 Institute of Archaeology, Beijing. 55 BL. 56bl WFA. 57al CL/CI; ar AP; c BM; b G&P Corrigan/RHPL. 58l Shaanxi Provincial Museum, Xian; c Ashmolean Museum, Oxford; cr Sichuan Provincial Museum, Chengdu; b China Pictorial, Beijing. 59a Jingzhou Regional Museum, Hubei; cl The Nelson-Atkins Museum of Art, Kansas City, Missouri; cr Henan Provincial Museum, Zhengzhou; b BM. 61l,cl&cr MFA, Denman Waldo Ross Collection. r BL. 63 MFA, Denman Waldo Ross Collection . 64a CL/CI; b Eileen Tweedy. 70 BM. 72 AP. 74a BL. 75b AP. 76al&r AP; b BM. 77 MFA, Denman Waldo Ross Collection. 78a CL/CI; bl WFA; br MFA, Caroline Balch Allen

and Cranemore Nesmith Wallace Funds . 79a&c AP; b WFA. 80 The Nelson-Atkins Museum of Art, Kansas City, Missouri. 81 Chinese Classical Architecture, 1979. 82 MFA, Denman Waldo Ross Collection. 84 MFA, Chinese and Japanese Special Fund . 85a RHPL; br CL/CI. 86a WFA; bl MFA; br The Nelson-Atkins Museum of Art, Kansas City, Missouri. 87 MFA, Denman Waldo Ross Collection. 88 BL. 89c Photo c.Bibliothèque Nationale de France, Paris; b NPM. 90 NPM. 90-91 IPM. 91 BM/WFA. 92al Royal Ontario Museum, Canada; ar Seattle Art Museum, Eugene Fuller Memorial Collection; b Wahbi al-Hariri, The Georgetown Design Group Inc. 93a Vatican Museums; b AP. 94c WFA/Courtesy Sotheby's, London; bl University of Pennsylvania Museum, Philadelphia; br AP. 95a Shaanxi Historical Museum, Xian; c Shaanxi Provincial Museum, Xian; b Morning Glory Publishers, Beijing. 96 BL. 97l Musée Guimet, Paris; r Colin Penn. 98a Shaanxi Historical Museum, Xian; b BL. 99 WFA. 100 AP. 101 AP. 102l AP; c WFA; b AP. 103a WFA; c&b Shaanxi Historical Museum, Xian. 104 BL. 105 Cheng Yan/ffotograff. 106c PW; bl Renuka Madan; br Shaanxi Historical Museum. Xian. 107a RHPL; b Staatliche Museen zu Berlin, © bpk. 108 BL. 109a Private Collection; b AP. 110 Morning Glory Publishers, Beijing. 111a Fujita Art Museum, Osaka; cl BM; cr&b AP. 113 BL. 114 l-r WFA. 115l WFA; b Shaanxi Historical Museum, Xian. 116 Gulbenkian Museum of Oriental Art, Durham. 117 AP. 119l&cl NPM; cr BL; r NPM. 121a CL/CI; b NPM. 123a NPM; b AP. 124 AP. 126 Musée Guimet, Paris. 127 AP. 128 IPM. 129 NPM. 131al NPM; ar AP; b NPM. 133a BL; c Museum für Völkerkunde, Berlin, © bpk; b Photo © Bibliothèque Nationale deFrance, Paris.134a Photo © Bibliothèque Nationale de France, Paris; b BM. 135br Percival David Foundation for Chinese Art, London. 137 BL. 138a NPM; bl Renuka Madan. 139a Ashmolean Museum, Oxford; b NPM. 140l NPM; r Freer Gallery of Art, Washington D.C. 141a NPM; c BM; b MFA. 143 IPM. 145 NPM. 146 AP. 147a BL; b BL. 149a NPM; b Courtesy, Asiatic Society of Bengal. 150a NPM; bl BL; br Colin Penn. 151 AP. 152c IPM; bl CL/CI. 153a&b AP. 154 NPM. 155 Copyright © 1997 by The Metropolitan Museum of Art, New York. Purchase, Lila Acheson Wallace Gift, 1992 (1992.54). 157a IPM; b Chinese Classical Architecture, 1979. 159l&cl NPM; cr IPM; r © The Cleveland Museum of Art, 1997, John L. Severence Fund, 1969.31. 160 BL. 161l&r AP; 162a BL; b AP. 164a PW; bl AP; br RHPL. 165a RHPL; b G&P Corrigan/RHPL. 166a Science Museum/Science and Society Picture Library; c CL/CI; bc Cambridge University Library; br Philadelphia Museum of Art: Given by John T. Dorrance. 167a NPM; b Cambridge University Library.168a Charles Aithie/ffotograff; c TW; b RHPL. 169a V&A Picture Library; b NPM. 171 V&A Picture Library. 172 AP. 173l NPM; b AP. 174 a NPM; b AP. 175 NPM. 176 Singer © BBC/RHPL. 177 NPM. 178 Gulbenkian Museum of Oriental Art, Durham. 179 AP. 180-181 NPM. 181 BL. 182 AP. 183 BM. 184al,ar&bl AP; br Sarah Martin and Renuka Madan. 185a,c&br AP; bl PW. 186a&br J.B. du Holde, Description of the Geography and History of China, 1735; bl John Thomson, Illustrations of China and Its People, 1873. 187 AP. 188br Private Collection. 189a Percival David Foundation of Chinese Art, London; c NPM; b Percival David Foundation of Chinese Art, London. 190 BL. 191a BL; b AP. 192 IPM. 193 IPM. 194a Musée Guimet, Paris; b BL. 195c IPM; b AP. 196 © The Cleveland Museum of Art, 1997, John L. Severence Fund, 1969.31. 197c Photo © Bibliothèque Nationale de France, Paris, b RHPL. 198a Musée Guimet, Paris; b AP. 199 Musée Guimet, Paris. 200a BM; b Private Collection. 201 BM. 203a

National Maritime Museum, Greenwich; b BL. 204 Hulton Getty. 206a IPM; b The Peabody Museum of Salem. 207a BL; bl BM; br National Maritime Museum, Greenwich. 208 J.M. Callery and M Yvan, History of the Insurrection in China, 1853. 209 L'Illustration, 22 December 1860. 210l John Thomson, Illustrations of China and Its People, 1873; b John Massey Stewart. 211a AP; b Tim Poole. 212 BL. 213 IPM. 214 WFA/Private Collection. 215 BM. 217 National Museum of Ethnology, Leiden

Sources of quotations

The quotations used in this book are taken from the following sources:

Beurdeley, Cecile and Michel Guiseppe Castiglione [London, 1972] (used on p. 192, p. 197).
Birch, Cyril ed. Penguin Anthology of Chinese Literature [Harmondsworth, 1965] (used on p. 104).
Cahill, James Chinese Paintings XI–XIV Centuries [Elek Books, London] (used on p.132).
Twitchett and Fairbank eds. Cambridge History of China vol. 3, part 1, Sui and T'ang China [Cambridge, 1979] (used on p. 89, p. 98).
Cameron, Nigel and Brake, Brian Peking, A Tale of Three Cities [New York and Tokyo, 1970] (used on p. 187).
Cameron, Nigel Barbarians and Mandarins [New York and Tokyo, 1970] (used on p. 196, p. 208).
Capon, Edmund Tang China [London 1989] (used on p. 106).
Carrington-Goodrich, L. A Short History of the Chinese People [London, 1948] (used on p. 120).
Carrington-Goodrich, L. ed. Dictionary of Ming Biography vol. 1 [Columbia University Press, 1976] (used on p. 163, p. 167, p. 170).
Chang Hsin-pao Commissioner Lin and the Opium War [Harvard University Press, 1964] (used on p. 207).
Cordier, H. Histoire Generale de la Chine vol 3 1920-21 (used p. 197).
Cotterell, Arthur The First Emperor of China [New York, 1981] (used on p. 20, p. 27).
de Groot, Jan Jakob Maria The Religious System of China [reprint Taipei, 1967] (used on p. 184).
Princess Der Ling Two Years in the Forbidden City [used on p. 214].
Dun, J. Li The Essence of Chinese Civilization [Toronto, 1967] (used on p. 28, p.36, p. 40).
Fitzgerald, C.P. China [London, 1935] (used on p. 66).
Giles, H. A. A Chinese Biographical Dictionary [London, 1898] (used on p. 88).
Guisso R. L. et al The First Emperor of China [London, 1989] (used on p. 16).
Hawkes, David transl. The Songs of the South [Harmondsworth, 1985] (used on p. 49).
Zhong, Luo Guan Romance of the Three Kingdoms vol 2, transl. C.H. Brewitt-Taylor [reprint Singapore, 1985] (used p. 63, p. 65).
Moule and Pelliott, Marco Polo [London, 1938] (used on p. 148).
Rossabi, Morris ed. China Among Equals [California, 1983] (used on p. 125, p. 142).
Spence, Jonathan Emperor of China: Self-Portrait of K'ang-hsi [Harmondsworth, 1974] (used on pp. 191–192).
Spence, Jonathan God's Chinese Son [New York, 1996] (used on p. 208).
Spence, Jonathan The China Helpers [London 1969] (used on p. 207).
Waley, Arthur Chinese Poems [London, 1971] (used on p. 106).
Waley, Arthur Anthology of Chinese Literature [Harmondsworth, 1967] (used on p. 108).
Wright, Arthur Buddhism in Chinese History [Stanford, 1959] (used on p. 80, p. 82).

Index

Page numbers in *italic* refer to illustrations on the relevant pages

(e) emperor

abacus 130
Aberhai, Manchu 190
Academy of Painting 134, 138, 140
acrobats 58
A-fang, palace 20, 21
Afghanistan 56
Aidi, Han (e) 14, 40, 42
Aidi, E. Jin (e) 60, 66, 69, 70
Aidi, Tang (e) 60, 112, 113, 117
Aisin Gioro Puyi *see* Puyi, Qing (e)
alcohol 37, 45, 152
Alopen, monk 93
Altan Khan 179, 180
Alute, Qing empress 212, 213
Ambassadors 96, 103, 161, 166, 202, 207, 212, *98, 127*
Amoy (Xiamen), Fujian 207
Amur 167, 193
Analects of Confucius 32
Andi, Han (e) 14
Andi, E. Jin (e) 60, 66, 69, 71
An Lushan, revolt 109, 112, 115
Annam 128, 153, 161, 167, 169
An Shigao, missionary 78
Antun (Marcus Aurelius Antonius) 56
Arabic, Arabs 96, 109, 117, 127, 139, 142, 166, 198
Aragibag, Yuan 156
Arigh Boke, Yuan 149, 156
Attiret, Denis, Jesuit 197
Austria 215
Ayurbarwada, Yuan (e) 118, 148, 156

Bactria 56
Bai Juyi, poet *108*
Baita si (White Dagoba temple) 153
Ban Chao, general 48
Banner system 190, 194
Baodingshan, Dazu 146
Bayan, Mongol general 146
Bayan, Mongol minister 157
Beijing, as capital: Jin 137, 147; Yuan (Dadu) 148, 150, 151; Ming 20, 161, 163, 164, 171; Qing 187, 214, 215
Belgium 215
Benoit, Michel, Jesuit 197, 199
Bezeklik 107
Bing Di, Song (e) 118, 136, 146–47
Bi Sheng (Song) 133
Board of Censors 125
Borneo, King of, 161
Boxer movement 214, 215
bridges 105, 150, *84, 150*

Britain, British 202, 206, 207, 208, 209, 212, 215
Buddha 48, 78, 79, 111, *86, 99, 101*
Buddhism, arrival and spread of, 56, 57,61, 69, 78–79, 80; imperial sponsors 73, 74, 76, 83, 87, 91, 99, 101, 113, 147, 151, 160, 167; pilgrims 70, 71, 87, 181; images *57, 78, 79, 80, 99, 110–11, 133, 146;* persecution of, 86, 116, 117, 151, 178
Burma 56, 68, 182, 198, 202
'Burning of the Books' 21, 31, 55, *26*

Cai Lun, inventor 53
calligraphy 134; examples of *69, 135 see also* Writing
canals 37, 82, 83, 87, 105, 149, 162 *see also* Grand Canal
Cang Wu Wang, Liu Song (e) 60, 67, 71, 72
Canton *see* Guangzhou
Cao Cao 55, 63
Cao Pi 55, 63
Castiglione, Giuseppe, Jesuit 197, 198, 199
Ceylon 143, 166
Chabi, Yuan empress 153, *154*
Champa *see* Vietnam
Chang'an, as capital 15, 29, 55, 56, 102, 107, *29, 30* (map), *106;* occupation of 44, 68, 109, 112, 117 *see also* Xi'an
Changling, Ming mausoleum 184, *185*
Changsha, Hunan 35
Changxin Palace 35
Chengde, Hebei (Jehol) 198, 199, 202, 205, 209
Chengdi, Han (e) 14, 40, 42, *41*
Chengdi, E. Jin (e) 60, 66, 69, 70
Chengdu, Sichuan 37, 121, 128,
Chenghua, Ming (e) 158, 170, 173–74, 178, 189
Chengzu, Ming *see* Yongle, Ming (e)
Chengzong, Yuan (e) *see* Temur Oljeitu
Chen She, rebel 27
Chongdi, Han (e) 14, 50, 51
Chong Mao, Tang prince 101
Chongzhen, Ming (e) 158, 170, 187
Christianity, Christians 151, 156, 183, 186, 197, 208, 209, 215 *see also* Nestorian Christianity
Chu, Kingdom of, 29
Chudi, Later Jin (e) 118, 120, 121
Chun II, Manchu prince 216
cities 9, 30, 102, *106,* 142, 150
Cixi, Qing empress 209, 210–16 *passim, 214*
Coal Hill, Beijing 165
Compass 130, 139, *166*
Confucius 6, 124, 172, *6, 32*
Confucianism 31–36 *passim,* 82; texts 65, 138; images *6, 32 see also* neo–Confucianism
Coromandel 161
currency 43, 48, 105, 117, 128, 143, 181

Dadu 150, 151, 153, 157, 164
Dai, Lady, tomb of, 35
Daizong, Tang (e) 60, 112–13
Dalai Lama 198
Dali *see* Yunnan
Dalien, Liaoning 212
Danyang 72, 76
Dao de Jing 32, 75
Daoguang, Qing (e) 158, 204, 205–06, 208, *206*
Daoism 8, 32, 69, 75; imperial sponsors 76, 87, 91, 101, 108, 115, 135, 151, 178–79; popular movements 54, 205; *189*
Datong, Shanxi 78, 79, 80
Dazu, Sichuan 146
Dehao, Song prince 144
Dengfeng, Henan 81, 151
Dezong, Tang (e) 60, 112, 113, *113*
Dezong, Qing *see* Guangxu, Qing (e)
Diamond Sutra 133
Difang *see* Xiaozong, Song (e)
Dingling, Ming mausoleum 184, *185*
Dong Hunhou, Qi (e) 60, 67, 73
Dorghon, Manchu regent 191
'Dragon Fleet' 87
Duan, Qing prince 215
Duanzong, Song (e) 118, 136, 146–47
Du Fu, poet 105, 108
Dujiang Weir, Guanxian, Sichuan 47
Dunhuang 57, 89, 97, 110, 111, 133, 198
Duzong, Song (e) 118, 136, 145, 146

East Africa 143, 166, 167
Eastern Tombs, Qing 191
East India Co. 202
Egypt 143, 166
elephants 94, 153, 177, 184
'Embroidered Brocade Guards' 162
envoy, foreign, 91, 144, 167, 182, 216 (*see* also Ambassadors)
Er Shi, Qin (Second Emperor) (e) 9, 17, 27
Esen Khan 170, 171
eunuchs, power of 15, 27, 50, 52, 113, 165, 167, 169, 171, 172, 178, 179; *coups* 51, 117; *115, 172*
Europe, European 166, 183, 186, 191, 208
Examinations 33, 45, 91, 105, 134, 142, 145, 156, 163, 212, 216

fabrics *57*
'factories' 207, *206*
Fa Men temple, Xi'an 110
Fan Guan, painter 140
Fan Min, tomb of 47
Fashions (clothing) 25, 92, 93, 95, 107, 114, 153, 172, 176, 182, 183, *25, 92*
Favier, Bishop 215
Fa Xian, pilgrim 70, 71
Feidi, Later Tang (e) 118, 120
Feidi, Wu (e) 60, 62
Ferghana 38, 39, 56

First Emperor *see* Shihuangdi
'Five Pecks of Rice' 54
Florence, Florentine 197
footbinding 135, 193, *135*
Flemish 151
Forbidden City 164–65, 176, 184; building of 163; *164–65, 210, 213, 216*
France, French 151, 197, 202, 207, 208, 209, 212, 215
Fujian 37, 75, 147, 180, 191
Fulin *see* Shunzhi, Qing (e)
Fuzhou, Fujian 147, 207

Galdan, nomadic chief 193
Gansu 17, 18, 38, 46, 56, 94, 110, 161
Gaochang, Central Asia 57
Gaocheng zhen, Dengfeng, Henan 151
Gaodi, W. Han, (e) 14, 28–31, 33, 44, 73, 160, *15, 28*
Gaodi, Qi (e) 60, 67, 72, 73
Gao Gui Xiang Gong, Wei (e) 60, 62, 63, 65
Gaozong, Qing *see* Qianlong, Qing (e)
Gaozong, Tang (e) 57, 60, 93, 94, 95, 96–97, 98, 99, 100, 102, 103
Gaozong, Song (e) 118, 136–138, 139, *119, 137*
Gaozu, Later Han (e) 118, 120, 121
Gaozu, Later Jin (e) 118, 120, 121
Gaozu, Tang (e) 60, 88–89, 109, *61, 88*
Gautama, prince, 78
Genghis Khan 144, 148, 152, 157, *152*
George III 202
German, Germany 197, 212, 215
Gobi 18, 38
Gongdi, E. Jin (e)60, 66, 69, 71
Gongdi, Sui (e) 60, 82, 87
Gongxian, Henan 80, 127
Gongzong, Song (e) 118, 136, 146–47, *147*
Grand Canal 13, 84–85, 151, 177, 183, 206, map *85*
Grand Secretariat, Secretaries 162, 169, 176, 178, 179, 182, *174*
Grand Tours 193, 194, 199, 202
'Greater Yan' dynasty 109
Great Goose Pagoda, Xi'an 97, 110, 111
Great Mosque, Xi'an 92
Great Wall 12, 13, 18–19, 20–21, 38, 83, 163, 171, 173, *18–19*
Greece 38
Guandi, God of War *65*
Guangdong 37, 147, 212
Guangzhou (Canton) 56, 117, 147, 191, 197, 207
Guang Wudi, Han (e) 14, 30, 44–48, *15, 44*
Guangxu, Qing (e) 158, 204, 213–16
Guan Yu (Three Kingdoms) *65*
Guangzong, Ming *see* Taichang, Ming (e)
Guangzong, Song (e) 118, 136, 143, 144
Guanlinmiao Museum, Luoyang 47
Guangxi 37, 174
Guanxian, Sichuan 47

Guanyin 111
Guilin, Guangxi Autonomous Region 163, *162*
Guizhou 210
Gu Kaizhi, painter 69, 70
gunpowder 147
Guo Shoujing, mathematician 151
Guo Xi, painter 140
Guo Ziyi, Tang general *89*

Hai Xi Gong, E. Jin (e) 60, 66, 69, 70–71
Hangzhou, Zhejiang 84, 119, 128, 132, 136, 138, 146, 151, 178, 181, 208
Harems 52, 65, 107, 169
Hart, Robert 212
Hebei 35
Hedi, Han (e) 14, 50–51
Hedi, Qi (e) 60, 67, 73
Heilongjiang 193
Henan 81
Heshan, Qing official 202, 204
Historical Records 13
Holland 212, 215
Hong Kong 147, 206, 207
Hongli, Qing *see* Qianlong, Qing (e)
Hongwu, Ming (e) 13, 157, 158, 160–63, 167, 172, 183, 217, *159, 160, 162*
Hongxi, Ming (e) 158, 160, 167–69
Hong Xiuchuan, Taiping 208, 209, *208*
Hongzhi, Ming (e) 158, 170, 174, *174*
Horses 39, 94–95, 114, 128, 131, 149, 171, 184, 198, *34, 39, 94–95*
Hou Jing, Liang 74, 76
Hou Zhu, Chen (e) 60, 62, 65, 67, 83, *61, 77*
Huai river 84
Huaidi, W. Jin (e)60, 66, 68
Huandi, Han (e) 14, 50, 51
Huangdi, Yellow Emperor *9*
Huang Zhao (Tang) 117
Huidi, Han (e) 14, 28, 31
Huidi, Ming *see* Jianwen, Ming (e)
Huidi, W. Jin 60, 66, 68
Huizong, Song (e) 13, 118, 122, 132–35, 136, 141
'Hundred Days' Reforms' 214
Hungary 152

Ibn Wahhab 106
Imperial Academy 37
Imperial Academy of Medicine 151
India 56, 70, 73, 81, 110, 111, 117, 142, 143, 161, 167, 201, 207
Indo-China 167
Indonesia 56
inscriptions 100, 105, 153
Irinjibal, Yuan prince 157
iron 37, 41, 45, 109
Irrigation 13, 47, 128, 199, 201
Islam 109
Isles of Penglai 21,
Istanbul 143
Italy, Italian 215

Jade 8, 9, 36, 56, 107, 116, 138, 142, 174, 184, *31, 34*
Jamal-al-Din, 151
Japan 45, 161, 167, 212, 216, 217; Chinese influence on 53, 128, 133, 151; trade with 142, 188; pirates 166, 180; wars with 153, 154, 182, 214, 215
Java 161, 167
Jehol *see* Chengde
Jesuits 93, 183, 186, 191, 193, 197, 198
Jiajing, Ming (e) 158, 170, 178–80, 183, 184, 188, *180*
Jiaqing, Qing (e) 158, 204–05
Jianling, Tang mausoleum 94
Jianwen, Ming (e) 158, 160, 163, 172
Jian Wendi, E. Jin (e) 60, 66, 69, 71
Jian Wendi, Liang (e) 60, 67, 74, 76
Jiangsu 12
Jiaohe 57
Jiayugang, Gansu 18
Jingdezhen kilns 181, 188, 200
Jin Kingdom 119, 128, 132, 135, 136, 144
Jingdi, Han (e) 14, 28, 33, 34, 44
Jingdi, Liang (e) 60, 67, 74, 76
Jingdi, Ming *see* Jingtai, Ming (e)
Jingdi, Wu 60, 62
Jing Ke 26
Jingtai, Ming (e) 158, 170–71, 188
Jingzong, Tang (e) 60, 112, 115, 116
Journey to the West, 81
Jurchen 173, 190
Juyongguan archway, Hebei 153

Kaifeng, Henan 109, 119, 129, 130, 132, 135, 136, 137, 138, 143
Kangdi, E. Jin (e) 60, 66, 69, 70
Kangxi, Qing (e) 158, 190–94, 195, 196, 197, 198, *5, 159, 192, 193*
Kang Yuwei, Manchu 214
Kashgar 56, 206
Kazakh 198
Khaishan, Yuan (e) 118, 148, 156, *5, 157*
Khitan 121, 124, 125, 128, 129, 132, 135, 137
Khoshila, Yuan (e) 118, 148, 156–57, *154*
Khotan 127
Khubilai Khan, Yuan (e) 12, 13, 118, 147, 148–53, 156, 164, *119, 149*
kilns 105, 181, 188, 200
Kong, Manchu prince 210, 212, *210*
Korea, Chinese contacts with 46, 53, 128, 133, 139, 142, 151, 169, 190, 198; envoys 98, 144, 161, 167, *127*; wars with 37, 87, 182, 214
Kowloon 207, 209
Kucha 48
Kunming, Yunnan 6

Lacquer 9, 36, 59, 142, 200, *35*
Lama, lamaism 151, 153, 156, 157, 176, 198
Lama Temple, Beijing 195

land reform 17, 41, 43, 81, 83, 129, 130, 161, 193
Laozi 32, 75, 101, 108, 115, *32, 75*
Legalism, Legalists 17, 31
Legation Quarter, Beijing 214, 215
Leshan, Sichuan 57, 111
Liao *see* Khitan
Liaodong, Liaoning 212
Liaoning 132, 190
Li Bai, poet *108*
Li Bing, Qin engineer *47*
libraries 76, 87, 130, 165
Li Hong, Tang prince 97
Li Linfu, Tang official 108
Lin'an (Hangzhou) 132
Lingdi, Han (e) 14, 32, 50, 51, 52–55
Lin Hai Wang, Chen (e) 60, 67, 77
Lintong, Shaanxi 24
Li Shimin *see* Taizong, Tang
Li Si, Qin minister 17, 27
Li Xian, Tang prince 95, 98
Li Yuan, Tang prince 87, 88
Lin Zexu, Qing official 207
Liu Bei 55, 65, *63*
Liu Bang *see* Gaodi, Han
Liubo 59
Liu He, Han prince 40
Liu Sheng, tomb of 34, *35*
Liu Ye, Liu Song prince 71, 72
Liu Yu *see* Wudi, Liu Song
Li Zicheng, Ming general 187
Li Zhe, Tang prince 97
Lizong, Song (e) 118, 136, 144–45, 146
Longqing, Ming (e) 158, 170, 180, 184
Longmen, Henan 80, 101, *79, 99,*
Lop Nor 18
Lu Buwei, Qin merchant 16
Luguoqiao, 150
Lu Hou, Han empress 14, 28, 31
Luoyang, as capital 15, 30, 44, 73, 80, 107, 142; sack of 55, 72, 87, 109

Macao 197, 207
Macartney, Lord George 202, 203, 207
Mahao, Leshan 57
Ma Hezhi, painter 138
Malaya 56
Mancheng, Hebei 35
Manchu 159, 173, 182, 187, 190–217 *passim*
Manchuria 12, 38, 109, 132, 167, 215, 217
Maoling, Han mausoleum 39
Mao Zedong, Chairman 165
Mappa Mundi 186
maps 130, 186, 193
Marco Polo *see* Polo, Marco
Mawangdui, Changsha, Hebei 35
Ma Yuan, Han general 45, 48
Mecca 166
Mediterranean 56
Meng Jian, Qin general 18
Mesopotamia 106, 143
Middle East 56, 114, 167
Mindi, W. Jin (e) 60, 66, 68

Mingdi, Han (e) 14, 44, 48–49
Mingdi, Wei (e) 60, 62, 63, 65
Mingdi, E. Jin (e) 60, 66, 69
Mingdi, Liu Song (e) 60, 67, 70, 71, 72
Mingdi, Qi (e) 60, 67, 73
Ming Huan *see* Xuanzong, Tang (712–56)
Ming Tombs 169, 184–85, 187, *184–85*
Min Ning *see* Daoguang, Qing (e)
minting 37, 48
Mingzong, Later Tang (e) 118, 120, 121
Mingzong, Yuan (e) *see* Khoshila
missionaries 78, 110, 197, 209
Modernists 41
Modi, Later Liang (e) 118, 120, 121
Modi, Wu (e) 60, 62, 65
Moggi, Bonaventura, Jesuit 197
monasteries 99, 131, 153, 160
Mongke Khan 149
Mongolia 12, 38, 48, 132
Mongols 12, 70, 128, 132, 144–47 *passim*, 148–57, 161, 166, 167, 169, 179, 182, *171*
monopolies 37, 41, 45, 48, 172
Muslims 92, 109, 151, 154, 156, 157, 166
Mount Tai, Shandong 99, 105
Mount Wu Tai, Shanxi 153
Mudi, E. Jin (e) 60, 66, 69, 70
Mukden (Shenyang), Liaoning 190
Muzong, Ming *see* Longqing, Ming (e)
Muzong, Qing *see* Tongzhi, Qing (e)
Muzong, Tang (e) 60, 112, 115, 116

Nan Chan temple, Wu Tai *117*
Nanchao *see* Yunnan
Nanjing, Jiangsu 128, 181, 208, 217; as capital 68–76 *passim*, 160, 209; tombs 65, 161
Nanjing, Treaty of 206, 207
Nanyue, Kingdom of 37
neo-Confucianism 123, 145, 190, 193, 212
Nepal 78, 153, 198, 202
Nestorian Christianity 93, 149, 151, 183
Ningpo, Zhejiang 207
Ningxia Hui Autonomous Region 18, 176
Ningzong, Song (e) 118, 136, 144
Northern Qi 81
Northern Wei 71–80 *passim*
Northern Zhou 77, 81, 83, 86
Nurhachi 182, 190

Opium 201, 206, 207
Opium War 206, 207
Oracle bones *12*
Ox, oxen 92, 109, *109*

pagoda *81, 86, 97*
palaces 9, 20–21, 26, 83, 93, 164, 202, *49, 106, 109*
Pamirs 38, 56, 198
Pan Ku, legendary creator 8

Pantoja, Jesuit 186
paper 53, 200, 201, *53*
paper money 128, 135, 143, 151, 156
Pearl Concubine, Qing 214
Pei Xu, cartographer 67
Persia 56, 93, 106, 117, 128, 151, 154
Persian Gulf 142, 143, 166, 167
'Phagsa-pa, 151, 153
Philippines 198
Pingdi, Han (e) 14, 40, 42
Pingyang, Sichuan 46, 76
polo 93, 103, 114, 115, 123, *95*
Polo, Marco 7, 84, 148, 150, 151, *150*
Poland 152
Potala temple, Chengde 198
Potala Temple, Lhasa 198
porcelain 13, 135, 169, 172, 174, 188–89, 200, *135, 139, 169, 188–89*; export of 142, 143 *see also* Kilns
printing 130, 133
Puyi, Qing (e) 158, 185, 204, 213, 216–17, *204, 216*

Qianling, Tang mausoleum 98, 100, 102–03, 115
Qianlong, Qing (e) 13, 158, 164, 195, 196–202, 203, 204, 212, *159, 196, 198*
Qiaoling, Tang mausoleum 101
Qingdao, Shandong 212
Qinghai 182
Qinzong, Song (e) 118, 122, 132, 134, 135, 136
Que (monumental towers) *46, 47, 76*
Qufu, Shandong 46, 124

Red Eyebrows 44
Red Sea 142, 166, 167
Red Turbans 160
Reformists 41
reign marks 169, 174, 188, *189*
Renzong, Ming *see* Hongxi, Ming (e)
Renzong, Qing *see* Jiajing, Qing (e)
Renzong, Song (e) 118, 122, 128, 129–30, *119, 129*
Renzong, Yuan (e) *see* Ayurbarwada
Republic, republican 216, 217
Ricci, Matteo, Jesuit 183, 186, 197
Rites Controversy 186
Romance of the Three Kingdoms 63, 64
Rome, Roman 6, 13, 38, 43, 48, 56, 186, 199
Rubruck, William of 183
Ruizong, Tang (e) 60, 96, 97–98, 101, 104
Russia, Russian 193, 198, 202, 212, 214, 215
Ruzi, Han (e) 14, 40, 42

salt 37, 41, 45
Sanbao Taijian 166
Sancai see Three-colours glaze
Sanskrit 153
Sassanid Kingdom 96
Schall von Bell, Adam *186*, Jesuit 191

Schreck, John (Terrentius), Jesuit 186, 187
scripts 154
Second Emperor see Er Shi
Seismograph 30
'Seven Sages in a Bamboo Grove' 69, 75, 75
shamans, shamanism 21, 151, 152
Shandong 18, 87, 202, 209, 212
Shang dynasty 8, 12,
Shangdi, Han (e) 14, 50, 51
Shangdu, Mongol capital 152, 161
Shanghai 207, 208
Shang Yang, Legalist 17
Shanhaiguan, Hebei 18
Shanyuan, treaty of 128,
Shaodi, E. Han (e) 51
Shaodi, Wei (e) 60, 62, 63, 65
Shaodi Hong, Han prince 31
Shaodi Kong, Han prince 31
Shao Yong, mathematician 130, 142
Shengzu, Qing see Kangxi, Qing (e)
Shen Nong, legendary sovereign 8
Shentong temple, Shandong 87
Shenyang, Liaoning 190
Shenzong, Ming see Wanli, Ming (e)
Shenzong, Song (e) 118, 122, 130, 132
Shidebala, Yuan (e) 118, 148, 156,
Shihuangdi, Qin (First Emperor) (e) 6, 7, 8, 9, 13, 14–26, 36, 43, 84, 15, 16
Shi Miyuan, Song official 144, 145
Shimonoseki, Treaty of 214
ships 87, 139, 143, 147, 162, 166, 167, 213, 84, 139, 180, 211
Shizong, Later Zhou (e) 118, 120, 121, 122
Shizong, Ming see Jiajing, Ming (e)
Shizong, Qing see Yongzheng, Qing (e)
Shizu, Qing see Shunzhi, Qing (e)
Shizu, Yuan (e) see Khubilai
Shu Kingdom 60, 63, 65, 121
Shundi, Han (e) 14, 50, 51
Shundi, Liu Song (e) 60, 67, 71, 72
Shundi, Yuan (e) see Toghon Temur
Shunzhi, Qing (e) 158, 190–91, 190
Shunzong, Tang (e) 60, 112, 113–15
Siberia 56, 167
Sichuan 13, 29, 37, 47, 54, 55, 56, 58, 70, 76, 87, 108, 109, 110, 117, 121, 161, 176, 191
Sicklepart, Ignatius, Jesuit 197
Siling, Ming mausoleum 187
Silk 8, 29, 36, 81, 107, 181; as export 56, 142, 188, 207; as tribute 128, 129, 136;
paintings 34, 97, 174, 177; texts 32
Silk Roads 19, 56–57, 80, 109, 110, map 57
Sima Qian, historian 13, 17
Sima Yuan see Wudi, W. Jin (e)
'Single Whip' tax reform 179, 181
Sixteen Kingdoms 70, 80
Sizong, Ming see Chongzhen, Ming (e)
Sogdiana 38
Song Yuan, envoy 73
Song Yue monastery, Henan 81

Sorghagtani Beki, Mongol empress 149
spirit roads 46, 102, 124, 161, 184, 191
Staunton, George 199
Stelae tablets 130, 78, 93, 100, 105, 161
Sumatra 161
Summer Palace, Beijing 197, 198, 199, 207, 209, 211, 212, 213, 214
Sun Quan, Wu kingdom 55, 63, 65, 63
Sun Yatsen, Dr. 216, 217
Su Song, inventor 129
Suzhou, Jiangsu 84, 174, 181, 208
Suzong, Tang (e)60, 94, 109, 112–13
Syria 93

Taichang, Ming (e) 158, 170, 183
Taiding, Yuan (e) see Yesun Temur
Tailing, Qing mausoleum 195
Tai Shan see Mount Tai
Taiping, Tang princess 101
Taiping rebellion 208, 209, 210
Taiwan 191
Taizong, Song (e) 118, 122, 123, 125–26, 127
Taizong, Tang (e) 57, 60, 88, 89–93, 94, 99, 102, 5, 90
Taizu, Later Liang (e) 118, 120, 121
Taizu, Song (e) 118, 122–25, 130, 139, 144, 5, 119, 123
Taizu, Later Zhou (e) 118, 120, 121
Taizu, Ming see Hongwu
Talas, battle of, 109
Tamerlaine, Mongol 167
Tangut 153
Tantrism 108
Targi, Yuan empress 156
Tarim 48, 56, 109
tea 128, 129, 142, 200, 201, 207
Temple of Heaven, Beijing 163, 164, 168, 177, 168
Temudur, Yuan minister 156
Temur Oljeitu, Yuan (e) 148, 154–56
Temujin see Genghis Khan
Ten Kingdoms 120–21
terracotta armies 13, 24–25, 58, 22–23, 34, 36
Terrentius see Schreck, John
Thailand 198
Three-colours glaze (sancai) 95, 105, 114
Tianjin, Hebei 217
Tian Lingzi, Tang eunuch 116
Tianqi, Ming (e) 158, 170, 183–87
Tianshun, Ming (e) 158, 170, 171
Tibet, Tibetan 19, 91, 97, 105, 112, 116, 124, 161, 176, 193, 202; lamaism 151, 153; campaigns against 97, 105, 113, 206
titles 13, 17, 37
Toba Wei see Northern Wei
tobacco 181
Toghon Temur, Yuan (e) 118, 148, 154–157
Tolui, Mongol, 148
tomb figurines 34, 58–59, 76, 92, 114–15, 58–59, 94, 95

tombs, Qin 24–25, 26; Han 36, 39, 58, 34–35; Three Kingdoms 65; Tang 94, 98, 102–03, 94, 102–03; Shu 121; Song 124, 127, 124, 127, 131; Ming 169, 184–85, 187, 184–85; Qing 210, 195
Tongzhi, Qing (e) 158, 204, 209, 210–13
Tong Zhongshu, Han 27,
Tongkking 202
Transoxania 167
triads 204, 205
Tripitaka, Buddhist 167
Tugh Temur, Yuan (e) 118, 148, 156–57, 154
Tuglug Temur, Mongol 157
Tungu, nomads 70, 132
Turfan 56
Turkestan 38
Turkic, Turks 70, 80, 91, 93, 102, 198

Uighur 89, 102, 107, 109, 150, 153, 154,
United States of America 181, 186, 212, 215

Venice, Venetian 151
Verbiest, Ferdinand, Jesuit 197
Victoria, Queen 209
Vietnam 37, 46, 48, 56, 124, 144, 147, 153, 161, 167, 198, 212

Wang Anshi, Song minister 129, 130, 131, 132, 134
Wang Chengen, Ming eunuch 187
Wang Jian, tomb of 121,
Wang Mang (e) 14, 15, 30, 40, 42–43, 44, 43
Wan Guifei, Ming concubine 173, 174
Wang Xizhi, calligrapher 69
Wanli, Ming (e) 93, 158, 170, 179, 180–83, 184, 185, 186, 7
War of the Three Feudatories 193
Warring States 16, 32
Water control 131, 182, 193 (see also Irrigation)
Wei, river 29, 30, 94, 179
Weihaiwei, Shandong 212
Wendi, Han (e) 14, 28, 33–36, 15
Wendi, Chen (e) 60, 67, 77
Wendi, Liang 76
Wendi, Liu Song (e) 60, 66, 71, 72
Wendi, Wei (e) 60, 62, 65, 61, 63
Wendi, Sui (e) 60, 77, 81, 82–86, 87, 61, 82
Wen Xuan 74
Wenzong, Tang (e) 60, 112, 115, 116
Wenzong, Yuan (e) see Tugh Temur
Wenzong, Qing see Xianfeng, Qing (e)
Western Hills, 165
Western Paradise 110
Western Tombs, Qing 195
Western Xia 129, 130
White Horse Temple, Luoyang 47, 78, 101
White Lotus Society 204
White Stag Notes 48

Writing 8, 9, 12, 13, 20, 91, 154; examples of *32, 53, 54, 69, 89 see also* Calligraphy
Wudi, Han (e) 13, 14, 28, 36–39, 46, 48, 56, 57, 180
Wudi, Chen (e) 60, 67, 76, 77
Wudi, Liang (e) 60, 67, 72, 73, 74, 76, *74*
Wudi, Liu Song (e) 660, 66, 71
Wudi, Qi (e) 60, 67, 73
Wudi, W. Jin (e) 60, 66, 67–68
Wudi, Wu (e) 60, 62, 63
Wuhan, Hubei 216
Wu Hou *see* Wu Zetian
Wu Kingdom 55, 60, 63, 65
Wu Sansi (Tang official) 101
Wu Sangui, Ming general 193
Wu Tai Mountains, Shanxi 110, 117
Wu Yue kingdom 125
Wu Zetian, Tang (e) 7, 60, 95, 97, 98–101, 102, 103, 104, 110, 210, *96, 98*
Wu Zhao *see* Wu Zetian
Wuzhu coins 48
Wuzong, Tang (e) 60, 112, 115, 116
Wuzong, Yuan (e) *see* Khaishan
Wuzong, Ming *see* Zhengde, Ming (e)

Xanadu 152
Xia dynasty 8
Xi'an, Shaanxi 15, 53, 107, 110, 135
Xia Nai, Dr. 184
Xian Bei, nomads 80
Xiandi, Han (e) 14, 50, 55, *55*
Xianfeng, Qing (e) 158, 204, 207, 208–09, 210, 213
Xianling, Zhongxian, Ming mausoleum 179, *179*
Xianyang, Shaanxi 20, 21, 28, 29, 34 145
Xiang Yu, general 27, 28, 29
Xianzong, Tang (e) 60, 112, 113, 115, 116
Xianzong, Ming *see* Chenghua, Ming (e)
Xiao Chen, Qing empress 210, 213
Xiao Daocheng *see* Gaodi, Qi (e)
Xiao Jing, Liang prince 72
Xiaoling, Ming mausoleum 161
Xiaoling, Qing mausoleum 191
Xiao Tong, Liang prince 74
Xiao Wendi, Northern Wei 80, 81
Xiao Yan *see* Wudi, Liang (e)
Xiao Wudi, E. Jin (e) 60, 66, 67, 69, 71, 72
Xiao Wudi, Liu Song (e) 60, 67, 71
Xiaozong, Song (e) 118, 136, 137, 139–43, 144
Xiaozong, Ming *see* Hongzhi, Ming (e)
Xidajiaocun cemetery, Henan 54
Xin dynasty 42
Xinjiang 19, 56, 57, 90, 157, 198, 206
Xiongnu 29, 37, 38, 48, 68, 80
Xizong, Tang (e) 60, 112, 116, 117
Xizong, Ming *see* Tianqi, Ming (e)
Xuande, Ming (e) 158, 160, 169, 177, 188, 189, *169*

Xuande, Shu 60, 62, 63
Xuandi, Han (e)14, 40, 41
Xuandi, Chen (e) 60, 67, 77
Xuandi, Qing *see* Puyi, Qing (e)
Xuanzang, Tang monk 97, 110, 111, 181
Xuanzong, Tang (712–56) (e) 60, 94, 104–09, 114, 140, *104*
Xuanzong, Tang (846–59) (e) 60, 112, 115, 116
Xuan Ye *see* Kangxi, Qing (e)
Xuanzong, Ming *see* Xuande, Ming (e)
Xuanzong, Qing *see* Daoguang, Qing (e)
Xue Huaiyi, monk 99, 101

Yangdi, Sui (e) 60, 82, 87, *87*
Yang Jian *see* Wendi, Sui
Yang Guifei, Tang concubine 104, 107, 108, 109, 114
Yangling, Han mausoleum 34
Yan Liben, painter 63, 77, 89, 91, 94
Yangshan quarry, Nanjing 161
Yangzhou, Jiangsu 84
Yangzi, river 12, 27, 68, 84, 87, 128, 146, 174
Yarkand 206
Yellow Emperor 8, 75
Yellow River 8, 12, 37, 43, 44, 49, 54, 67, 84, 105, 109, 150, 151, 179, 204, 209
Yellow Turbans 54, 75
Yesun Temur, Yuan (e) 118, 148, 156
Yide, Tang prince 106
Yindi, Later Han (e) 118, 120, 121
Yinchen *see* Yongzheng, Qing (e)
Ying Yang Wang, Liu Song (e) 60, 66, 71
Yingzong, Ming *see* Zhengtong, Ming (e)
Yingzong, Song (e) 118, 122, 130
Yingzong, Yuan (e) *see* Shidebala
Yinreng, Qing prince 194
Yizhun *see* Xianfeng, Qing (e)
Yizong, Tang (e) 60, 112, 116, 117
Yonghe Gong (Lama Temple), Beijing 195
Yongle, Ming (e) 158, 160, 161, 163–67, 169, 172, 178, 184, 185; *frontispiece, 159, 167*
Yongtai, Tang princess 103
Yongyan *see* Jiajing, Qing (e)
Yongzheng, Qing (e) 158, 190, 194, 195, 197, *195*
Yu, Xia king 8
Yuandi, Han (e) 14, 40, 41–42
Yuandi, E. Jin (e) 60, 66, 68, 69, 70
Yuandi, Liang (e) 60, 67, 74, 76
Yuandi, Wei (e) 60, 62, 63, 65
Yuanmingyuan *see* Summer Palace
Yuan Shikai, President 168, 216
Yue Fei, Song general 137, 138, 139
Yungang, Datong 78, 79
Yunnan 19, 56, 109, 110, 113, 124, 144, 149, 161, 166, 191, 210 *see also* Dali
Yu Zhang Wang, Liang (e) 60, 67, 74, 76

Zen Buddhism 191, 195
Zeng Guofeng, general 210
Zhangdi, Han (e) 14, 44, 48–49
Zhang Fei (Three Kingdoms) 65
Zhang Heng 30
Zhanghuai, Tang prince 103, 115
Zhang Qian 38, 39, 56
Zhang Zeduan, painter 143
Zhaodi, Han (e) 14, 40–41
Zhao Gao, Qin eunuch 27
Zhao Heng *see* Zhenzong, Song (e)
Zhao Hongyin, Song 123,
Zhao Kuangyin *see* Taizu, Song (e)
Zhaoling, Ming mausoleum 184
Zhaoling, Tang mausoleum, 102
Zhao Shu *see* Yingzong, Song (e)
Zhaoxuan *see* Aidi, Tang
Zhao Zhen *see* Renzong, Song (e)
Zhao Zicheng, Song 143
Zhaozong, Tang (e) 60, 112, 117,
Zhengde, Ming (e) 158, 170, 176–78
Zheng He, admiral 166, 167, 172
Zhejiang 37
Zhen Jin, Mongol 154
Zhengtong, Ming (e) 158, 166, 170–72, 173, 188
Zhenzong, Song (e) 118, 122, 126, 128
Zhezong, Song (e) 118, 122, 127, 130–32
Zhidi, Han (e) 14, 50, 51
Zhongzong, Tang (e) 60, 96, 97–98, 101, 103
Zhou dynasty 8, 30, 31, 41
'Zhou dynasty' (690–705) 101
Zhuangzong, Later Tang (e) 118, 120, 121
Zhuangzi 32, 75
Zhuge Liang, Three Kingdoms 65
Zhu Chanle *see* Taichang, Ming (e)
Zhu Di *see* Yongle, Ming (e)
Zhu Gaozhi *see* Hongxi, Ming (e)
Zhu Houcong *see* Jiajing, Ming (e)
Zhu Houzhao *see* Zhengde, Ming (e)
Zhu Jianshen *see* Chenghua, Ming (e)
Zhu Qiyu *see* Jingtai, Ming (e)
Zhu Qizhen *see* Zhengtong, Ming (e)
Zhu Wen, Tang official 117
Zhu Xi, Confucian philosopher 145, *145*
Zhu Yizhen *see* Wanli, Ming (e)
Zhu Yuanzhang *see* Hongwu
Zhu Yujian *see* Chongzhen, Ming (e)
Zhu Yujiao *see* Tianqi, Ming (e)
Zhu Yunwen *see* Jianwen, Ming (e)
Zhu Yutang *see* Hongzhi, Ming (e)
Zhu Zaihou *see* Longqing, Ming (e)
Zhu Zanyi, Ming prince 163
Zhu Zhanji *see* Xuande, Ming (e)
Zuling, Ming mausoleum 172